2007 Microsoft®
Office System and
Your Windows®-Based PC:

A Real-Life Guide to Getting More Done

PUBLISHED BY
Microsoft Press
A Division of Microsoft Corporation
One Microsoft Way
Redmond, Washington 98052-6399

Copyright © 2009

Library of Congress Control Number: 2009925532

Printed and bound in the United States of America.

1 2 3 4 5 6 7 8 9   QWT   4 3 2 1 0 9

Distributed in Canada by HB Fenn and Company Ltd.

A CIP catalogue record for this book
is available from the British Library.

Microsoft Press Books are available through booksellers and distributors worldwide. For further information about international editions, contact your local Microsoft Corporation office or contact Microsoft Press International directly at fax (425) 936-7329. Visit our website at **www.microsoft.com/ mspress**. Send comments to **mspinput@microsoft.com**.

All images in this book are supplied by Jupiter Images Ltd (www.jupiterimages.com) or Future Publishing Ltd.

With grateful thanks to the following people and organizations for their contributions to the content of this book:
Joe Cassels, Richard Cobbett, Katharine Davies, Dan Grabham, Karl Hodge, Gary Marshall, Alec Meer, Neil Mohr, Adam Oxford, Tamsin Oxford, Nick Peers.

Access, Aero, BitLocker, DirectX, Excel, Fluent, Groove, Hotmail, InfoPath, Internet Explorer, Microsoft, Microsoft Press, MSN, OneCare, OneNote, Outlook, PivotTable, PowerPoint, ReadyBoost, ReadyDrive, SharePoint, SideShow, SkyDrive, SmartArt, SpyNet, SuperFetch, Visio, Windows, Windows Live, Windows Media, Windows Mobile, Windows Vista, Xbox, and Xbox 360 are either registered trademarks or trademarks of Microsoft group of companies. Other product and company names mentioned herein may be the trademarks of their respective owners.

Acquisitions Editor: Juliana Aldous
Developmental Editor: Sandra Haynes
Project Editor: Rosemary Caperton
Operations Editor: Jo Membery, Future Publishing
Art: Seth Singh & John McAllister, Future Publishing
Section Editor: James Stables, Future Publishing
Editor-in-Chief: Adam Ifans, Future Publishing

Body Part No: X15-66440

2007 Microsoft Office System and Your Windows-Based PC

Welcome

to your comprehensive guide to using Windows Vista and the 2007 Microsoft Office system! The team behind *Windows Vista: The Official Magazine* has, in conjunction with Microsoft, compiled this book to show you how you can be as productive as possible.

Introduction

This book covers every aspect of Microsoft's user-friendly operating system and suite of programs – Windows Vista and the 2007 Office system. From initial set-up basics, you can progress to find out how Windows Vista can help you to get the most from all your PC requirements. Like Windows Vista, the Office release covers all bases, too – from humble text documents, to savvy presentations and organized lives! The two combine to create a powerful backbone to your PC that can assist and enhance your working day and family time.

Get Started

New to Windows Vista? Never opened an Office document? Then this is your starting point. Get to grips with setting up the operating system exactly how you want it and familiarize yourself with the top features of the 2007 Office suite. It doesn't take long to feel right at home...

Explore

Once you've had a good look around, you'll be itching to find out more! In this section, you'll find an in-depth look at how Windows Vista and the Office suite can make every aspect of your life more organized and, in turn, more constructive, whether you're using your PC for work or leisure.

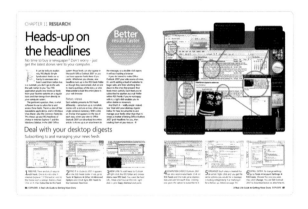

Do More

Now you've conversant with the workings of Windows Vista, and acquainted with the flexibility and power of the Office programs, it's time to launch into some projects. From working on the move to discovering creative talents, this is where things get productive – and fun!

Contents

Get Started

Explore

Contents

Chapter 20 Friends & family

Chapter 15 Work projects

Appendix

Installation

Get Started

It won't take long to see the benefits of working with Windows Vista and the 2007 Microsoft Office system

CHAPTER 1 **INTRODUCING...**

"Wow"

12 reasons why you'll love Windows Vista

A guide to the most outstanding elements
in this latest Microsoft operating system

(1) The new interface looks amazing

■ The Windows Aero interface manages to be both eye-catching and unobtrusive. Much of this is down to the Aero Glass transparency effects on window borders and menus – you can now see exactly what's where on the desktop. And the frosted look gives it a futuristic feel, but without ever getting in the way.

There's a whole bunch of new effects, such as Flip3D, which shows every running application in a scrollable 3D stack of windows. You can actually see movies and games still cheerfully playing back, but in thumbnail form.

(2) Simple but powerful Photo Gallery functions

■ Photos are treated like VIPs. The core function of the new Windows Photo Gallery tool is clear, but it's the way that you can arrange things that makes it great – organizing photos by tags you assign to them rather than by location. So you can tag a bunch of related photos scattered across your hard drive with 'dog's wedding anniversary' and find them all under that tag, rather than only being able to group them together by putting them all in the same folder. There are also some photo-fixing tools, plus the options to burn pictures to CD/DVD or upload them to the web. And the way image files are displayed is improved, with a whole selection of different modes and thumbnail views available.

BIGGER PICTURE Now you can order prints online or even make movies from your pics

(3) Foolproof to set up

■ Insert DVD, press Install, turn brain off. The set-up process in Windows Vista is no more taxing than installing a game, and no longer stops halfway through to ask you an asinine question about which currency symbols to use at which times.

(4) Speed up in a flash

■ Windows Vista offers an easy way to eke more life out of a laboring PC, and all without taking the side off the case. ReadyBoost is an instant adrenaline infusion, and all you have to do is plug in a ReadyBoost-compatible flash drive or digital camera memory card. Because these can read and write data very quickly, they can act as surrogate memory, so the PC can do more at once without grinding to a halt. It's like using steroids, but without the expense, health risks or any fear of an Olympics ban.

SPEED UP You decide how much space on your USB drive is required for ReadyBoost

(5) Windows Media Center can be built in

■ **Windows Media Center is now a component part of the Windows Vista Home Premium and Ultimate editions. Its advanced from-your-own-sofa television recording, scheduling and time-shifting capabilities mean** that, for many of us, all other forms of recording TV and movies will quickly become obsolete. It's also a great way of managing a bewilderingly huge music and photo library – again, all from sedentary comfort.

ENTERTAINMENT TIME Windows Media Center turns your PC into an easy-to-use, complete home entertainment system

(6) All you need for top class gaming

■ **DirectX – the part of Windows that handles games – has been upgraded to version 10, exclusively available with Windows Vista. It means both improved graphics for upcoming stuff and better performance for existing games. In DirectX 10's wake, consoles look like the day before yesterday's news. Windows Vista also offers safe passage** through the problem of working out whether a game will run on your PC. The Performance Index tool checks out what hardware is in your system, then assigns a number to it that you can compare to the one on the back of a game box. If your PC's number is equal or better, you can play it – kind of like a rigged lottery, but with better graphics.

(7) Parental controls

■ At last, you can ease back on some of the worry about what your little rugrats are up to on the computer. Windows Vista has a collection of very straightforward ways to keep non-patronizing tabs on your kids' computing, such as setting strict time limits on how long they can use the PC for, what age-rating of game they're allowed to play, or restricting specific sites and types of site so they can't ever clap innocent eyes on them. This is all easily and simply tied into the individual User Accounts that you can create and set up with Windows Vista, not only providing a personal space for your children, but a space that you can place responsible limits on as well.

(8) Windows Sidebar

■ **Handily, all the essentials (and plenty of entertaining non-essentials) of the modern PC experience have been crammed into one neat little column that resides discreetly on the desktop. Headlines from websites, your inbox, the local weather, a TV guide, a photo gallery, a notepad, Sudoku – pretty much everything that you care to mention has either already had a 'gadget'** made for it, or will do very soon. Microsoft has created a handy gallery of gadgets so it's easy to browse, select and install exactly what you need.

MOVEABLE FEASTS Sidebar gadgets can also be detached and dragged across to the desktop if you want to up the scale

(9) Supremely fast file-searching facilities

■ The new operating system has a constantly-updated database, which keeps tabs on every file as it's created, changed or deleted. Whenever you type in a search term (whether it's a filename, the sender of an email, name of a song, or a million other possibilities), the results will be presented instantly, as you type.

(10) Mobile computing

■ Available in Premium editions, the Windows Mobility Center puts efficient laptop power usage at the heart of Windows Vista. There are three configurable power plans that enable users to opt for different levels of performance or battery life. Alongside this, a new battery meter makes it easier to track how much longer a laptop can run for. Also, a number of mobile-centric features have been implemented to make connecting to networks on the move easier and safer.

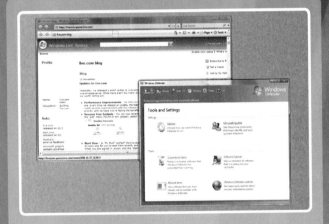

(11) The best networking

■ To make everyone's life easier, a new Network and Sharing Center has been introduced. It provides a visual breakdown of your network, where you can check the connection status, view network devices and the PC, as well as troubleshoot problems. This data is provided via the Network Map that lets you see instantly if the network can find the internet, and provides a summary of all this information. For problems, the new Network Diagnostics and Troubleshooting provides easy-to-understand reports and advice. Windows Vista is also designed to work with the newest wireless networks and offers the latest in security support for WPA2. So it's far easier and safer to use in conjunction with wireless hotspots.

(12) A secure safety net for you to perform over

■ Security is a major focus this time around. As well as it being designed in a fundamentally different way to Windows XP – meaning that the most significant vulnerabilities simply no longer exist – Windows Vista keeps a beady eye open for online threats at all times, giving you a gentle nudge if it spots anything out of the ordinary. The new Security Center, meanwhile, documents just what's been going on. It can give your system a thorough scour for anything that shouldn't be there, then restore it to squeaky-clean status and let you know via an easy-to-understand interface.

10 things you'll love about the 2007 Microsoft Office system

There are plenty of great new features in the 2007 Office release – here are 10 of the best

(**1**) Fluent interface

■ The Fluent interface is used across all the applications in the suite and breaks up the commands into obvious groups. Flick between them and you'll see things neatly laid out – Clipboard, Font, Paragraph and so on. Create polished projects faster, saving time and frustration.

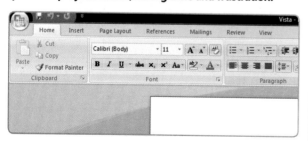

RIBBON TABS The new interface makes navigation a pleasure

(**2**) Live Preview

■ Not only is it quicker and easier to create your documents in Microsoft Office Word 2007, but you can now experiment with documents and check the results instantly with the Live Preview facility. Being able to check your work as you go along is a huge time-saver, and particularly beneficial when you've got a tight deadline.

(3) SmartArt

■ SmartArt offers a large library of standard charts, quick formatting tools and several diagram types. It's now easy to change the look of different sections, add 3D effects or assign colors. Other SmartArt layouts handle text, structuring data in clean, professional tables.

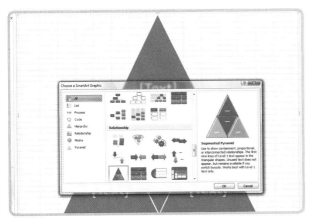

SPICE IT UP Add visuals, from Venn diagrams to 3D effects

(7) Image manipulation

☐ Import your image and you'll get a whole Ribbon panel devoted to making it look better. You can alter the brightness and contrast within the application, convert an image into a lightly washed background, and add 3D effects to shapes to bring a piece of information straight off the page. Needless to say, you should use these options sparingly because such tricks are best used to highlight what really matters.

(9) Private

■ New to the Microsoft Office system is the Document Inspector. This highly valuable tool can search for and remove personal comments or identifiable information, so that no embarrassing or sensitive information is accidentally passed on.

(4) Organize notes

☐ Office OneNote 2007 has to be the perfect student accessory. It's a digital notebook for recording a variety of information – lecture notes, web grabs, audio and video recordings, even typed text. Notes can be organized and searched far more efficiently, so a piece of research is always instantly accessible.

(5) Easy formatting

■ Easy editing makes for smart projects. Document Themes, available throughout the suite, give your work a consistent, tailored appearance. Plus Microsoft Office Excel 2007 is packed with features and an improved visual representation of data to help bring numbers to life.

(6) Save as .pdf/.xps

☐ Although not built into the 2007 Office release, you're only one click away from adding support for .pdf and .xps formats. These guarantee that everyone can read your file and the document appears on their screen exactly as it does on yours. Go to www.microsoft.com/downloads.

(8) Better blogging

■ Microsoft Office Word 2007 has a dedicated blogging mode, capable of hooking directly into blog engines. Another reason why you never have to leave the 2007 Office system to get things done, and an easier way to put your words online than creating an entire website.

(10) Help!

☐ Usability is key to the Office 2007 suite, so if you need help, improved ScreenTips and links are just a mouse click away. Online tutorials and ready-made templates are on-hand to make your life a little easier, too. Go to www.office.microsoft.com for more...

Introducing Windows Vista

Discover the new features of Windows Vista, and personalize the settings to your liking

The first excitement Windows Vista offers is its glossy new look – load it up, and you'll immediately want to play around with the new Start menu, flick through the Games Explorer, and impress any passers-by with Flip 3D (press the **Windows** key and **Tab**). Having given all this the once-over, your first port of call needs to be Windows Update, which you can search for in the **Start** menu. It's always worth checking if there are any new downloads, and if you've plumped for Windows Vista Ultimate edition, you may have some Ultimate Extras to soak up a bit more of your time before getting on to the rather more mundane business of importing all of your old

files. Mind you, if you've gone for the Windows Easy Transfer route, then there's very little to worry about when setting up your new PC. However, if you've used the backup tool in Windows XP, you need to use a special tool to convert the files so that Windows Vista can open them. Open **Backup** from the **Start** menu, click **Restore**, then click **Learn how to restore from backups created on older versions of Windows**.

Safety first

Over the course of installing and restoring, you'll notice many system options are now behind a security prompt, flagged with a little shield icon. You need to click through the prompt (or enter your password) to continue.

It can be a chore during the early stages, but once you've got your PC set up, you see these far less frequently, and your PC is much safer. If you really must – although it's not recommended – you can turn it off by clicking the icon above your name on the **Start** menu and choosing **Turn User Account Control on or off**. It's behind a security prompt...

The next few pages are dedicated to the most common startup needs, but there isn't room for everything. If you can't see the advice you need here, click **Start → Help and Support** in Windows Vista for lots of useful help. You can also find further guidance on common requirements or problems at the website for *Windows Vista: The Official Magazine* – www.windowsvistamagazine.com.

"Wow"

Variable volume

To set different levels for your music and email alerts, click the speaker icon, then **Mixer** – and you can adjust the volume of the system alerts so they don't disturb your listening

The Get Started five-minute guide...

Everything you need to know about personalizing Windows Vista

1 WELCOME Making Windows Vista look the way you want is easy. Click **Show all...** in the **Getting Started** section of the **Welcome Center**, then select **Personalize Windows** to begin.

2 CHANGE VIEW Click **Desktop Background** to choose a new background. Then follow the **Screen Saver** link to replace the Windows logo with something more entertaining.

3 ADJUST ICONS If the desktop looks a little bare, click **Change desktop icons** to add some. Here you may choose to add icons, perhaps to your documents, Control Panel or Computer.

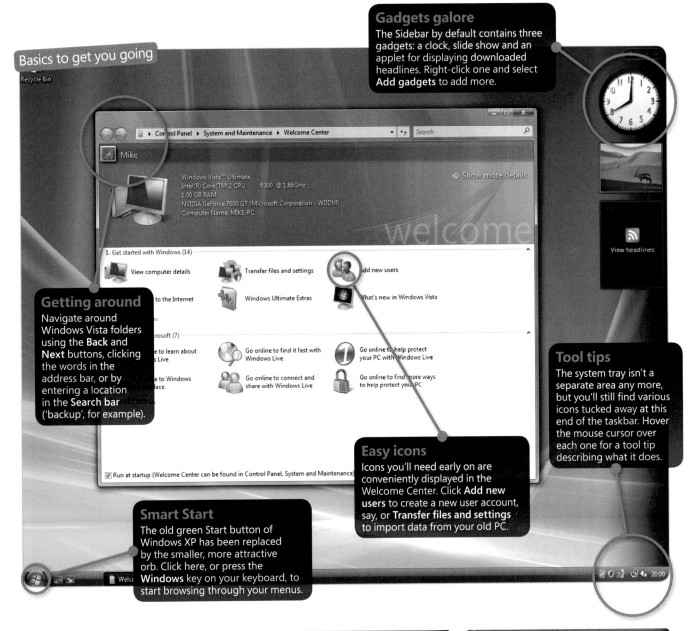

Gadgets galore
The Sidebar by default contains three gadgets: a clock, slide show and an applet for displaying downloaded headlines. Right-click one and select **Add gadgets** to add more.

Recycle Bin

Mike

Windows Vista™ Ultimate
Intel(R) Core(TM)2 CPU   6300 @ 1.86GHz
1.00 GB RAM
NVIDIA GeForce 7600 GT (Microsoft Corporation - WDDM)
Computer Name: MIKE-PC

Show more details

welcome

View headlines

1. Get started with Windows (14)

View computer details   Transfer files and settings   Add new users

to the Internet   Windows Ultimate Extras   What's new in Windows Vista

Getting around
Navigate around Windows Vista folders using the **Back** and **Next** buttons, clicking the words in the address bar, or by entering a location in the **Search bar** ('backup', for example).

crosoft (7)

e to learn about   Go online to find it fast with   Go online to help protect
s Live   Windows Live   your PC with Windows Live

e to Windows   Go online to connect and   Go online to find more ways
ace   share with Windows Live   to help protect your PC

Tool tips
The system tray isn't a separate area any more, but you'll still find various icons tucked away at this end of the taskbar. Hover the mouse cursor over each one for a tool tip describing what it does.

☑ Run at startup (Welcome Center can be found in Control Panel, System and Maintenance)

Easy icons
Icons you'll need early on are conveniently displayed in the Welcome Center. Click **Add new users** to create a new user account, say, or **Transfer files and settings** to import data from your old PC.

Smart Start
The old green Start button of Windows XP has been replaced by the smaller, more attractive orb. Click here, or press the **Windows** key on your keyboard, to start browsing through your menus.

Welc   20:00

4 CONNECT If you're connected to the internet through a network or router, you should have a connection; if not, click **Connect to the Internet** from the **Welcome Center** and follow the steps.

5 ADD GADGETS Open **Windows Sidebar** from the **Start** menu and click the '+' symbol at the top to see the available gadgets, then drag what you want on to the sidebar or the desktop.

6 GO FURTHER Click **Get more gadgets online** for a wider range. If you want the Sidebar to appear when you start up, right-click the '+' symbol in the bottom-right and choose **Properties**.

The Welcome Center

Now that you're familiarized with Windows Vista, it's time to start exploring all the nooks and crannies of customizing this good-looking operating system

 You've switched on your Windows Vista PC, so now it's time for you to become acquainted with your shiny new operating system. As well as looking radically different to Windows XP, Windows Vista works differently, too. In this section, you'll find your way around the interface and discover how you can tweak it to fit your own particular preferences.

Welcome indeed
The first thing you'll see when you run Windows Vista is the Welcome Center – and it should make you feel very welcome indeed. Not only is it there when Windows Vista loads, but you'll also spot it on the Start menu and find it in Control Panel. To prevent the Welcome Center from loading every time you switch on your PC, you can uncheck the **Run at startup** box to kill

it, but don't do that just yet, because you can learn some key things about Windows Vista just by looking at it.

Basics first
At the top of the Welcome Center there's some basic information about your computer and the current version of Windows Vista, and that information is accompanied by a link to more details (this opens the **System and Maintenance → System** application). Below this you'll find links to User Accounts, Easy Transfer and other features; while only six icons are displayed, there's also a hyperlink that you can use to show all available items. If you click on this, the Welcome Center expands to show you some further destinations including Windows Media Center and the Ease of Access Center. This is very much part of the Windows Vista style; by default you're shown a

limited selection of key information, and related features are just a click away.

Below the 'Get started with Windows' pane you'll find Offers from Microsoft for many of its latest products.

User Accounts
Before closing the Welcome Center there's one last thing to try. Click on **Show more details** in the top panel, and look for the link in the Computer Name section that says **Change settings**. When you click this, up pops a User Account Control window asking you to confirm or cancel your actions – until you choose an option, your entire system freezes. Welcome to User Account Control, which is telling you to proceed with caution. If you find this a little too intrusive, it is possible to turn this off. Find out more about User Account Control on page 102 or do a search for it at www.microsoft.com/windows/windows-vista.

YOU'RE VERY WELCOME The Welcome Center is the first thing you see when you launch Windows Vista; it's an easily navigable window to introduce you to the system

In real life...
Intuitive input

Adam Ifans,
Editor,
Windows Vista:
The Official Magazine

While the default interface on Windows Vista requires a certain level of hand-eye coordination, if you don't get on with it, or you have a physical impairment, it's easy to adjust the basic input controls.

Options such as slowing the mouse speed, changing the size of the on-screen text or requesting Visual Notifications rather than audio ones, can make your PC experience a great deal more intuitive.

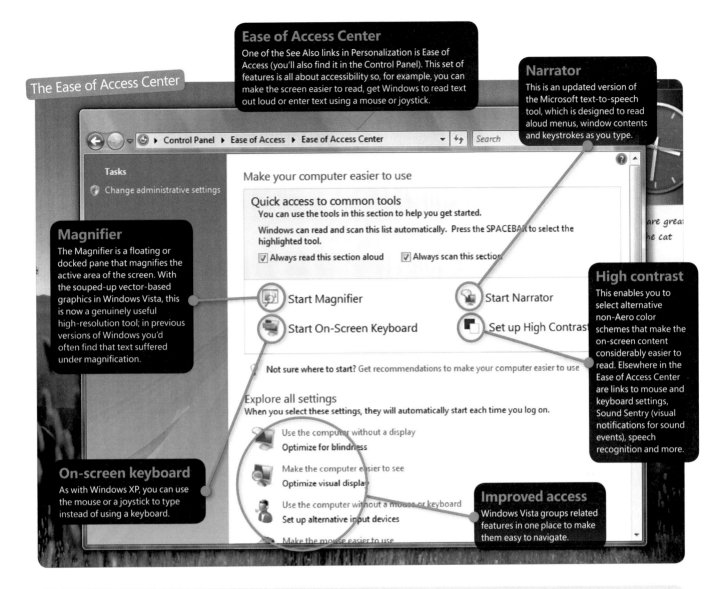

The Ease of Access Center

Ease of Access Center
One of the See Also links in Personalization is Ease of Access (you'll also find it in the Control Panel). This set of features is all about accessibility so, for example, you can make the screen easier to read, get Windows to read text out loud or enter text using a mouse or joystick.

Narrator
This is an updated version of the Microsoft text-to-speech tool, which is designed to read aloud menus, window contents and keystrokes as you type.

Magnifier
The Magnifier is a floating or docked pane that magnifies the active area of the screen. With the souped-up vector-based graphics in Windows Vista, this is now a genuinely useful high-resolution tool; in previous versions of Windows you'd often find that text suffered under magnification.

High contrast
This enables you to select alternative non-Aero color schemes that make the on-screen content considerably easier to read. Elsewhere in the Ease of Access Center are links to mouse and keyboard settings, Sound Sentry (visual notifications for sound events), speech recognition and more.

On-screen keyboard
As with Windows XP, you can use the mouse or a joystick to type instead of using a keyboard.

Improved access
Windows Vista groups related features in one place to make them easy to navigate.

Introducing the Address bar

It hides more power than you might imagine, so use it wisely...

Windows Vista uses 'breadcrumb' navigation. Look at the contents of the Address bar: System and Maintenance is to the left of the Welcome Center, the current location, indicating their relationship. The Welcome Center is located within System and Maintenance.

To open System and Maintenance, point at the name in the Address bar – it glows blue – and click. The window changes to System and Maintenance and you're in the heart of the toolkit. The breadcrumb in the

Address bar is now Control Panel, as it's the parent of System and Maintenance. To get back to the Welcome Center, click the back arrow left of the Address bar. It's essentially a web browsing approach, with Address bar breadcrumbs, hyperlinks and arrows.

If you point at the arrow between any two connected entities in the Address bar, you get a drop-down menu providing links to key features within the parent. If you click the double chevron at the far left of the Address bar, you can trace through the

NIFTY NAVIGATION The Address bar is now an interactive navigational tool, with clickable buttons and drop-down menus

hierarchy and jump to key locations, including your user profile. Finally, you'll see a search box beside the Address bar. Search is everywhere in Windows Vista.

The Start menu and the Windows Sidebar

It's time to hit Start and see what's on offer – and maybe saunter over and order something from the Sidebar...

It's time to Start! As in Windows XP, you'll find a Pinned Programs section at the top of the left menu; this retains permanent links to programs while the rest of the menu updates dynamically. Pinned Programs comes with internet (Internet Explorer 7) and email (Windows Mail) links by default, but you can add other programs by right-clicking and selecting **Pin to Start Menu**. You can also drag and drop folder shortcuts here.

The menu displays the programs you've used most recently, with the most commonly used programs at the top. This approach means that Start menu shortcuts are more relevant to your current habits. However, if you want to deactivate this, right-click the **Start** button, select **Properties** and uncheck **Store and display a list of recently opened programs**. You can do the same for recently opened files, too.

In Windows Vista, All Programs opens within the left side of the Start menu with a vertical scroll bar. When you click

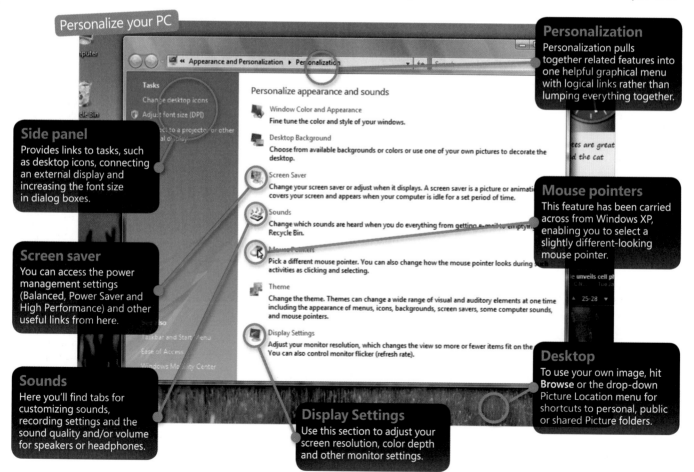

Personalize your PC

Personalization
Personalization pulls together related features into one helpful graphical menu with logical links rather than lumping everything together.

Side panel
Provides links to tasks, such as desktop icons, connecting an external display and increasing the font size in dialog boxes.

Mouse pointers
This feature has been carried across from Windows XP, enabling you to select a slightly different-looking mouse pointer.

Screen saver
You can access the power management settings (Balanced, Power Saver and High Performance) and other useful links from here.

Sounds
Here you'll find tabs for customizing sounds, recording settings and the sound quality and/or volume for speakers or headphones.

Display Settings
Use this section to adjust your screen resolution, color depth and other monitor settings.

Desktop
To use your own image, hit **Browse** or the drop-down Picture Location menu for shortcuts to personal, public or shared Picture folders.

Personal touch
Organize the Windows Sidebar and its gadgets

1 ALWAYS ON If you want the Sidebar to launch every time you turn on your computer, type 'sidebar' into **Start Search**. Now open **Windows Sidebar Properties** and check **Start Sidebar when Windows starts**.

2 STAY ON TOP To lock open windows against the Sidebar, click **Start → Control Panel → Appearance and Personalization → Windows Sidebar Properties** then check **Sidebar is always on top of other windows → Apply.**

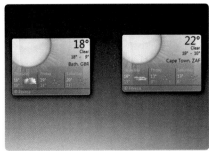

3 NEW TOYS Right-click on the Sidebar, choose **Add Gadgets**, then double-click a gadget. You can add the same gadget repeatedly, so you could load two weather gadgets – one for your hometown, one for a holiday destination.

4 MOVE ON Gadgets can be moved around your desktop. Right-click the gadget, select **Detach from Sidebar** and drag it where you want. If you want to move gadgets inside the Sidebar, drag them in the order you prefer.

a folder icon within All Programs, it expands the contents in a drop-down list. Click **Back** at the bottom of All Programs to return to the Start menu.

The Start menu can be customized by right-clicking the **Start** button, **Properties**, then **Customize** in the Start Menu tab. For instance, you can convert the Control Panel to a menu rather than a link. Here, because the link is the right side of the Start menu, you do get a fly-out menu. You can also ditch the Windows Vista menu's behavioral pattern completely by reverting to a Classic – Windows XP – menu style.

From the Start menu you can also change the appearance of Windows Vista, go to **Appearance and Personalization**, then **Personalization** and you can change your screen saver, cursor, desktop backgrounds; alter the screen resolution and monitor settings and customize sounds.

The Windows Sidebar

The Windows Sidebar sits on the side of your screen, organizing and managing your gadgets – mini programs that give access to frequently-used tools. A number of Sidebar gadgets come included with Windows Vista, including the incredibly useful Weather, Calendar, Clock and Currency converter.

Installing, adding and managing gadgets is simple. Use the guide (top right) then, once you've got the hang of moving gadgets about and getting

them to display information, you can go to Windows Live Gallery (gallery.live. com) or simply click **Get more gadgets online** in the Sidebar; you'll find a plethora to choose from. To download, just click on **Download → Open** and follow the prompts.

If you end up downloading loads of gadgets, don't worry about running out of space – if your Windows Sidebar starts to overflow, it will automatically create a new Sidebar that you can access by

pressing the arrow keys at the top. You can also use 'hotkeys' to cycle through gadgets. Pressing the **Windows** key and **Space** bar at the same time will bring all your gadgets to the front and select the Windows Sidebar. Pressing the **Windows** key and **G** will cycle through the gadgets and you can manipulate the one that is highlighted – pressing **Alt** and **F4** closes it. The gadgets can sit on your desktop if you prefer, but some may resize and take up more room.

Exploring the 2007 Microsoft Office system

Tap into the power, flexibility and user-friendliness of the 2007 Microsoft Office system to get the most out of your computer

The 2007 Microsoft Office system will revolutionize the way you write documents, create spreadsheets or organize your business.

When you fire it up for the first time it's hard not to be drawn towards the Microsoft Office Fluent interface and, in particular, the command Fluent Ribbon at the top of the screen. But don't think that it's mere eye candy – the Ribbon successfully brings to the fore all those tools and features you never knew existed in Microsoft Office.

It's not just about making existing features more visible though – the 2007 Office release boasts plenty of features that will quickly become indispensable. It's also designed to make it easier to share your documents with others, whether you're sending an invitation to friends or passing on a work-related file to colleagues.

It dovetails superbly with Microsoft Windows Vista, too; the instant search technology found in Microsoft Office Outlook 2007 is based on the Windows Vista desktop search tools, while the interface has been designed to complement the look and feel of Windows Vista.

The following pages will point you towards some of its best features and help you to get familiarized with a new, simplified way of working. ⊞

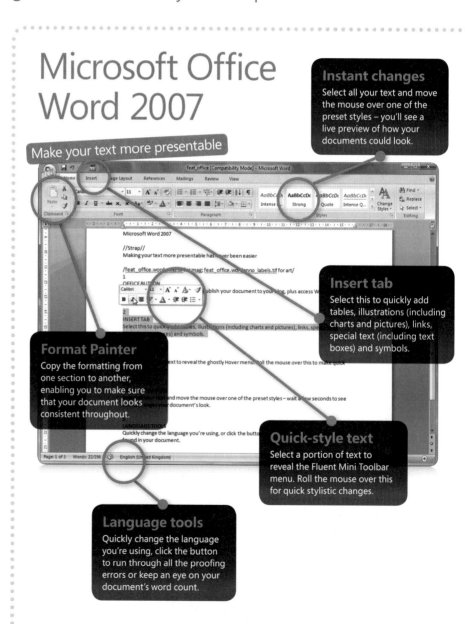

Microsoft Office Word 2007

Make your text more presentable

Instant changes
Select all your text and move the mouse over one of the preset styles – you'll see a live preview of how your documents could look.

Insert tab
Select this to quickly add tables, illustrations (including charts and pictures), links, special text (including text boxes) and symbols.

Format Painter
Copy the formatting from one section to another, enabling you to make sure that your document looks consistent throughout.

Quick-style text
Select a portion of text to reveal the Fluent Mini Toolbar menu. Roll the mouse over this for quick stylistic changes.

Language tools
Quickly change the language you're using, click the button to run through all the proofing errors or keep an eye on your document's word count.

Microsoft Office Excel 2007

Present data in an eye-catching way

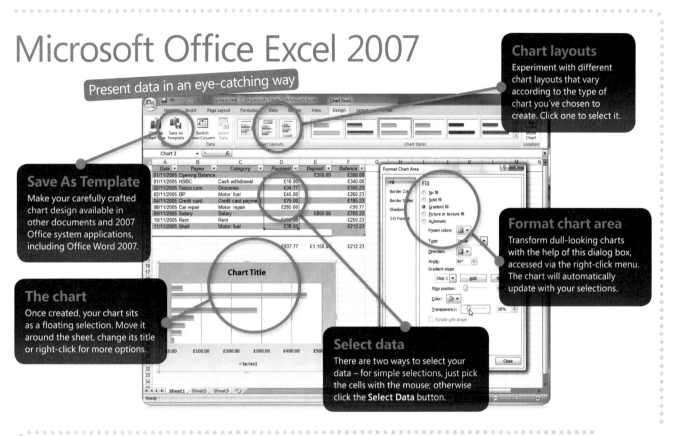

Chart layouts
Experiment with different chart layouts that vary according to the type of chart you've chosen to create. Click one to select it.

Save As Template
Make your carefully crafted chart design available in other documents and 2007 Office system applications, including Office Word 2007.

Format chart area
Transform dull-looking charts with the help of this dialog box, accessed via the right-click menu. The chart will automatically update with your selections.

The chart
Once created, your chart sits as a floating selection. Move it around the sheet, change its title or right-click for more options.

Select data
There are two ways to select your data – for simple selections, just pick the cells with the mouse; otherwise click the **Select Data** button.

Microsoft Office Outlook 2007

Tap into Outlook 2007's features

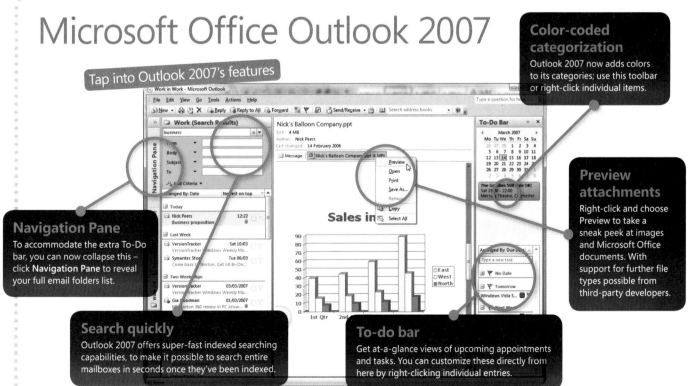

Color-coded categorization
Outlook 2007 now adds colors to its categories; use this toolbar or right-click individual items.

Preview attachments
Right-click and choose Preview to take a sneak peek at images and Microsoft Office documents. With support for further file types possible from third-party developers.

Navigation Pane
To accommodate the extra To-Do bar, you can now collapse this – click **Navigation Pane** to reveal your full email folders list.

Search quickly
Outlook 2007 offers super-fast indexed searching capabilities, to make it possible to search entire mailboxes in seconds once they've been indexed.

To-do bar
Get at-a-glance views of upcoming appointments and tasks. You can customize these directly from here by right-clicking individual entries.

Prepare your documents

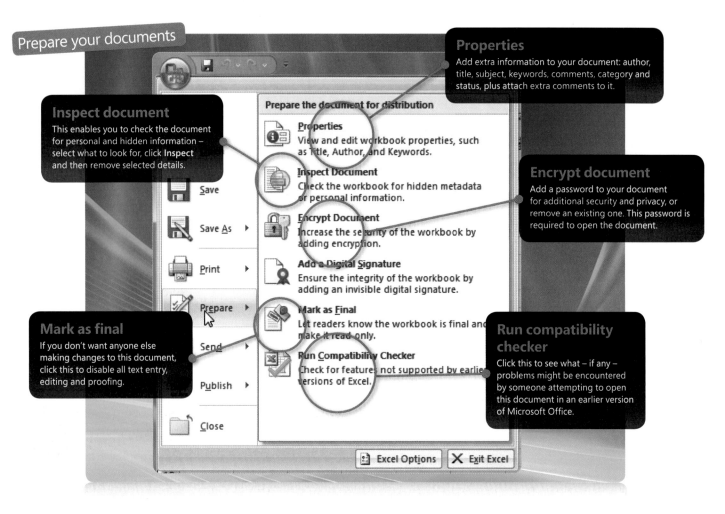

Properties
Add extra information to your document: author, title, subject, keywords, comments, category and status, plus attach extra comments to it.

Inspect document
This enables you to check the document for personal and hidden information – select what to look for, click **Inspect** and then remove selected details.

Encrypt document
Add a password to your document for additional security and privacy, or remove an existing one. This password is required to open the document.

Mark as final
If you don't want anyone else making changes to this document, click this to disable all text entry, editing and proofing.

Run compatibility checker
Click this to see what – if any – problems might be encountered by someone attempting to open this document in an earlier version of Microsoft Office.

Prepare the document for distribution

Properties
View and edit workbook properties, such as Title, Author, and Keywords.

Inspect Document
Check the workbook for hidden metadata or personal information.

Encrypt Document
Increase the security of the workbook by adding encryption.

Add a Digital Signature
Ensure the integrity of the workbook by adding an invisible digital signature.

Mark as Final
Let readers know the workbook is final and make it read-only.

Run Compatibility Checker
Check for features not supported by earlier versions of Excel.

Save
Save As
Print
Prepare
Send
Publish
Close

Excel Options   X Exit Excel

Sharing documents

If you're going to be sharing documents with others, consider the capabilities of their PC before doing so. If they'll need to edit the document, consider saving it in a format that will open in earlier versions of Microsoft Office (choose **Save as** from the Office button). If they just need to read or print the document, click the **Office** button and choose **Save as ➜ Find add-ins for other file formats**.

Download the Save as PDF or XPS plug-in and install; you can now convert documents to either format and attach them to an email via **Office ➜ Send menu**. Choosing either format ensures it will look the same on any PC. For more on sharing files, turn to page 180.

Publish your document

The 2007 Office system's Publish feature makes it easier than ever to share documents in a variety of different ways. You can burn your PowerPoint 2007 presentation to CD or post a Word 2007 document as a blog entry, for example.

To convert a Word 2007 document into a blog entry, click the **Office** button and choose **Publish ➜ Blog**. Follow the instructions to set up access to your existing blog account or sign up for a new account. Your document will appear in a new window with a Blog Post tab containing tools you can use to tweak your entry before uploading. For more on different ways of blogging, turn to pages 92, 94 and 150.

The quick access toolbar

You'll notice that there's a small toolbar sitting to the right of the Office button. This gives quick and easy access to the Save, Undo and Redo buttons. It can also be customized further to give access to just about any other command.

To add more options, simply right-click the **Office** button and choose **Customize Quick Access Toolbar**. To quickly add less visible options to the toolbar, select **Commands not in the ribbon**.

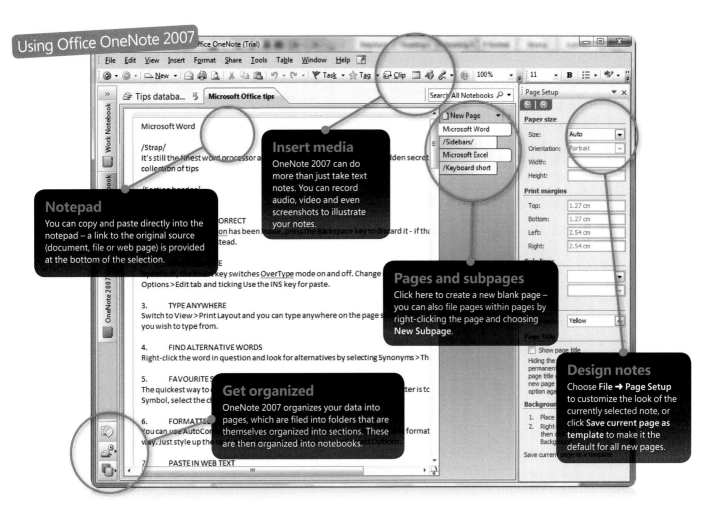

Using Office OneNote 2007

Notepad
You can copy and paste directly into the notepad – a link to the original source (document, file or web page) is provided at the bottom of the selection.

Insert media
OneNote 2007 can do more than just take text notes. You can record audio, video and even screenshots to illustrate your notes.

Pages and subpages
Click here to create a new blank page – you can also file pages within pages by right-clicking the page and choosing **New Subpage**.

Get organized
OneNote 2007 organizes your data into pages, which are filed into folders that are themselves organized into sections. These are then organized into notebooks.

Design notes
Choose **File ➜ Page Setup** to customize the look of the currently selected note, or click **Save current page as template** to make it the default for all new pages.

One for all

Sharing between Outlook 2007 and OneNote 2007 works both ways, so you can transfer emails, appointments and so on into new notes. After installation, OneNote 2007 places an icon next to the **Send/Receive** button in Outlook 2007. Clicking this creates a new note with the currently selected email message, plus any attachments. Similarly, right-clicking any appointment and choosing **Meeting Notes** creates a note with a link back to the original Outlook item.

Integrate OneNote with other programs

It's possible to transfer selected notes to other programs – you can insert notes into Outlook 2007 appointments and calendars by selecting **Tools ➜ Create Outlook Item**, for example; use the **File ➜ Send To** menu to attach the notes to an Outlook email or open them in Word as a document or blog entry. You can even publish notes as web pages using the **File ➜ Publish** option.

You'll find some of these options are also available by right-clicking different elements – for example, you can right-click a page and choose **Blog This** to transfer it to Microsoft Office Word 2007's blogging tool.

Scribble down notes

Office OneNote 2007 works with tablets and pens, enabling you to write notes instead of typing them; it works with a mouse, too, but the results are less impressive. The options you need can be found on the **Tools ➜ Pen Mode** sub-menu – you can scribble notes, make handwritten drawings or do a combination of both. If your writing is legible enough, you can then convert it into normal text by selecting **Tools ➜ Convert Handwriting to Text**.

To customize your pen in OneNote 2007, select **Tools ➜ Writing Notes ➜ Pens**. Then simply pick one of the Highlighter pens to quickly highlight parts of your notepad.

Explore

Now you're acquainted
with Windows Vista
and Microsoft Office,
it's time to see how
they can help you

The new way to keep in touch

Web mail users don't have to stick with two-dimensional online mailboxes. Get all the benefits of web mail but with the power of Windows Live Mail

In the early days of the internet, web mail helped change the face of email. It democratized the inbox for the masses, bringing email to those who accessed the web at libraries, cafés or work – not just those who paid premium rates.

A decade on, web mail is more important than ever. Services such as Windows Live Hotmail aren't just for email; they're essential for online messaging and can unlock a wealth of other uses. Unfortunately, one thing hasn't changed – the online mailbox.

Desktop mail users can enjoy the luxuries of new email notifications, synchronizations with web pages, easy organization, calendars, RSS feed readers and a variety of email enrichments. In most cases, web mail users can only dream of this kind of functionality. But you can now import Windows Live Hotmail into desktop mail clients...

On the lookout

If you're using Microsoft Office Outlook 2003 or 2007, you can download the Outlook Connector software, which enables you to import any Windows Live Hotmail or Office Live web mail account. Downloading the connector software is the only way to pair your Windows Live Hotmail account with Office Outlook.

It's easier to work with other web mail services, such as Yahoo! and Gmail, as these offer POP3 email settings that

allow you to connect with an existing client. In Office Outlook, just go to **Tools → Account settings**, then **Add accounts**. You will be asked to supply the POP3 and SMTP settings. These differ for each service, but for step-by-step guides head to office.microsoft.com.

If you're not using Office Outlook, you don't have to miss out on all the great functionality. If you're keen to bring web mail on to your desktop, Windows Live Mail is the software for you.

While Windows Mail, which ships with Windows Vista, was capable of handling most types of email, it wasn't able to handle Windows Live Hotmail accounts. Mail has now been superseded by Windows Live Mail, a new desktop client that can natively support Windows Live Hotmail accounts. You can also add any POP3-based web mail service, exactly the same as in Office Outlook.

In real life...
Take account

**Matt Hanson
Writer,
*Windows Vista: The Official Magazine***

While free web-based email allows me to have more than one account, checking my mails can be a protracted process of logging into each website to view my inboxes. Fortunately, I can now set my desktop mail client to connect to all web mail accounts, so I can view all my inboxes from the same location, without having to individually log in. Most desktop clients such as Microsoft Outlook will also display any inbox that has an unread email in bold, so you can check for new emails at a glance.

Learn the lingo

It's all easy to use, once you get your head round the abbreviations...

Web mail
Email services accessed by logging into a website are known as web mail. Popular services are Hotmail, Yahoo! and Gmail, but your Internet Service Provider (ISP) may also have a web mail service where you can log in to get your mail, as well as receiving it through Windows Mail or Microsoft Office Outlook.

POP3
Post Office Protocol version 3 lets you retrieve email from a remote server. (Your email provider holds your emails on its server.)

SMTP
Simple Mail Transfer Protocol is the standard for sending emails. Your email program is configured to know your ISP's SMTP address.

Get web mail on your desktop

Use Microsoft Office Outlook Connector to import your account

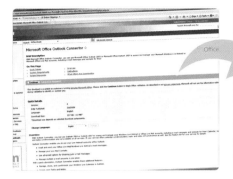

1 **DOWNLOAD** Head to www.microsoft.com/downloads and search for 'Microsoft Office Outlook Connector'. Download the software and install. Make sure that Microsoft Office is closed while you're installing the Outlook Connector.

2 **SET UP** When you load up Office Outlook, you'll see a menu that asks for the login details of your Windows Live Hotmail account. Enter your username and password, and press **OK**. You'll then need to restart Office Outlook.

3 **CONNECT** When you restart Office Outlook you'll see your Windows Live Hotmail added to the list. Your messages will be synchronized automatically. (To synchronize calendars and notes, you'll need the paid subscription version.)

Desktop mail users can enjoy the luxuries of notifications, synchronizations, RSS feeds and a variety of enrichments

4 **ADD MORE** In Office Outlook you'll also notice a new addition to the menu. The Outlook Connector tab enables you to add more Windows Live accounts or to manage your existing ones. Go to **Outlook Connector → Add Account** to add a Windows Live Hotmail or Office Live email account.

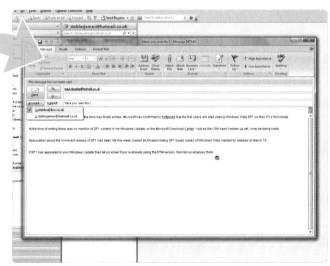

What a picture!

Sending photographic attachments used to slow delivery, clog up a recipient's inbox or stop mail getting through; Windows Live Mail sends a thumbnail that can be clicked on to view a full size image online.

5 **SEND** When you compose a new message, you can choose which account you want to use by clicking the drop-down option in the top corner. The list of email addresses will be displayed, so just click on the one you want to use.

Fulfilling the role of divine messenger

Why pay for a phone call when you can chat for free – and more – via Windows Live Messenger?

So Windows Live Mail is the answer to your email dreams, but how about spontaneous repartee? Windows Live Messenger complements Live Mail perfectly, enabling you to chat and share photos – instantly – with friends and family all over the world.

Like Windows Live Mail, Live Messenger is multi-account friendly, so if your friends are on Facebook or Bebo (or other social network sites) you can sign them up to your contacts in Messenger. And if you have a webcam, you can chat face to face, so no matter how far away your friends are it'll feel like you've just hooked up with them in the local coffee house. If you frequently suffer from bad hair days, though, you could invest in a microphone and speakers or a headset, and just chat as though you were on the phone – for free! (Or call their landline or cell number at a very low rate.) What if your friend happens to be away from their PC? Well, you can just text your message to their cell phone number.

Windows Live Messenger is not just about instantaneous chat, though...

If you're using Live Messenger as a kind of a conference call facility, for instance, your colleagues can also gain access to selected files of yours. And as part of its social network armory, whenever a friend updates their profile in Windows Live Spaces, you'll see an icon appear next to their name in Windows Live Messenger, keeping you informed of when they upload photographs or add a new blog post, so you won't be the last person to know when something's happening.

Not in the mood for idle gossip or a lengthy work discussion? Well, if you're simply feeling a little playful, why not challenge your friend to an online game, such as chess or Uno?

More Messenger

Windows Live Messenger enables you to communicate in many ways

■ **FACE TO FACE** If you have a webcam, Windows Live Messenger can deliver high-quality video chat.

■ **ID PARADE** The latest Windows Live Photo Gallery beta identifies faces in pictures, so you can tag them using your Windows Live Messenger contacts.

■ **GAME ON** Challenge a friend to one of the many free online games that come with Live Messenger.

■ **TEXT CHAT** If you'd rather not get into an instant chat, text your message to a cell phone instead.

■ **PERSONAL PROFILE** Change your message backgrounds, choose a photo or even add crazy noises to catch your friends' attention.

STAY IN TOUCH Windows Live Messenger makes it easy to keep in contact with friends

In real life...
Talk is cheap

**Nick Odantzis
Writer,
Windows Vista: The
Official Magazine**

Using Windows Live Messenger is so easy, as I can contact friends just by searching for their email address. The really great thing about Windows Live Messenger is that it comes with built-in video calling. When I start a conversation with someone else with a webcam, I just click the Video button at the top of the menu and we can see each other while we're chatting. I can even watch it in full screen to really see what's going on!

Eye-to-eye contact

Meeting up with friends, the easy way

1 WINDOWS LIVE INSTALLER This automatically installs everything you need for Windows Live Messenger. When you load Live Messenger you're asked to sign in. If you don't have a Windows Live ID, click **Sign up for a Windows Live ID**.

2 SIGN IN In the 'Sign in as' drop-down list you can change how you appear when you sign in. The default is Online, which means your contacts can see that you're online and available to talk. Other options include Away and Busy.

3 MAKE CONTACT Click **Add a contact**. You can add the email address of the person you want to add as a contact. If they don't have a Windows Live ID, you can invite them to install Live Messenger and create a Windows Live ID.

No matter how far away your friends are, it'll feel like you've just hooked up with them in the local coffee house

4 SEE YOUR FRIENDS Once you've added your contacts, or they have added you, you'll be able to see who is online at the time. Double-clicking your contact's name will bring up the conversation window, from where you can launch your video call. Click **Start Video Call** to begin a webcam chat.

Download it now!

Go to get.live.com/messenger to download Windows Live Messenger for free. From here you can also check out the new features in the latest version. Once downloaded, the Windows Live Installer program runs.

5 GET TALKING For best results make sure your webcam is positioned correctly, and the room you're sitting in is well lit. If you're using a microphone, make sure you're sitting the right distance from it, and that you talk clearly. To adjust any of the webcam settings, go to **Show → Tools → Webcam settings**.

Keep in contact the easy way

Keep communication simple yet versatile with the handiest address book – Windows Contacts

You can use Windows to keep track of people you need to stay in touch with by using the address book that comes with it – Windows Contacts. Enter the details, then when you need to look up a friend's email address or phone number, you can open your Contacts folder and find it there.

No surprises. But Windows Contacts goes a step further. You can also add copious notes to people's profiles. No matter what type of contact information you want to remember about someone, you can put it in the Contacts folder – even a picture. The photo element is great for when you can't put a face to a name before picking up the phone or typing a new message. And the notes element makes sure you look as informed as possible when dealing with business associates, customers or even friends. If you're simultaneously working on a number of projects with different contacts at the same company, you can make sure you never send an email to the wrong person. Alternatively, you can add minutiae such as 'prefers to take calls after lunch' or 'Friendly guy I met in bar the other night, has contacts in

the outside catering trade – may be good contact for Jenny's party'. The sort of thing that you can't always tap into the contact details on a cell phone, for example...

Obviously, the Contacts folder also functions as the address book for Windows Mail. When you create an email message in Windows Mail, you select the recipient from your Contacts folder. In fact, even if you don't use Windows Mail as your email program, you can still use Windows Contacts to store information about people you correspond with.

You can also create contact groups, which combine individual contacts into a single group. This collection of contacts simplifies the process of sending email to multiple addressees, especially if you find yourself sending to the same group of people on a regular basis.

In addition to using Windows Contacts to address your own email messages and store information, you can also easily send contacts to other people. There's no need to manually type a bunch of telephone numbers, addresses and other contact information into an email message – just send them a contact profile containing all the information you want to share.

Compile a profile

Windows Contacts can be a mine of information

■ **EMAIL ADDRESSES** Store as many email addresses as you want for a contact, and set one as the preferred address.
■ **CONTACT PHOTO** Adding a picture of a contact can help you remember the person.
■ **PHONE NUMBERS** Store home, work, cell phone, and fax numbers for a contact.
■ **ADDRESSES** You can store both home and work street addresses for a correspondent.
■ **FAMILY INFORMATION** You can enter information here about a contact, their spouse or partner, children, gender, birthday and wedding anniversary.
■ **WEBSITE LOCATIONS** You can store both home and work website URLs for a contact.

Create a contact list

How to make and amend your correspondents

1 OPEN UP Open Windows Contacts by clicking on the Start button, clicking **All Programs**, and then clicking **Windows Contacts**.

2 ADD NEW Click **New Contact**, and then type the information you want for the contact in any of the boxes on the available tabs.

Get it together

Create a group to speed up sending mail to multiple recipients

1 GROUP GENERATION Click **New Contact Group**, type in a group name, then fill in the Contact Group tabs.

2 ADD PEOPLE To add existing contacts, click **Add to Contact Group**. To create new contacts, click **Create New Contact**.

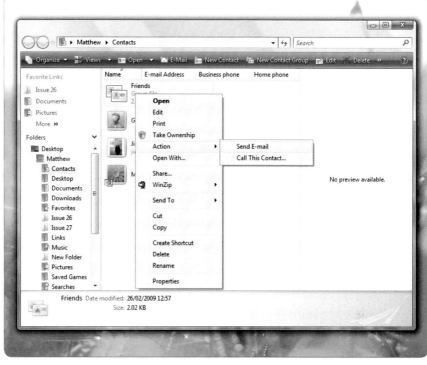

3 MULTI SEND You can now send an email message to a group that you've created using Windows Mail. Open Windows Contacts, right-click a contact group, point to **Action**, and then click on **Send Email**.

3 MAKE AMENDS Double-click the contact you want to change. Click the tab where you want to add info, and then type in any of the available boxes.

4 ADD PICTURE Double-click a contact. In the **Name and email** tab, click the picture, then **Change picture**. Locate the image you want; click it and click **Open**.

Network choices

There are several cutting-edge technologies you can use to network with Windows Vista...

If you've got more than one computer in your household, Windows Vista can help them talk to each other, and this will open up a whole new world of PC and internet convenience. A Local Area Network (LAN), is easier to connect and configure than ever using Windows Vista, thanks to the unified Network and Sharing Center. This feature intelligently configures network devices, setting up most connections automatically, and provides a central place for monitoring connections and hardware.

With a home network you can share

You can share an internet connection and swap files

one internet connection between several computers, see shared folders on connected machines and swap files. You can use connected devices like printers, and stream movies and music from one computer to another. All you need to do is choose the hardware configuration.

Here's a look at the three most common network configurations available; starting with wired connections, moving on to wireless networks and rounding off with a look at the world of powerline devices. Each set-up has its own strengths and weaknesses – detailed here so you can make an informed choice for your home.

If you're concerned about networking because of a lack of PC knowledge, it's worth noting that Windows Vista boasts a simple Network Map that provides a visual report on connected devices. If a device does not appear, it is not working, and you can then investigate the problem further. (If you experience internet issues, turn to page 32 for more advice.)

"Wow" At your service

Since the introduction of the Windows Vista Service Pack 1 upgrade, browsing and sharing files over your network can be up to 50 per cent faster

Learn the lingo

If you're thinking of linking, it's worth knowing the terminology

TCP/IP
A set of network communication protocols that enable your computer to communicate with others over a network. The abbreviation stands for Transfer Control Protocol/Internet Protocol.

LAN
A Local Area Network is a collection of networked computers within a geographically small area, like your home or office.

DHCP
Dynamic Host Configuration Protocol. This system, built into network routers and Windows Vista, allocates your computer a unique numerical address.

Megabit
A megabit is a unit of data equivalent to 125kb – about 60 pages of raw text.

Firewall
A program that restricts access to sections of a network by unauthorized users or software.

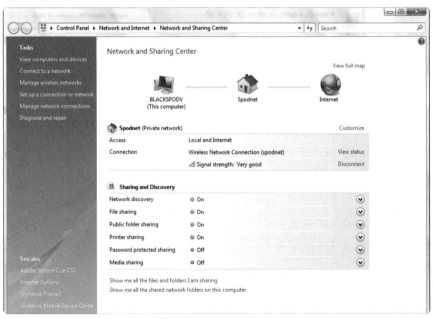

HIGH COMMAND The Network and Sharing Center is a central hub for all your network needs

Wired networking

Easy and reliable, just watch out for all those wires...

In Windows Vista, the easiest network to set up is, generally speaking, a wired network. If your machine is up to Windows Vista specifications it will almost definitely have an Ethernet port. Ethernet is a well established technology for connecting a LAN using cables. Older Ethernet cards are capable of moving data at 10 Megabits per second (Mbps) – a little faster than the average 8Mbps broadband connection. Newer 'Fast Ethernet' cards are 10 times faster, transferring data at 100Mbps – fast enough to stream high-quality video. The top speed for home computers is Gigabit Ethernet – operating at 1,000Mbps.

You can create an 'ad-hoc network' by connecting two computers with Ethernet ports and an Ethernet cable. 'Plug and Play' networking takes care of the rest.

A more reliable way to network is to use a 'router'. This is a device with multiple Ethernet ports that manages your network for you. It does this by assigning a unique numerical address to each of your connected machines. This process uses the same protocol as your internet connection – known as TCP/IP – to get your computers talking. Many internet service providers (ISPs) supply you with a router that doubles as a broadband modem. Several ISPs supply routers with four Ethernet ports – giving even more flexibility. If you're on broadband but were supplied with an ADSL modem instead, you should be able to replace it with a modern ADSL router. Many routers now boast wireless capability.

The alternative to a router is a 'switch'. This is a similar device but with fewer features. While a modern home router will usually have internet connectivity and a built-in firewall, a switch simply enables you to connect multiple machines on a network via the Ethernet. (Additional Ethernet cables can be bought cheaply enough.)

For and against

Pros

✔ Wired networks offer the fastest, most reliable data transfer rates. Gigabit Ethernet can be used for up to 100m using copper wire cables.

✔ Ethernet is more secure than other networking methods. The only way in for an intruder is through a computer on your network, or an open port over the internet.

Cons

✘ Ethernet networks mean trailing cable – the more computers connected, the more internetti spaghetti.

✘ You need additional hardware to set up an Ethernet network.

INS & OUTS Some routers offer four Ethernet ports and a built-in ADSL modem for internet connectivity

Setting up a wired network

Configure an Ethernet-powered network with the Network and Sharing Center

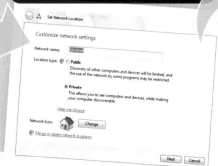

1 SET-UP Follow the network router's installation instructions. You should be prompted to connect an Ethernet cable to a port on the router, with the other end plugged in to your computer's Ethernet port. Switch on the device.

2 NAMING NAMES You should be prompted to configure your network. Fill in a network name and choose the **Private** checkbox. This will enable other computers connected to the network to find your machine.

3 GOING LIVE Don't worry if the Network dialog box doesn't appear. Go to Start and choose **Network ➔ Network and Sharing Center**. Your network should be live – you can access the configuration dialog by clicking **Customize**.

Wireless networking

Freedom from wires but there are limits

With wireless networking – often called Wi-Fi – data is transferred between your machines over radio waves. To set up your own Wi-Fi network you'll need a wireless router or hub and Wi-Fi adaptors in each connected machine.

A wireless router is very like a wired Ethernet router. It does the donkey work of configuring your network, assigning numerical addresses to connected machines. However, a wireless router can connect more Wi-Fi enabled machines together – as many as 70 in some cases.

Wi-Fi adaptors enable your computer to send and receive data to/from the wireless router. You may have one already built into your machine. If not, you have a couple of choices... The first is to fit a Wi-Fi card into a spare slot in your desktop computer, which involves opening up your machine and manually fitting the hardware. Cards can be bought for as little as $30. Although fairly easy

to fit, you need to know the exact specifications of your motherboard and the slot types before you buy the card. Most cards will fit into a spare PCI slot.

Alternatively, you can opt for a less invasive USB adaptor; these are similarly priced to Wi-Fi cards.

The most common networking protocol for wireless devices is known as 802.11. The most widespread version at the moment is 802.11g – a wireless standard that allows data rates of up to 54Mbps with a range of 35 meters. Devices using the newer version of the standard – 802.11n – are available; they're more expensive, but are five times faster and have double the effective range of the older protocol.

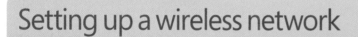

N FOR NEW Combine a wireless USB adaptor with your 802.11n wireless router to add high-speed Wi-Fi capability

For and against
Pros
✔ With a wireless adaptor installed in your laptop, you can connect to public Wi-Fi 'hotspots'. Find them with online help from Wi-Fi-FreeSpot (www.wififreespot.com).

✔ Wireless networking is the clutter-free solution, with no trailing wires or cables to trip over.

Cons
✘ Your network will have a limited range and the signal may not penetrate well through thick internal walls.

✘ Wireless is the least secure networking method. It's difficult to capture or crack the password encryption but dedicated hackers can do it.

Setting up a wireless network

Secure Wi-Fi connections in just a couple of clicks with Windows Vista

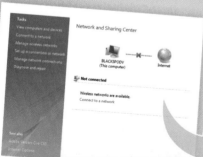

1 OPEN SESAME Some Wi-Fi adaptors ship with proprietary software. If you're prompted to use this to connect to your network, click **No**. Instead, open up the Network and Sharing Center.

2 FIND THE LOCK Click on the link labeled **Wireless Networks are Available: Connect to a Network**. A box appears listing your router's network. Select it and click **Connect**. You'll be prompted for a security key.

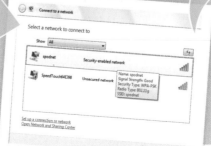

3 TURN THE KEY Check your router's documentation for the default security key – a sequence of numbers and letters – and enter it. Once connected you will see the network enabled, with an icon showing the Wi-Fi signal strength.

Powerline networking
An adaptable and powerful plug-in option

While Wi-Fi dominates the network market, there's an economical alternative that combines the range of an Ethernet system with the mobility of wireless. Powerline networking uses an electrical mains loop to transfer data. You don't need a router or switch; you need a HomePlug device (a separate device is required for each computer).

A typical HomePlug device looks like a mains adaptor and, indeed, plugs directly into any 240-volt power point. This means you can quickly install a network point wherever there's a heavy-duty electrical outlet. You can also use it in combination with other methods; for example, you might use a Wi-Fi capable HomePlug to extend the range of your wireless router.

There are several different powerline protocols in use, but the most popular HomePlug standard comes in two speeds. HomePlug 1.0 Turbo enables data transfer rates of up to 85Mbps. The newer HomePlug AV can manage 189Mbps, making it ideal for streaming video files.

Typically, a HomePlug device creates a closed ring – but there is a possibility that data could be accessed by others close by. To help secure your network, HomePlug devices come with built-in password protection; to access your network, you need to enter the password.

HomePlug devices may also ship with an extra program that enables you to access the plug's internal software and change passwords, set-up a default IP address or monitor your HomePlug network. Otherwise, configuring and setting up a HomePlug network on Windows Vista is similar to setting up any other wired or wireless network.

POWER PACK These simple plug-in devices manage to offer both range and mobility

For and against
Pros
✔ Powerline devices offer great flexibility and range, with network access points available wherever you have a mains socket.

✔ You can easily extend an existing Ethernet or Wi-Fi network to any part of your living space using a HomePlug device.

Cons
✘ Some devices can get very hot over long periods of use. Watch out for flimsy construction as cases can crack over time.

✘ Most HomePlug devices ship with built-in, fixed addresses and additional, bespoke software is required to configure them.

Setting up a fixed IP
Create network connections and Windows Workgroups with fixed IP addresses

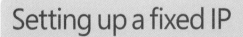

1 TEAMWORK If the computers on your network fail to find each other, make sure they share the same 'workgroup' name. Go to Start, right-click **Computer**, choose **Properties** and click **Change Settings** to rename the workgroup.

2 PROTOCOL Set a fixed IP for your main machine. Go to the Network and Sharing Center and click **Manage Network Settings**. Right-click on the **Local Area Connection** (click **Continue** when prompted). Choose **Internet Protocol v4** and click **Properties**.

3 CATCH THEM ALL Here you can enter a fixed IP address – try 192.168.2.1. Click the **Subnet mask** link to auto-fill it. On connected machines, set their IP address to 192.168.2.2, 192.168.2.3 and so on – setting the gateway field on these to 192.168.2.1.

Solve network niggles

Sorting out network problems can seem like a black art. Unveil the mystery by following these simple steps when connectivity fails you

The ubiquity of broadband means that many of us now own a router – essentially a network in a box. Reliability is improving, but sometimes things can go wrong...

There are three potential 'fail points' with a connection to the internet. Firstly, there's the connection itself – a problem with your phone line or ISP, for example. Secondly, there's the router and how it's configured. Is it set up correctly? Finally, there's the PC settings – how it connects to the router and how it's configured.

If you connect to your router via a wired connection, it's likely the problem will be with your internet connection or the router, rather than the PC. Wireless connections are more tricky.

Fortunately, networking within your computer is handled in Windows Vista, which uses The Network and Sharing Center as a nexus where you can set up, troubleshoot and modify connections.

Before starting, it's important to know that the problem might not be with your PC or router at all – there may be a problem at your ISP's end, with your local exchange, or even your phone line (check with your line supplier for slow or poor connection issues). Equally, if you've only tried to access a single website, the problem might be with the site itself. Try other sites and your email, too.

If you still can't connect to the internet, look for the networking icon – the two mini computers – in your system tray. A globe here indicates an internet connection, so the problem is likely to be with your PC's settings. If there are just the computers and the globe is missing, then you have a connection to the router, but not to the internet, so the problem is likely to be with your router. If there's a cross by the two computers, your connection is broken; unfortunately, in this case, the problem could lie anywhere.

The first thing you should try is restarting your router. Networking connections can sometimes 'drop out' unexpectedly. After that, if you think you've diagnosed the problem to be within Windows Vista, right-click the networking icon and select **Diagnose and Repair** from the menu. The powerful Windows Networking Diagnostics feature should be able to determine most issues with your PC.

Common wireless issues

If you connect to your wireless network with a laptop, it's worth checking to make sure your wireless on/off switch hasn't been accidentally turned off. Windows only sees itself as connected or disconnected, so it won't tell you if this is the problem. The switches are usually found on the side of your laptop or designated a function key shortcut.

You should also check your signal. To find out how strong your signal is, hover over the network connection icon in your system tray; a bar graph will appear indicating strength. This shouldn't be the issue unless you have a very weak signal, but factors such as wall thickness and proximity to other wireless devices can affect performance.

It's also possible that there's a hardware fault with your PC, although it's unlikely if you've connected wirelessly before. However, if you've recently installed new hardware, ensure that you've done everything in the order the instructions tell you to and you've checked for software updates.

These solutions will solve most common problems, but if you're still stuck, log on to support.microsoft.com or check out the forum at www.windowsvistamagazine.com. ⊞

Firewall issues

Keep connected: how to let useful programs through

Firewalls can pose a real hurdle to connectivity. If your browser, email client or other internet-bound application isn't allowed through your security, it isn't going to work. Third-party firewall applications, from the likes of McAfee or Norton, can seem particularly aggressive in this regard, as they will initially block even common programs such as Internet Explorer.

It's essential that you configure the firewall you've installed to let useful programs through. The same is also true of the Windows Firewall in Windows Vista. The first time you run a new application that needs internet connectivity, Windows Firewall may ask if you want to allow it through; you'll need to go to the Firewall settings in Control Panel and click **Allow a program through Windows Firewall**. You'll be able to allow the application and the program will be able to access your internet connection.

Problem with surfing the web?

If your connection looks fine but you can't view pages, try this

1 NOT CONNECTED? IPv6 (Internet Protocol version 6) is a relatively new technology supported by Windows Vista, but it's not common in other devices. Don't worry if your router doesn't support IPv6, because it can be disabled.

2 DIAGNOSTIC CHECK Check your connection using Windows Network Diagnostics. Right-click on your network connection in the System Tray, then select **Diagnose and Repair**; this may well solve your difficulties.

3 CONNECTIONS If that's unsuccessful, go to the Network and Sharing Center and click **Manage Network Connections**. Or go to **Control Panel → Network and Internet → Network Connections** to see all your different connections displayed.

4 SELECT THE PROBLEM Find the connection you're trying to use from the options; right-click on its network adaptor and select **Properties**. When the User Access Control prompt appears, click **Continue**.

Select Diagnose and Repair: the Windows Networking Diagnostics feature should be able to determine most issues

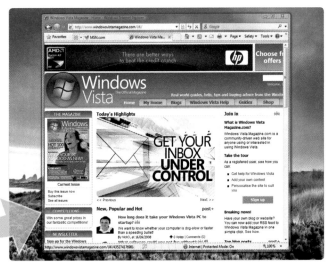

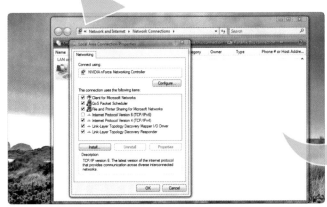

5 CLEAR THE BOX In the Properties box that appears, clear the check box next to 'Internet Protocol version 6 (TCP/IPv6)'. It's found in the component list under 'This connection uses the following items'.

6 CAN YOU SURF? Finally, click **OK**. (If at any time you should need to re-enable IPv6 for the connection, you can always return to **Properties** and check the box again.) You should now be able to surf the web normally, but if you're still unable to see pages, the problem lies elsewhere.

You *can* make a spreadsheet sparkle!

Number crunching doesn't have to be laborious. With Office Excel 2007 you'll find an array of features that will bring clarity and interest to your calculations

The spreadsheet no longer has to be a limited, lifeless list of figures. Excel 2007 addresses any former capacity issues and brings a range of visual tricks to the table (ahem). Spreadsheet capabilities have been expanded to cope with over a million rows and 16,384 columns in a single worksheet, smashing the previous 65,536 row and 256 column limits. Excel 2007 can also handle longer text values and more complex formulas. And if you want to push the application, it supports multiple-core processors, dividing up tough tasks between the cores for the fastest processing possible.

While these technical background enhancements are impressive, the interface hasn't been overlooked. The charts feature, for instance, has had a complete overhaul. While in past versions this has been comprehensive, the end results looked a little ancient, so the style update transforms the look.

In a similar vein, Conditional Formatting has evolved into a simple yet more powerful feature. It's now easier than ever to add formatting based on the values in cells. This is further enhanced with icon-based options and data bars that are sized depending on the range of data.

The Styles system found in Word 2007 appears within Excel 2007 in two guises; styles can be applied to elements of a spreadsheet such as tables, charts and other objects, while themes can be applied to the entire spreadsheet enabling you to quickly style up a document or keep a coherent style within a company.

In addition to all these features, Excel 2007 also provides assistance. An improved Page Layout mode keeps a document better formatted for printing; PivotTable allows multiple layers of data to be drilled down through the data, and improved filtering, sorting and AutoFilter are welcome. A resizeable Formula bar that supports Function AutoComplete is the fancy bow on this impressive parcel of improvements. ⊞

Top features

With Excel 2007, your finances will be looking good

■ CAPACITY Supports worksheets with over one million rows and over 16,000 columns
■ FORMAT Enhanced Conditional Formatting offers colors scales, icons and data bars
■ CONTROL Column titles display mini toolbars to control layout
■ VIEW Page Layout view displays worksheets as they will print
■ CHART New charting engine supports advanced formatting and 3D rendering, transparencies and soft shadows
■ CREATE Easy to use PivotTables with improved data layer support
■ HELP Formula Autocomplete means that you write the correct syntax every time
■ FILTER Improved sorting and filtering, such as multi-select in AutoFilter functions
■ SHARE Use Excel services to more securely share spreadsheets and data with others

FUNCTION AND FLAIR Use Excel 2007 to convey your data with clarity and creativity

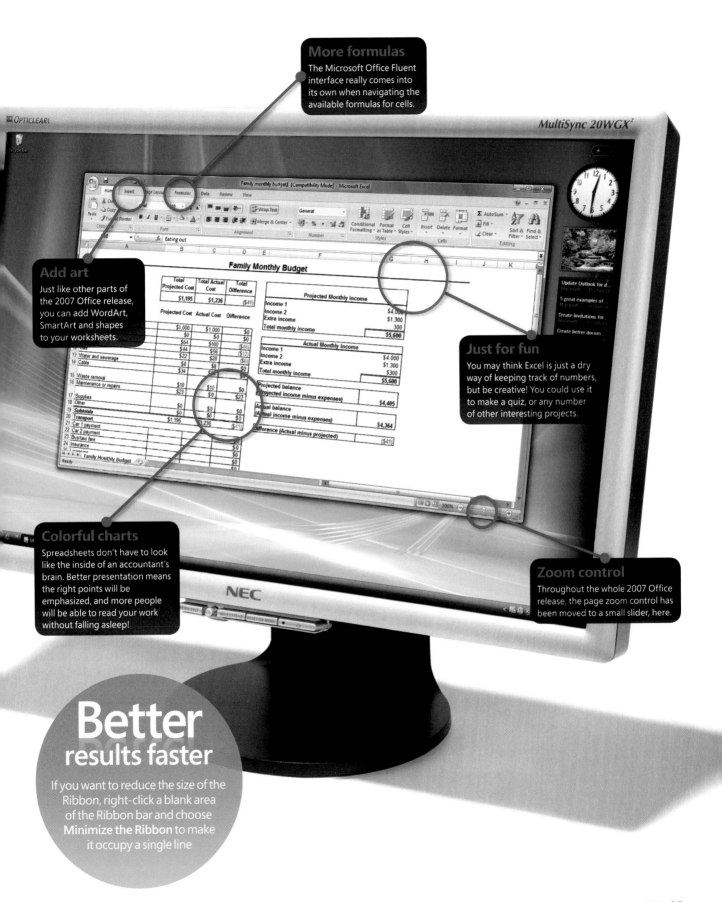

More formulas
The Microsoft Office Fluent interface really comes into its own when navigating the available formulas for cells.

Add art
Just like other parts of the 2007 Office release, you can add WordArt, SmartArt and shapes to your worksheets.

Colorful charts
Spreadsheets don't have to look like the inside of an accountant's brain. Better presentation means the right points will be emphasized, and more people will be able to read your work without falling asleep!

Just for fun
You may think Excel is just a dry way of keeping track of numbers, but be creative! You could use it to make a quiz, or any number of other interesting projects.

Zoom control
Throughout the whole 2007 Office release, the page zoom control has been moved to a small slider, here.

Better results faster
If you want to reduce the size of the Ribbon, right-click a blank area of the Ribbon bar and choose **Minimize the Ribbon** to make it occupy a single line

Give your clients quality quotes

Microsoft Office Excel can produce quick quotes but it's not just businesses that benefit from spreadsheets

Microsoft Office Excel 2007 is a flexible program but many people want to know about one particular way of making the most of it... one reader, Ken Woodhouse, contacted *Windows Vista: The Official Magazine* to ask about using Excel 2007 to produce a quote.

Ken, who runs a framing business, explains: "I need to present customers with a quote based on materials and time, which I usually prepare by hand, but I'd like to be able to do this more quickly. I've got the 2007 Office release and wondered if I could use Excel to generate my quotes. I'm not a computer genius so I need something that's simple to use but that will still look good when I present it to clients."

Well, Ken couldn't have chosen a better time to get acquainted with Excel because the 2007 Office release provides the most streamlined design so far. It's particularly good for novices because while Excel 2007 has loads of features,

the Microsoft Office Fluent interface ensures you only see the tools that you're likely to be using at any particular time. A stocklist for building a quote is an ideal use for a spreadsheet because, once you've got the basics, you simply select the items that you need and it does all the number-crunching for you.

Supply and demand

Assuming you have a limited number of materials that you regularly use, and you need to charge for your time, your spreadsheet should list each material and the cost of each item by unit. In ➡

Spread better

Make your spreadsheet look professional to impress your clients

You can quickly make a spreadsheet look nice using a couple of tools on the Fluent interface. Highlight all the cells by clicking and dragging over them. Now select the Design tab. Choose **Quick Styles** from the Table styles section. Roll the mouse over each style and you see a preview on your table. When you find a style you like, click it to apply it.

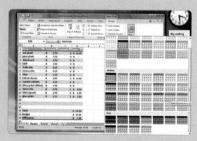

LOOKING GOOD Use Table styles to give your spreadsheet a professional sheen

HOME PLAN You can use Excel 2007 to budget for anything – including redesigning your home

Better results faster

If your spreadsheet goes beyond one page but you want to see all the totals, go to the **View** tab. In the **Window** area, click the button to the right of **New Window** to split the screen into handy scrollable parts

You thought Excel was just for the office...

An Excel 2007 spreadsheet can be applied to a number of jobs

1 TAKE-OUT MENU Enter your favorite dishes and prices from your local restaurant and the amount of money you have to spend on your meal to make sure you make the most of your budget.

2 HOLIDAY COSTS If you prefer planning your own holiday rather than using a travel agent's package deal, use a similar spreadsheet to keep track of hotels, travel fares and other expenses.

3 PC BUDGET Planning to put together your own PC? Use the spreadsheet to list the cost of the components that you'll use and make sure that you stay within your computer-building budget.

A budget is the ideal use for a spreadsheet because Excel 2007 does the number-crunching for you

4 STATE OF YOUR WALLET Want to invest in some state-of-the-art home entertainment? Why not use the spreadsheet to help you work out the best technology for your budget, where to shop from and what you might have to save up for?

Get connected

Why not connect your Excel 2007 spreadsheet to an Access 2007 database, linking data, such as prices, between the two? When the database is updated, so is your spreadsheet, so your quotes are always correct.

5 CHILDREN'S PARTY Your little one's having a party and you need to make sure that all 12 guests get an equal favor bag. Use the spreadsheet to try out different combinations of candy and toys without blowing your expenses.

the case of time this can be per hour, and any other item can be costed in the quantities usually charged by your supplier (by the foot or a particular weight, for instance).

Having listed each of these along with your costs, you supply the quantities required and can then work out a cost for each item based on its quantity. By using the right formula, in this case =B2*C2, you can get Excel 2007 to work this out, multiplying the unit price by the quantity.

Having worked out the cost of each item required, all that's left is to add them up to get a total. The Autosum tool is ideal for this because it simply adds up all the items in a particular column or row. The walkthrough below shows how to put together a simple spreadsheet based on these requirements.

In the real world, most people are asked to create a quote based on a budget, so you should make sure that this is listed on the spreadsheet, too. With a further formula, you can get Excel 2007 to work out whether you're over or under budget as you go. Enter the formula =[cell containing the budget]-[cell containing the total]. If you do come in over budget, you can always look at cutting back on

materials or requesting an appropriate increase in the overall budget.

By using conditional formatting you can make the difference between the total cost and the budget appear in red if you've gone over budget. Select the cell with this figure in and click **Conditional Formatting** above Styles. Now choose **Highlight Cells Rules ➜ Less than**. This opens a dialog box. Enter the figure zero below the label **Format cells that are LESS THAN**. Select the formatting you want from the drop-down list. You can choose red text, though light red fill with dark red text is effective. Click **OK** to confirm. Now this cell shows you at a glance if you're over budget or not.

Freeze frame

If you often use more materials than can comfortably fit on one screen, you may need to ensure that the header row is visible at all times. You can do this by freezing that portion of the pane, and allowing the rest of the sheet to scroll independently. Select cell A2 and then move to the View tab above the Fluent interface. In the section marked Window, select **Freeze panes ➜ Freeze top row**. You can now flick through the rest of the spreadsheet without losing the top row.

In real life...
Chart your progress

Adam Oxford Contributor, *Windows Vista: The Official Magazine*

I only really started using Excel 2007 after I learnt how to work with multiple worksheets at once. Comparing budgets for projects at work was so much more straightforward when I could fill in each as a separate worksheet, and then instantly call up a graph comparing the two. It's amazing how quickly you gain competence when you start experimenting.

The spreadsheet designed in this example can be used for almost any stock budgeting exercise you need to do. The principle of dealing with unit prices, quantities and totals applies in many different situations.

Many people find dealing with money intimidating and worry about getting their sums right, but you don't need to be a genius to set up this spreadsheet and get it working for you. ⊞

Do quote me on that
Set up your basic quote spreadsheet from scratch

1 CREATE HEADINGS Starting with a completely blank spreadsheet, enter the following headings into the top cells of columns A to D: Item, Unit Cost, Quantity and Cost.

2 PRICE LIST Now enter the data that will remain the same each time you use the spreadsheet. In column A enter each material you use plus one entry for labor. Put the prices in column B.

3 CURRENCY FORMAT To get the prices to appear as money, highlight column B by clicking the **B** at the top. Above Number on the Fluent interface, click the **Currency button**.

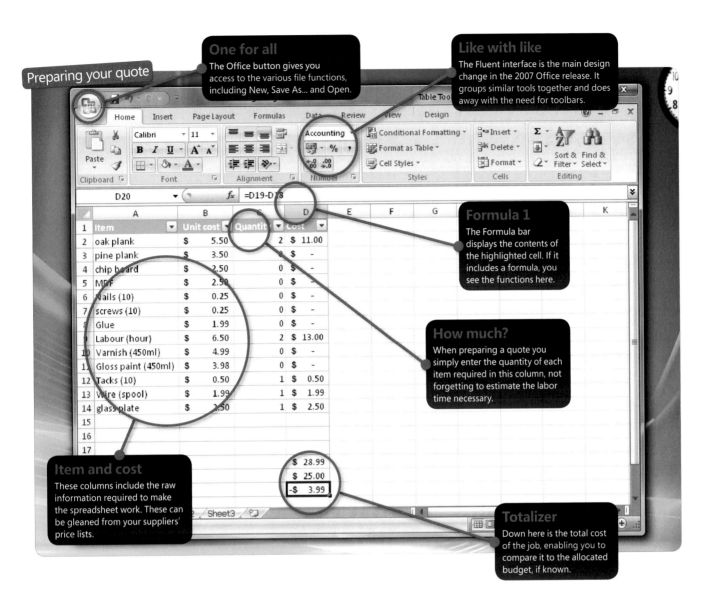

One for all
The Office button gives you access to the various file functions, including New, Save As... and Open.

Like with like
The Fluent interface is the main design change in the 2007 Office release. It groups similar tools together and does away with the need for toolbars.

Formula 1
The Formula bar displays the contents of the highlighted cell. If it includes a formula, you see the functions here.

How much?
When preparing a quote you simply enter the quantity of each item required in this column, not forgetting to estimate the labor time necessary.

Item and cost
These columns include the raw information required to make the spreadsheet work. These can be gleaned from your suppliers' price lists.

Totalizer
Down here is the total cost of the job, enabling you to compare it to the allocated budget, if known.

4 CALCULATE COST In the Quantity column enter zero for each for now. Select cell D2 and enter the formula =B2*C2. Press Enter and this value is worked out. Format this as currency, too.

5 COPY FORMULA Now extend this formula to each cell below D2. Move the pointer to the bottom-right of the cell and click and drag over the cells you want. Release the mouse button.

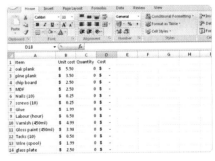

6 TOTAL COST In column A add labels for Total, Budget and Difference. Select the column D cell opposite Total. Above Editing, click **Autosum ∑**. Click and drag over column D and press **Enter**.

Chart toppers

Microsoft Office Excel isn't just about keeping track of numbers – it's about presenting information in the best way possible

The *raison d'être* for Microsoft Office Excel is its ability to handle complex tables and formulas, keeping track of numbers to help with planning and budgeting at home and work. With its simple gridded interface, though, it's easy to forget that Excel isn't just there to be a functional method of analyzing figures. Whatever kind of information you're tracking in a spreadsheet, you're never more than a couple of clicks away from turning it into a powerful overview of your data.

This may sound like you're just adding window dressing to the important business of tables and spreadsheets, but the way information is presented is vital to helping your audience quickly understand what it is you're showing them. There's a whole discipline dedicated to the subject of 'visual analytics', kickstarted by experts like political scientist Robert E Horn who pioneered a technique called

It's easier to spot patterns in numbers when presented as images

'information mapping', which overlays images with data to help people take in and understand a large amount of information at once.

It's the same idea that spawned other visual aids, like Venn diagrams, flow charts and more. You can see examples of Horne's work in spheres as diverse as public spending and geopolitical

controls at www.stanford.edu/~rhorn/. Essentially, his success boils down to one principle – it's easier for your eyes to spot patterns in numbers when they're presented as images. A picture doesn't just say a thousand words, it can count a thousand numbers too.

The fact is that this is just as true for analyzing your household expenses or making a business presentation as it is for working out how to deal with nuclear waste – just one of the many 'info-murals' on Horne's site.

Fixtures and figures

While your project may not require the complexity of some of Horn's examples, Excel 2007 does come with a very powerful suite of charting tools which can help you get started with presenting visual data comparisons.

This isn't as arcane or advanced as it sounds. If you're planning to refit your kitchen, for example, you might break ●

Further format

Make your figures look good

While changing the style and layout of your charts is easy with the Ribbon tools, you may want to go further by right clicking on the tools and using the Format options. You can change the way bars are drawn and shadowed, and change the 3D rotation.

FORMAT You can delve even deeper into a host of presentation options

MOVE ON From sticky notes with different prices on; clarify your financial research in Excel

Get the chart right

As with any tool, using the right chart for the right information is crucial

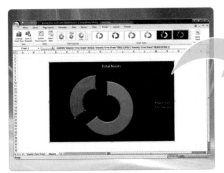

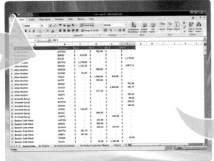

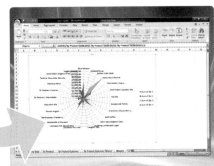

1 TWO DIMENSIONS From a simple two-column table, you can create all kinds of easy charts. Doughnuts are a simple and fun way of comparing two straightforward data sets, like regular and overtime hours in a working week.

2 DATA RELATION If your data is a bit more complicated, you need to consider your chart options. If you're just trying to clarify your own figures, you could stick to a 'flat' display, like a bar chart or radar graph (see next step).

3 ON THE RADAR Radar graphs are often used in statistical analysis. This restaurant example shows a large spike in cheese orders during the Fall months, so the business can order appropriately. However, the data could look prettier...

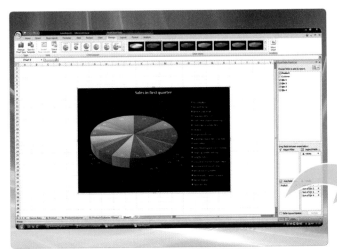

4 ORDER MORE PIE So if you're looking for a clear overview of which product sold best over each quarter, you may want to consider going 3D! This kind of pie chart is a great choice – it's easy on the eye and the best sellers are immediately obvious.

While your project may not require complexity, Excel 2007 comes with a powerful suite of charting tools

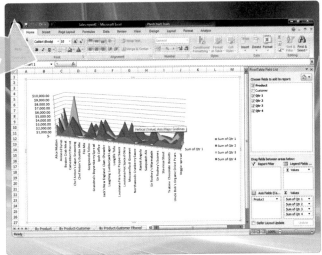

5 AREA MAP By combining the advantages of line graphs – which connect points together to map trends – and the solid colouring of bar graphs, area graphs are a very useful visual tool for comparing sets of data.

Link your charts

To use a chart you create in Excel in a different Office application, right-click on the chart and **Copy**. When you paste the chart into a new document, use the Paste Options command and link the two together, so when data changes in Excel, your new document is updated.

CHAPTER 6 **BUDGETING**

down all the materials you want into a simple table and then price them up at your local hardware store. That's just two columns in a simple spreadsheet to create – not a task that requires a certification in accounting. The easiest way to then compare prices from different sources across the range of parts – down to the last screw – is to copy and paste the table into a new worksheet for a different store. Comparing pages and pages of figures to see which fixings to buy from where is no fun, though, and this is where Excel charts come in. A quick, color-coded table will show at a glance what you're best buying from where, saving you time and money over the course of a project.

IT'S A TOUGH JOB But whatever your project, Excel can help you to budget for it

Chart progress

Certain forms of graphical interpretations are so instinctively easy to understand that they've become a standard part of our visual lexicon. In other words, you can clearly see what proportion of your money goes where in a pie chart of your monthly expenses, instead of trying to make sense of a large table of figures.

Excel has historically always been very good at taking your data and charting it, and because it's part of the Microsoft Office system it's also easy to export graphs and images into other programs like PowerPoint or Word, and even actively link them so that if you need to update a spreadsheet, your presentation or document will also update to the latest information.

Excel 2007 takes things a step further... As well as new types of charts, that range from simple bar graphs to scatter diagrams, there's a whole range of highly customizable visual effects you can apply to your charts.

There are loads of predefined templates with different designs and layouts for bar charts, line graphs, columns, doughnuts, bubble graphs and more, but each element can be tweaked to add color and advanced 3D effects like soft shadowing and anti-aliasing. Whatever you're working on, Excel 2007 can help add clarity and pizzazz!

Creating a chart from scratch

A simple guide to 3D price comparisons

1 NEW PROJECT Say you need to price up a simple, low-cost PC... Start by drawing up a list of components in Excel and then get prices from your local component store.

2 MORE STORES To compare the costs from a variety of sources, fill in the same shopping list based on prices from different stores. Each new store is added to the table by inserting a column.

3 NEW SHEET As the number of stores increases, it's worth starting a new worksheet by clicking on the tab at the bottom of the page. If you go to the **Insert** tab you can create a 3D bar chart.

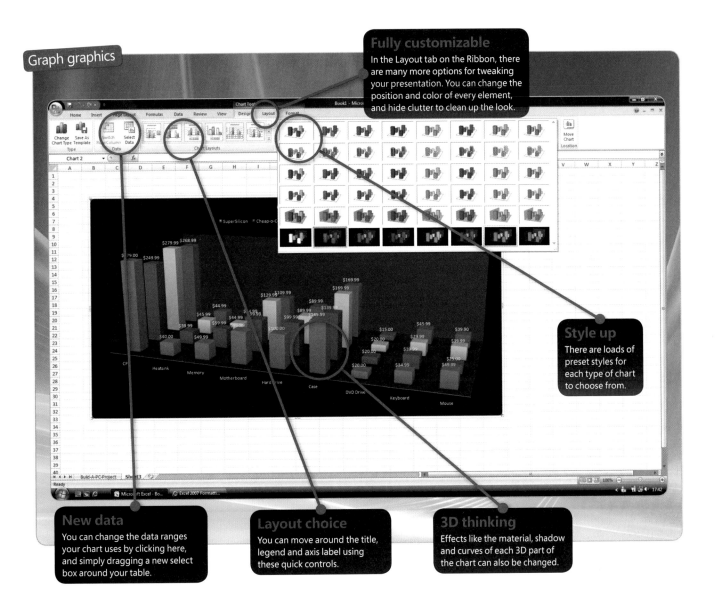

Fully customizable
In the Layout tab on the Ribbon, there are many more options for tweaking your presentation. You can change the position and color of every element, and hide clutter to clean up the look.

Style up
There are loads of preset styles for each type of chart to choose from.

New data
You can change the data ranges your chart uses by clicking here, and simply dragging a new select box around your table.

Layout choice
You can move around the title, legend and axis label using these quick controls.

3D thinking
Effects like the material, shadow and curves of each 3D part of the chart can also be changed.

4 DATA SELECT When you select a chart, a dialog box pops up asking which data to include. Go back to the first sheet and drag the box round the table to include all the information.

5 NAME AND NUMBER Clicking back through to the second worksheet, the graph has been completely plotted out. You can clearly see which shop is cheapest for which component.

6 THERE'S MORE Changing the color scheme can make your charts look even more impressive or easy to read, and fit in with any document or presentation you're copying them to.

Financial control

Get on top of your accounts with this free program – you'll be in control of your spending for the coming year and could reduce your accountancy fees

While Excel 2007 works well for a variety of costing exercises, if your finances are a little more complicated there is a free solution that may be more suitable for your needs.

Microsoft Office Accounting Express 2009 is primarily designed for the small business user who wants to produce invoices, receipts and process purchases in an easy-to-use system.

And Office Accounting Express has plenty of other uses outside of small business requirements, too... If you're an eBay vendor, and want to get your finances in order and produce professional receipts for your buyers,

then this is the perfect program. The software is designed to integrate with PayPal business accounts, by accepting a .csv file which can be downloaded from the history link on the site. This file holds all of your transaction details, and can be used in Office Accounting Express or Office Excel, where you can publish or store reports. You can also manage payroll and accept credit cards with affordable add-on services.

To get started, go to http://office.microsoft.com to download. The step-by-step wizard means you'll be able to get working in no time, and you'll then find Office Accounting Express incredibly easy to use. One of the greatest benefits

is the program's ability to recognize data from programs like Excel 2007, and vice versa. And you can share information – with your accountant, for example – through Office Live Small Business.

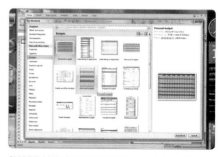

SHARE AND SHARE ALIKE Share data with other Office programs, such as Excel 2007

Office Accounting Express 2009

Organize your accounts with this easy program

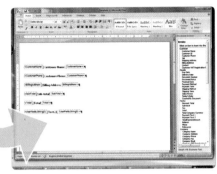

1 GOOD COMPANY Load up Office Accounting Express and you should see the welcome page. If you're a first time user, select **Start a new company** from the list. Otherwise, simply load your business from this screen.

2 SET UP You can add all the details of your business, including tax details, so your tax returns can be calculated by the program. You will then be transported to the Quick Start menu, for your day-to-day activities.

3 ADD DETAIL You'll need to give the program information about your business; details of employees, products, suppliers and customer lists. You can import these from an Office Excel 2007 spreadsheet or add them manually.

4 CUSTOMIZE You can create invoices from scratch using the Quick Start Menu or by designing them in Office Word, but there is a much easier way...

Office Accounting Express is primarily designed for the small business user who wants an easy-to-use system

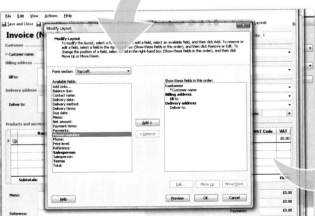

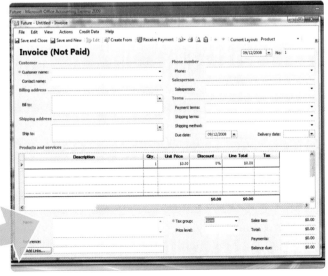

5 MODIFY In the invoice menu, click the small arrow by **Current Layout** on the toolbar and then **Modify Layout**. You can add or remove fields from each section of the invoice depending on the information your business requires.

6 BUSINESS Once all your details are added, it's time to get down to business. Click on **Create an invoice** and use the drop-down menus to select your employee, product and customer information. It even works out the tax for you.

Microsoft boosts its word power

The most high-profile application in the 2007 Microsoft Office system has a very responsible position. Thankfully, it's both intuitive and dependable...

Office Word 2007 is synonymous with Microsoft Office – it's a core program that appears in every version of the suite. Office Word 2007 has to function well; if not, it would have an impact on the usability of the entire system. Thankfully, the new Microsoft Office Fluent interface groups common tasks and tools in an intelligent manner. For those more used to cascading menus, this can be a shock, but it doesn't take long to appreciate the design elegance it brings.

Microsoft Office Word 2007 adds context-sensitive tabs that appear and disappear depending on the object you're editing, offering easier access to common functions. A good example is the way you handle images. Drop in an image and a Picture tab appears. This shows off Office Word 2007's graphical features, such as easy drop shadows, transparencies and other effects.

The Styles section provides instant visual feedback on available font styles and provides access to entire new style sets, making it easy to completely change a document's typeface. The drop-down Gallery that appears can be totally user defined with new types.

Greater customization is available through Quick Parts, a simple but powerful tool that manages commonly used document parts, be it a single line of text or an entire calendar.

A key addition for Office Word 2007 is near complete blogging support. Tap a few thoughts into Office Word 2007 and you can have your latest blog entry and images uploaded directly to your blog.

Office Word 2007 is also a little more conscious of your feelings, as improved grammar and spell checkers help avoid embarrassing mistakes. Exclusion and custom dictionaries can now be made global for the entire suite. The grammar checker has improved context-sensitive checks, so it can now make a better judgment on using 'their' or 'there'.

Extra enhancements cover greater collaboration with new review modes, improved marking of final drafts and scanning documents for hidden metadata before publishing them. Most reassuringly, Word 2007 is even better at protecting work in case of a crash. ⊞

Top features

The latest version of Microsoft Office Word has lots new to offer

- **FLUENT INTERFACE** The interface maximizes program features
- **TEMPLATES** Preformatted elements, including page designs and typeface styles
- **GALLERY** Drop-down Gallery elements for instant feedback
- **IMAGES** New charting, diagram and enhanced image effects
- **BLOGS** Integrated and direct blogging uploads
- **STYLES** Instant document-wide style changes
- **ACCURACY** Enhanced spelling and grammar checker
- **REVISION** Enhanced document revision system with new view
- **EXPORTS** Support for PDF and XPS document exporting
- **SECURITY** Reduced final file size and enhanced security

WORDS WORTH Transforming your words into presentable, eye-catching documents is easy

Symbols and formulas

They were once hidden away but now it's really easy to add symbols and mathematical formulas to your documents via the Insert tab.

Fast review

The new tri-panes review tool lets you see versions of the same document side by side before confirming any changes.

Quick templates

There are hundreds of document templates you can add before you start a document – or even while you're part way through. Just check the Office Fluent Gallery.

New format

Goodbye .doc, hello .docx. Office Word 2007 now saves your work in a more transferable format that can easily be recovered if a file gets corrupted.

Better
results faster

Click the Style group's dialog box launcher to get a further list of Quick Styles that can be floated on the desktop for easy access. Check the **Show Preview** box for an instant preview

Turn your words into works of art

Reports don't need to look dull – create colorful Office Word 2007 documents with ease

Better results faster

The Microsoft Office Online website can help you do anything, from designing a tutorial to saving home-made invitations as PDFs. Go to office.microsoft.com and grab a download

You've typed up your text and all the salient points are in. Now you just need to give your report a bit of visual pace and gloss. This stage often gets left to the last minute because of a lack of confidence in what can be done... Do you often find yourself doing something complicated and time-consuming with images or formatting when you're facing a deadline? It's OK, making vivid documents in Microsoft Office Word 2007 is really easy.

It can take a while to format text, themes and headings as you change each element into the colors and fonts of your choice. If you want to make an impression, Themes really make a difference. In Word 2007 you can use a series of predefined themes that include colors, fonts and effects with one click of the mouse. Go to **Page Layout ➔ Themes** and choose from the drop-down menu. If you can't find anything that suits, go to Microsoft Office Online (http://office.microsoft.com) where there are over a hundred variations available.

Pictures are fantastic for juicing up boring documents or creating cards and invitations. For ideas on designing invitations go to Office Online where there are several templates and images.

If you used earlier versions of Microsoft Office then you probably spent time fiddling with image sizes, getting them to fit around the font and so on. Now SmartArt graphics make it easy to insert all kinds of images. Go to

Insert ➔ Illustrations ➔ SmartArt and choose the type and layout you want. Then click on a shape in your SmartArt graphic and type your text. Try different combinations of SmartArt styles and colors until you find the ones you like; if you change the layout, the SmartArt style and colors will stay with you. You can also add animations, which is particularly good for email invitations.

The best thing about SmartArt is that you can use it in most 2007 Office system applications. You can create graphics in Microsoft Office Excel 2007, Microsoft Office PowerPoint 2007 and even in emails using Microsoft Office Outlook 2007.

Say goodbye to fiddly frustration and hello to hours of creative fun!

Be Smart with your Art

Spice up your documents with a few well placed SmartArt graphics

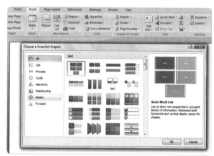

1 SMART GRAPHICS Go to **Insert ➔ Illustrations ➔ SmartArt**, and in the **Choose a SmartArt Graphic** box choose the type and layout of SmartArt graphic, such as a list, cycle or matrix.

2 TEXT MESSAGE To enter text, click in a shape then type, or click **Text** in the Text pane and type or paste your words. To copy text from another program, click **Text** and paste it into the Text pane.

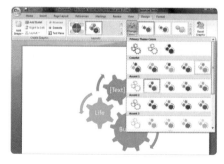

3 COLOR IT IN To apply colors, to match stationery or letterheads, click on the SmartArt graphic then, under SmartArt Tools on the Design tab, click **Change Colors** and select the colors.

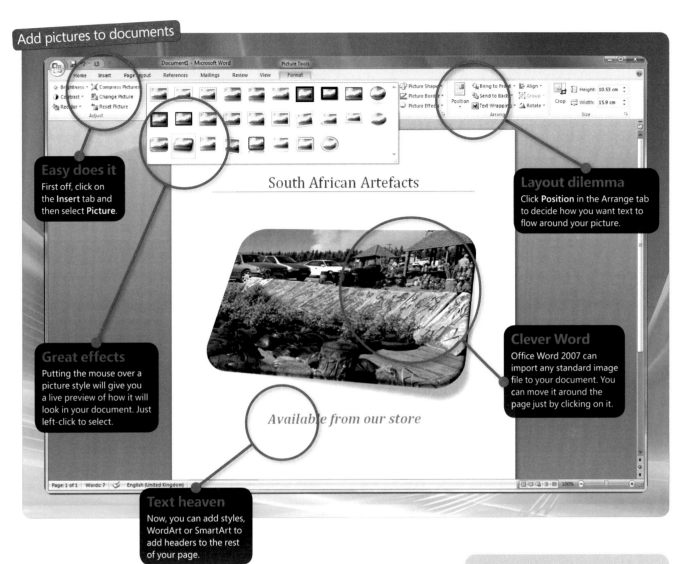

Add pictures to documents

Easy does it
First off, click on the **Insert** tab and then select **Picture**.

South African Artefacts

Layout dilemma
Click **Position** in the Arrange tab to decide how you want text to flow around your picture.

Great effects
Putting the mouse over a picture style will give you a live preview of how it will look in your document. Just left-click to select.

Clever Word
Office Word 2007 can import any standard image file to your document. You can move it around the page just by clicking on it.

Available from our store

Text heaven
Now, you can add styles, WordArt or SmartArt to add headers to the rest of your page.

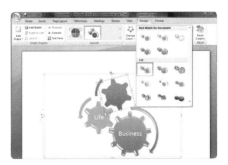

4 ADD STYLE You can now add various effects, such as 3D. Simply click the SmartArt graphic and, under SmartArt Tools on the Design tab, select a style. To see more styles select **More**.

5 MIGHTY MORPHS You can customize your SmartArt by adding individual shapes, removing shapes and more. Go to the Format tab, click on **Change Shape**, then select the style you want.

Planning is key

Decide on what you want to say and how you want to say it...

Before starting your presentation, you should consider what type and layout are the best for showing your information and what you are trying to convey with your images and graphics. For example, if you want to show steps in a timeline then a process graphic would be the best choice. Also, keep the amount of text in each graphic down so you just convey key points as this will have more impact.

Style stamp

You don't actually have to spend tons of cash to create your own brand identity...

If you've started your own business or regularly send out literature for a project you're involved in, you'll know how important it is to stand out from the crowd with a defined brand. You need something that embodies your business services or enterprise ethos: a strong brand will help to develop customer or volunteer loyalty.

The following pages focus on the business side of things, but the tips apply to any frequent themed communication.

Fortunately, there's plenty of information out there on how to create a powerful brand; you can research different color combinations and their psychological effects and examine other brands. What have other companies that offer similar services to your own done with their logo or company letterhead?

Be individual though! Don't get too caught up in everybody else's ideas and the dictates of the experts. If your business personality can carry off bright pink and red, go ahead and do it. Once you've established color schemes, you can look at how to incorporate them into your company identity.

For things like your logo, letterheads, email signatures and newsletters, you need to decide what levels of color you plan to use and what fonts. These need to be easy to read, memorable and easily reproduced across other formats such as flyers or T-shirts. You can design your own logo using Microsoft PowerPoint or you set up an online competition challenging young artists and designers to come up with a logo. Not only does this drive traffic through to your site, but you'll gain the advantage of a stunning logo for the price of your first prize. ➲

Better results faster

If you're short of time, use a pre-made Word 2007 template as it has already been formatted and can quickly be used to create what you need. Go to office.microsoft.com

Text-tastic!

Text boxes are useful and easy to implement and customize

Text boxes are ideal for positioning copy and images in specific places. You can use them to display pictures, control the flow of your text (especially handy if you are doing a newsletter) and to create effects.

To insert a text box go to the Insert tab, click **Text Box ➜ Draw Text Box** and drag the cursor to create the shape and size you want. To format your box, click on the **Format** tab, or right-click the text box itself, to adjust the colors, layout, text controls and fill effects.

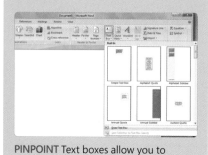

PINPOINT Text boxes allow you to position copy exactly where you want

RESEARCH AND REFINE Take a look at designs you like to start your search for a brand identity

Keep in touch, keep in style...

Create an email newsletter with Word 2007

1 **RIGHT TEMPLATE** Download a template from http://office.microsoft.com. This will automatically open up in Word 2007. Add your company logo, change the colors and include your business information.

2 **GOOD VIEW** Use the Web Layout view when creating your newsletter as this is how your customers will see the final version. Never use more than two or three fonts as this becomes confusing and can look very amateur.

3 **FEATURE PERFECT** At this stage, you need to delete any features that you don't want to use from the original template and add any standard copy or features that you plan to use on a regular basis within your newsletters.

4 **TOTAL TEMPLATE** Save the newsletter as a Word template. Go to **File → Save As → Save as type** and select **Document Template**. Give it a title and accept the default to store in the Templates folder, click **Save**.

If your business personality can carry off bright pink and red, then go ahead and do it!

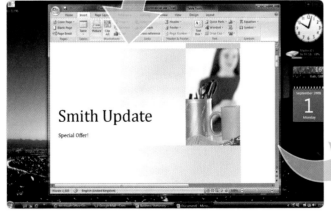

5 **WRITE WORDS** Make sure you keep your text down to short and interesting bite-size pieces of information. Use images to break up the text and think in terms of keeping the reader's eye moving down the page.

6 **LINKED UP** To really stamp your identity on the newsletter, include links to your company website whenever you can. To do this select the text or image you want to link, go to **Insert → Hyperlink** and under Link to, click **Existing File** or **Web Page**. Then type in the web address you want and click **OK**.

Once you've got your logo in the bag, you can move on to the letterheads and email signatures. A unified look creates a strong impression, so use Word 2007 to apply your brand by using Themes.

Themes present options of color, font and formatting that work together to create a professional design and take away the anguish of painstaking fiddling. All you need to do is adjust the colors and fonts until they match up to your logo design and overall business style.

Word also includes new templates and tools that make it extremely easy for you to reuse content and to preview any changes you make before you commit to them. It certainly makes it a lot quicker than repeatedly selecting Undo.

FONT OF ALL OPTONS Click on the font tab to pick and choose from a variety of typefaces

THEME DREAM Themes enable you to form a coherent look to your business literature

Staying in touch with your customers is essential – it encourages them to come back again and again, and people like to feel they are important to your business. Newsletters are a great way to do this and they deliver valuable information such as special offers, new services or products, directly into the inbox.

Now, before you think that this extra work will only end up ignored, think again. If a newsletter is crisp and clean, with the information easily accessible and easy to read, you'll find that people will be drawn to read it. Word 2007 is a powerful ally in this field as it has all the tools you need to create an email newsletter with powerful visual impact. See the walkthrough on the previous page for six easy steps to producing a newsletter. You can also use the Header and Footer feature in Word 2007 to

create your own letterheads by selecting the fonts and colors you've already chosen. Once you've finalized your letterhead, you'll want to include your company logo, so simply follow the steps on the walkthrough opposite.

Finishing touches

Now you've got all the elements in place and selected the fonts and styles you want to carry your brand forward, you can use Word 2007 to design your own business cards. There are plenty of set templates that you can customize to suit at office.microsoft.com. Just click **Download** and you can get started on fine-tuning the layout of your choice. So instead of feeling overwhelmed by the volume of fonts, formats and rules out there, you can create an entire business image portfolio and enjoy doing it!

Image control

Inserting your logo, and other company images, is easy...

Take the headache out of inserting and positioning images. To include an image in a Word 2007 document, drag the image file from wherever it's saved directly on to the page. Alternatively, use a text box or a table cell; once you've created the text box, click on Insert and drag down to Picture, then choose where to get the image from (eg Clip Art, SmartArt or from your own files).

If you then right-click on the image, you'll find lots of options to tailor how it appears, such as text wrap and artistic effects.

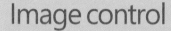

CONTENT CONTROL Use Picture Control to format an image like any other object

FEEDBACK Get feedback from your colleagues before launching your business logo

Letterhead logo

It's easy to keep your logo predominant

1 SETTING UP Control-click on the image and select **Format Picture** from the drop-down menu that appears, then select the wrapping style – **Behind Text** – and click **Advanced**.

2 FORMAT IT In Advanced Layout you can position your logo in relation to the page. Set the Absolute position based on where you want the logo to sit. Test the position by printing the page.

3 ADVANCED MOVES In Advanced Layout you can position your logo in relation to the actual page. Set the Absolute position based on where you want the logo to sit.

4 HEADER SET To set your logo into the header, simply click **View → Header and Footer**. Then use the settings to determine if you want the logo to appear on every page, or every alternate page.

Top tips for images

How to keep your documents looking good

1 RESOLUTION Use an image resolution of 72dpi for online viewing but always go for the highest resolution of 300dpi for professional printing purposes.

2 INTEGRITY If you format your images to be relative to the page it will help maintain the integrity of your own design if someone else then modifies them.

3 COHESION Don't group multiple images in separate locations on a page, only do this if they form one cohesive image or form a single design element.

4 CROP You can crop an image using the cropping tool in Word 2007. When you're done, compress the image to remove the cropped areas and then reduce the file size.

5 NO ACCIDENTS If you place an image behind text it will prevent accidental repositioning or resizing by colleagues.

In real life... Multiple mail-outs made easy!

Matt Hanson,
Writer,
Windows Vista: The Official Magazine

While I don't own a business empire just yet, I have created newsletters – both in printed and email form – for other non-business activities, and it really is a doddle!

Using Word 2007, I can create great looking documents in a fraction of the time it used to take me, and I can take advantage of the powerful mail merge tools, so I can send out my newsletter – through email or regular mail – to recipients quickly and easily. All I need to do is supply a list of the addressees and then Word 2007 does all the rest of the hard work for me – like printing address labels and sending the emails through the desktop mail client (such as Windows Live Mail). I've just discovered that you can also use mail merge to include each contact's title and name in the newsletter, which is great for adding that personal touch to high-volume communications.

All publicity is good publicity

Microsoft Office Publisher 2007 helps you get noticed in print, on the web and via email

Despite the growth of the internet, the printed page is still key in promoting a business, a product or your birthday party. Microsoft Office Publisher 2007 enables you to get maximum impact from your message whether it's on paper, the web or email.

Recognizing that not everyone is blessed with the design gene, Microsoft has made sure that Office Publisher 2007 comes with a range of templates. These have been developed to help you create stunning results with the least amount of hassle. The templates have reusable details, so if you've put a company name in one template it can be automatically transferred to another.

To help make the finished publication as slick as possible, Office Publisher 2007 comes with a raft of suggestions while a design is being put together. Publisher Tasks, for instance, are step-by-step guides that show you how to get the most out of a marketing campaign.

If the campaign you're planning is distributed via email, Office Publisher 2007 can optimize the publication for sending over the internet, while the Catalog Merge Wizard handles multiple mailing lists with ease.

Regardless of whether you're planning to use snail mail or email, Office Publisher 2007 happily switches, so you can transfer information and graphics from a catalog to a newsletter or web page. This saves the time and effort of starting from scratch for each format. And frequently used elements can be placed in the Content Library; this enables items such as logos, lists, services, testimonials and maps to be stored in a central location for reuse.

When it comes to printing, Publisher 2007 supports a variety of options. Full PDF support is implemented with CMYK, spot and process color options. Publisher 2007 can make you aware of any potential problems, and the Pack and Go Wizard can let you know of any potential issues with a publication before it's sent for commercial printing.

With Office Publisher 2007 handling your publicity, you can focus on ensuring your event goes with a bang.

Top features

The essential elements of Office Publisher 2007

■ FILL Templates are automatically filled with information, such as a company name and logo wherever applicable
■ STORE Frequently used content can be kept in Content Store for quick access
■ CONVERT Documents support automatic conversion from one type to another, such as newsletter to web page
■ PRINT Save as PDF supports commercial printing quality
■ RETRIEVE Catalog Merge can create content by retrieving data from an external source
■ CHECK Improved Design Checker to find design inconsistencies
■ PREVIEW Improved print preview for even greater accuracy
■ LIST Simplified list management can work with Excel 2007, Access 2007 and Outlook 2007

GOING PUBLIC Not only is Office Publisher 2007 quick and easy to use, it can also guide you

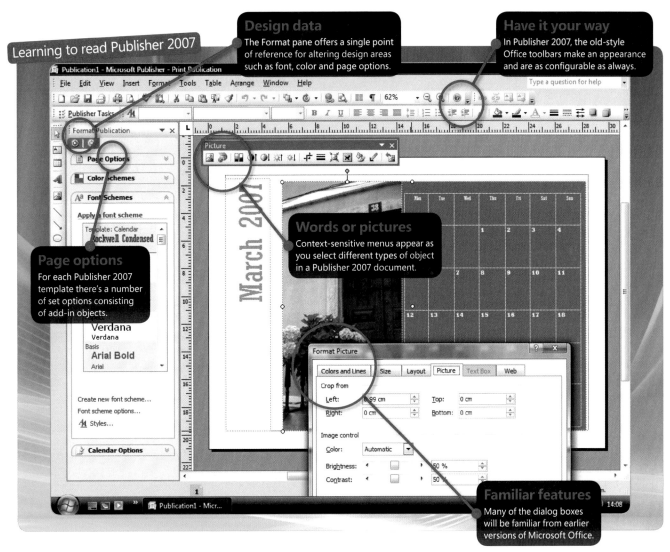

Learning to read Publisher 2007

Design data
The Format pane offers a single point of reference for altering design areas such as font, color and page options.

Have it your way
In Publisher 2007, the old-style Office toolbars make an appearance and are as configurable as always.

Page options
For each Publisher 2007 template there's a number of set options consisting of add-in objects.

Words or pictures
Context-sensitive menus appear as you select different types of object in a Publisher 2007 document.

Familiar features
Many of the dialog boxes will be familiar from earlier versions of Microsoft Office.

Spread the word
Creating and printing a flyer takes minutes in Publisher 2007

1 CREATIVE DESIGNS You can see how versatile and complete the new set of templates are. Each of the hundreds of designs can be customized with color schemes, font schemes and paper sizes.

2 INSIDE PUBLISHER Despite offering all the power and features of a full DTP package, Publisher 2007 can feel as easy to use as a word processor – with tools geared towards print publishing.

3 READY TO PRINT A host of powerful print features are available. Print at home, package the document for a commercial printer, or transform your design for use online.

How to show off all your hard work

Adding pizzazz to presentations is easier and faster than ever thanks to Microsoft Office PowerPoint 2007. Get ready to wow your audience

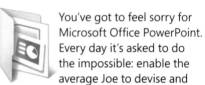

You've got to feel sorry for Microsoft Office PowerPoint. Every day it's asked to do the impossible: enable the average Joe to devise and design the most graphically sumptuous and impressive presentation ever seen by his colleagues or clients. And while this core Microsoft Office application has always managed to do a good job of holding your hand through the design process, Microsoft Office PowerPoint 2007 takes things to a new level.

With new design tools based around the Microsoft Office Fluent interface, it offers a cornucopia of themes, styles and color schemes. The new themes are slicker than ever and the color schemes eliminate eye-watering combinations. Of course, if none suit you, your own design and styles can be added. Even better, as they are consistent throughout the 2007 Microsoft Office release, all your documents can have the same look.

On the subject of visual flair, the new SmartArt tool is insanely easy to use and results in the slickest buttons, shapes and diagrams imaginable. A couple of clicks and you have a professional-looking, customizable, rendered 3D diagram.

Reusing designs and objects is easy in PowerPoint 2007. Whether you want to update an existing presentation or reuse a previous design, PowerPoint 2007 has tools to help you manage designs and objects for easy repurposing.

A huge addition is the ability to import and use tables easily from Microsoft Office Excel 2007. This is beside the general table creation improvements.

A number of technical improvements help keep PowerPoint 2007 up to date with display advancements. Multiple monitor support is improved for on-the-fly editing in presentations. Widescreen slides are also an option now that such displays and projectors are common.

As with other 2007 Office products, PowerPoint 2007 can detect and remove unwanted comments, hidden text and personal data from documents before they're shared. It can also add a digital signature to prevent documents being changed without an author's permission.

It seems the only thing PowerPoint 2007 can't do is write a presentation for you. Perhaps that's coming next time.

Top features

Just look at what the latest release of Office PowerPoint offers...

- RENDERING Improvements to text rendering to support text-based graphics
- 3D Support for 3D graphics
- TABLES Support for tables and enhanced support for table pasting from Excel 2007
- PRESENTATIONS Slide Library, which enables you to re-use any slide or presentation as a template
- LIBRARIES Any custom-designed slide library can be saved
- SECURITY Presentations can be digitally signed
- VIEWS Improved Presenter View
- WIDESCREEN Added support for widescreen slides
- PLACEHOLDERS Allows addition of custom placeholders
- DIAGRAMS New SmartArt tool for easy creation of diagrams

PRESENTING POWER Office PowerPoint 2007 takes the stress out of giving presentations

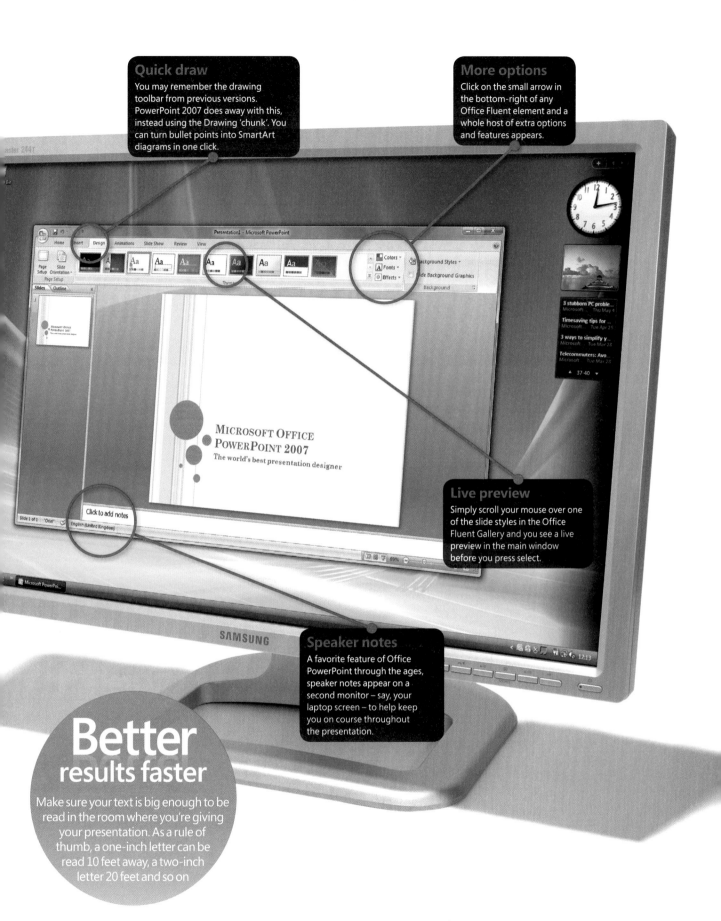

Quick draw
You may remember the drawing toolbar from previous versions. PowerPoint 2007 does away with this, instead using the Drawing 'chunk'. You can turn bullet points into SmartArt diagrams in one click.

More options
Click on the small arrow in the bottom-right of any Office Fluent element and a whole host of extra options and features appears.

Live preview
Simply scroll your mouse over one of the slide styles in the Office Fluent Gallery and you see a live preview in the main window before you press select.

Speaker notes
A favorite feature of Office PowerPoint through the ages, speaker notes appear on a second monitor – say, your laptop screen – to help keep you on course throughout the presentation.

Better results faster
Make sure your text is big enough to be read in the room where you're giving your presentation. As a rule of thumb, a one-inch letter can be read 10 feet away, a two-inch letter 20 feet and so on

CHAPTER 8 **PRESENTATIONS**

Presentation is everything

The 2007 Microsoft Office system could help you seal the deal with a flawless presentation

Better results faster

You can set up your show to run by itself. At the Slide Show tab select **Rehearse Timings**. Work through the show at the pace you want; press **Esc** to end. Choose **Set up Slide Show** and pick **Browsed at a kiosk**

Microsoft Office PowerPoint 2007 is an excellent tool for communication. And it's particularly useful if you need to talk to a group of people, as you can use it to guide a presentation as well as display important information.

Many people find public speaking nerve-racking but, with the 2007 Microsoft Office release, your pitch should be less traumatic. PowerPoint 2007 is designed to make creating slides for a presentation as easy as possible and you can make them look professional without any design training.

PowerPoint has always been intuitive, but with the 2007 Office release the Microsoft Office Fluent interface makes it even easier. The screen breakdown on page 61 gives you an overview of the interface, and the walkthrough opposite takes you through the process of setting up slides for a simple presentation.

After you've created a basic slide show you can try to lift areas to emphasize

certain points. Animations can be helpful here, and you can apply these to the change between slides or to individual slide components. It's effective to use simple animations with bullet-point lists or blocks of text so you can introduce each point one at a time, helping to focus the audience's attention.

To do this, select the slide you want to use the animation on and click the first object you want to animate. Move to the Animations tab on the Fluent interface and, above Animations, choose **One** ➜

Using templates

Need a ready-made presentation? There may be a template for you...

Themes take the headache out of applying a uniform design to your slides but they don't help with the content. However, a template could contain all you need. Click the **Office** button, select **New** and choose **Presentations**. Under **Microsoft Office Online**, decide on the kind of presentation you want, then choose a template. All you need to do now is replace the sample content with your own.

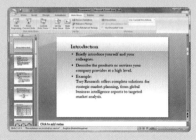

READY MADE Ready-made presentations are merely a click and a text paste away!

RUN THROUGH Think you've gone overboard on your presentation? Ask for some opinion

Powerful show

Simplicity is key; follow these steps for a clear presentation

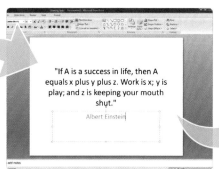

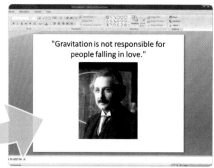

1 GETTING STARTED Start by launching PowerPoint 2007. You're shown a blank title slide. Add text to it by clicking the title or subtitle and typing it in. This kind of slide works well for quotations, with the subtitle showing the author.

2 ENTER THE QUOTE We're going to put together a selection of quotes from great historical characters throughout the ages. Enter the quote in the title section and the name of the author in the subtitle section.

3 NEW SLIDE We now need to add another slide. Choose **New Slide → Title and content**. Now click the picture icon on the slide and browse to the right picture. You can find plenty of royalty-free images on the internet.

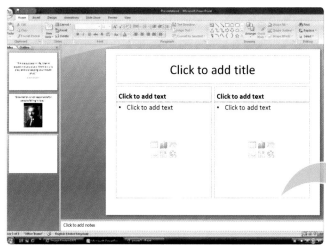

A blank title slide works well for quotations, with the subtitle showing the author

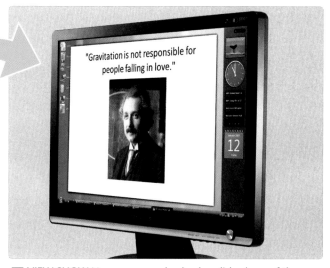

4 NEXT QUOTE Enter the next quote that you want to use into the title section of the slide. Continue adding slides until you're happy, then click the disk icon in the top left-hand corner to save your work. Provide a filename and location – make the file name something obvious so you can find your work later.

Working together

One of the joys of using an integrated suite is that you can copy things from one application to another. Grab a chart from Excel and put it into PowerPoint; updates to the spreadsheet are made in the presentation.

5 VIEW SHOW Now you can play back a slide show of the words of wisdom. Move to the Slide Show tab and, above Start Slide Show, click **From Beginning**. Each slide is shown full screen so you can see exactly what your audience will see, and you can move to the next one with a left mouse click.

by one. Rest the mouse pointer over one of the slide transitions to see a preview. If you're happy with it, click the transition button you've chosen to confirm it.

It's possible to further customize the way you animate individual items. Choose **Custom Animation** to open a new task pane. In this pane you can choose the effect you want to use – if it's a wipe, select the direction it comes from and the speed that it's applied.

You can also set the animations to advance according to a set time but it's probably more effective to opt to start on the mouse click so you can remain in charge of timings while you speak.

Click **Play** in this pane to see a preview of the animation that you've set up; click

Slide Show to see the slide in context in a full-screen view.

You can add sounds to animations. In the Transitions section of the Fluent interface under the Animations tab, you can select the sound to play on the current transition. The drop-down list gives you access to a number of sounds but you can apply your own sound file by choosing **Other Sound** and browsing to the file that you want to use.

Remember that not all presentation setups include sound equipment and many of the most commonly used sounds can become irritating. When in doubt, opt for no sound. Be sparing with animations, too. In moderation they can draw attention to important points; if each slide contains a complex animation, they may just annoy your audience.

Having set up your slide show it's a good idea to rehearse the presentation before you see your clients. This gives you a chance to practice what you're going to say and get the timings right for advancing each slide. Don't stick too rigidly to what you've rehearsed; people may have questions to ask as you speak.

Rehearsal also helps you to remember what you have to say and leaves you more prepared for problems like the projector bulb expiring. Good luck!

ART SMART Adding images and diagrams to your presentation is easy with SmartArt tools

Other ideas

PowerPoint 2007 lets you make slide shows for any occasion

TEAM TALK Use a presentation to motivate your staff. Highlight areas where the company is doing well and where you must improve.

CALENDAR It's easy to create a slide per month and use it to track a project or print it out.

CREATIVITY GROUP Use a presentation for brainstorming. It can help to ensure that all areas are covered without needing to appoint a draconian chairperson.

ON TIME Use PowerPoint 2007 to make a calendar, with each month on a new slide

Adding the extras
You know the basics, now you can make the finishing touches

1 DESIGN If your slide show looks plain, experiment with the Design tab on the Fluent interface. Move the mouse over a theme to see the current slide preview it, then click to apply it.

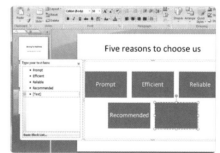

2 ADD A LIST You can add graphics to enhance the look of your slides. Go to **Insert** and select **SmartArt**. We've chosen a basic block list to highlight key words but there are many options.

3 ANIMATED BEHAVIOR Have fun playing around with the different options in SmartArt. Pick a graphic, then go to the **Animations** tab and select an animation from the list.

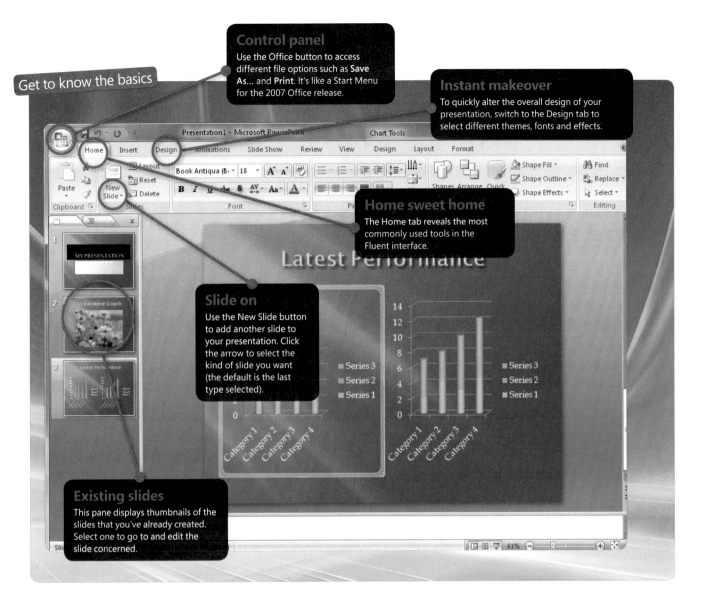

Get to know the basics

Control panel
Use the Office button to access different file options such as **Save As...** and **Print**. It's like a Start Menu for the 2007 Office release.

Instant makeover
To quickly alter the overall design of your presentation, switch to the Design tab to select different themes, fonts and effects.

Home sweet home
The Home tab reveals the most commonly used tools in the Fluent interface.

Slide on
Use the New Slide button to add another slide to your presentation. Click the arrow to select the kind of slide you want (the default is the last type selected).

Existing slides
This pane displays thumbnails of the slides that you've already created. Select one to go to and edit the slide concerned.

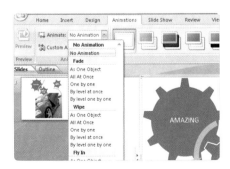

4 ONE STEP FORWARD The options depend on the layout. We've chosen **One by one** so each shape is animated individually; you can animate everything at once, but don't go OTT!

5 ONE STEP BACK Right-click **Custom Animation** and choose **Effect Options**. Click **SmartArt Animation → Reverse order** and it runs backwards. Other effects can be added here.

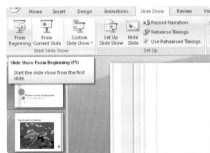

6 PRESENT THE SHOW When finished, save the presentation. Move to the Slide Show tab. Above Start Slide Show, choose **From Beginning** to start. Left-click to advance each slide.

Take the frustration out of formatting

If you want to add finesse to your documents, the 2007 Office system has plenty of tricks up its sleeve

So you want to be the formatting expert in the office. The one who can take a troubled document and line up bullet points, re-number lists and make the text wrap around the picture. Well, the 2007 Microsoft Office system can help you to achieve such iconic status.

Some document drafters may already know the buzz of making a change to a style and seeing the entire document update without the need to manually reformat every header. For those still going back and forth to the toolbar to format one paragraph, this style insight will prove an invaluable timesaver.

Office Word 2007
Bring some style

In Microsoft Office Word 2007, a new blank document is simply a copy of a template named Normal.dotx (or Normal.dotm if it includes macros). In previous versions of Microsoft Office, if you changed Heading 1 and closed the document without saving changes to the template, the changes made to Heading 1 weren't available in any new documents.

Now you can open a new document and transfer styles from another – it doesn't have to be a template. Click the **Office** button, click **New** and select **New from existing**. When your file directory opens, select a document where you edited the styles or customized bullets, double-click that file name, then click **Create New**. Office Word 2007 creates a new document based on the existing file. Just delete the text and start again, knowing your favorite styles are in your Quick Styles gallery on the Office Fluent interface. When you save the new file, the application prompts you to rename it; your other document won't be affected.

Visit the gallery

On the Home tab, you'll find the Styles group. This is your Quick Styles gallery (see screen on next page) and you can add the styles you want to access most often to this gallery. If you want to access styles that are not in the Quick Style gallery, click the arrow in the bottom-right of the Styles group to expand the Styles pane. Right-click the style you want, click **Add To Quick Style Gallery** and then close the Styles task pane.

While you cannot drag and drop styles around the Quick Style gallery, the gallery will hold its position on a particular line as long as you're on the Home tab. If you leave the Home tab and come back again, the top line of the Quick Style gallery will be visible.

To create a new style and add it to your Quick Style list, click the diagonal down arrow to open Styles and click the **New Style** icon. Name your style and select the formatting you want to apply. Confirm that **Add to Quick Style List** is checked and select **New Documents Based On This Template**.

Automatically Update is what you would check if you were reformatting an existing style and you wanted all the other instances of that style to update. Click **Format** if you want to format the paragraph spacing or add a fill or border. When you are finished, click **OK**.

Once you have your Quick Styles gallery the way that you want it, click **Change Styles** then **Set As Default**. ➔

Taking it further

Recommended reading

This article is adapted from a chapter in another very useful guide book *So That's How! Timesavers, Breakthroughs & Everyday Genius for 2007 Microsoft Office System* by Evan Archilla and Tiffany Songvilay. It's published by Microsoft Press and is available from good booksellers, including Amazon.com and Barnes & Noble online. Every major application in the 2007 Microsoft Office release is covered, with tips and walkthroughs for every occasion. From basic Microsoft Office Word 2007 commands through advanced PowerPoint 2007 design tips to using SharePoint Server 2007, it's a truly comprehensive guide. And it comes with a CD of video tutorials. Find out more about this book and other training titles at www.microsoft.com/learning/books.

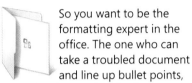

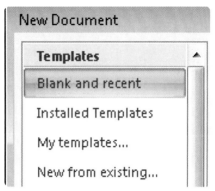

NEW FOR OLD When opening a new document, **New from existing** saves time

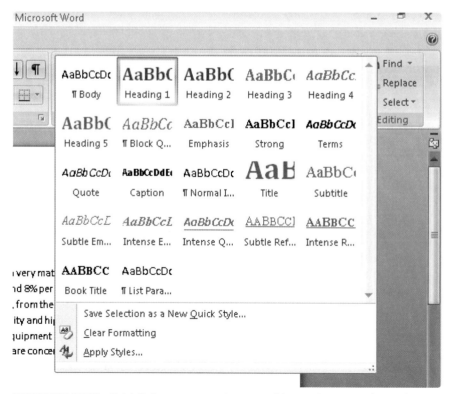

Better results faster

Text not behaving? Select the text and click **More** (next to Quick Styles), then **Clear Formatting**. Now you have a clean slate for this section of the document

If you skip this step, the Quick Styles gallery will reset the next time you open Office Word 2007.

With Live Preview you can see how your document will look if you let Office Word 2007 apply styles that look good. On the Home tab, click **Change Styles**, move the mouse over **Style Set**, then hover over Distinctive, Elegant, Formal and so on to preview styles (see screen opposite). Use Quick Styles and Style Sets when you don't have time to tidy,

You can always be one click away from your favorite formatting

or as a basis for documents. Here's how you can create your own Style Set and make it available in all your documents...

Open the Styles pane by clicking on the diagonal down arrow in the Styles group on the Office Fluent interface. Add or remove styles by either clicking the **New Style** icon or right-clicking and removing styles. When you have a list of styles you like, click **Options** (bottom of the pane), select **New Documents Based On This Template** and click **OK**.

Close the Styles pane and click **Change Styles** on the Office Fluent interface. Click **Style Set ➜ Save As Quick Style Set**. Give the Style Set a file name, then **Save**. Click **Change Styles**, select **Style**

Set and look for your name. Your styles are now available every time you open a new document in Office Word 2007.

Dream themes

Like picking out clothes in the morning, themes in Office Word 2007 ensure that color choices complement each other within a document.

In previous versions of Microsoft Office, you had to pick colors from a

honeycomb-looking palette and go back and forth, consult a color wheel, then finally settle on something you'd never be able to match again.

Click the **Page Layout** tab on the Office Fluent interface and then click the arrow under Themes. Try Flow. On a blank page you won't notice a difference but, to see what it's done, click the down arrow next to Page Color in the Page Background group. Notice the theme colors? Go back to Themes and choose Verve. Click **Page Color** again. Notice that the blues of Flow have changed to the purples of Verve? Themes limit your options to prevent you from making color choices that clash.

It's not just page color; these themes also apply to other features in your document. Go back to the Home tab and click **Change Styles ➜ Colors**. Notice the list of themes available. If you incorporated colors into your styles – such as the shading of a text box – then selecting a document theme will automatically update the colors in your

SNAPPY STYLING The Quick Styles pane can sort you out with some instant text formatting

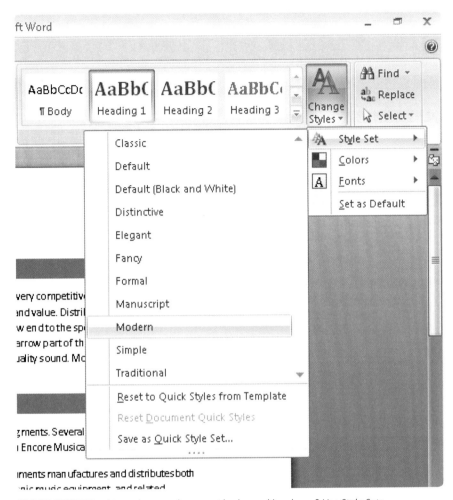

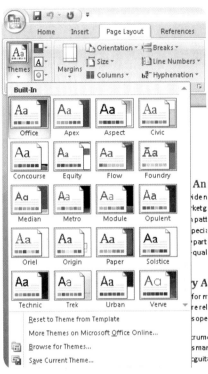

HUE AND CRY Document themes will help to keep your color choices tasteful

FAST FASHION Need to make your document look good in a hurry? Use Style Sets

Better results faster

Format Painter copies format rather than text. Highlight text, find the Paintbrush in the Clipboard (under Home); double-click **Paintbrush** and select other sentences to apply the style

styles. Now you can have the styles you want updated automatically to match the colors used in other elements of your document.

With styles, themes and a little help from Live Preview, you can make your documents look like a million dollars in half the time.

Building blocks

Have you ever spent so much time picking apart the way a handout looks that you don't bother to read it at all? Or made a judgment about someone you've never met by how professional their resumé looks? As much as we'd like to think that everything we write is going to be carefully considered by our readers, the reality is that we are

all influenced by the visual appeal of a document or presentation.

Building Blocks are reusable chunks of content you can incorporate into any document. Think of them as virtual LEGO that you can use to build your document. No more fumbling around with invisible tables, indentations and the like. With Building Blocks (also known as Quick Parts), great-looking documents are child's play.

Let's start at the top of the page with a header. Click the **Insert** tab, click **Header** in the Header & Footer group, and then select Tiles from the gallery. Notice the Design tab that appears (below-left). From here you can change the location of the header on the page and insert a company logo. Double-click off the

header to exit the Design tab, and double-click the header to return to it.

For a full list of Quick Parts, click the **Insert** tab on the Office Fluent interface, then click the **Quick Parts** button in the Text group. Go to Building Blocks Organizer. Scroll to Page Numbers under the Gallery column and choose Circle Right. Then click **Insert**.

To edit the number in the circle, highlight the number, then right-click and a brief menu will appear; you can ➡

Better results faster

To make a table of contents, click the **References** tab on the Fluent interface, then **Table Of Contents**. Use **F9** in the table to update headings and page numbers

	January	February	March	April	May	June	July	August	September	October	November	December	N
Column1													
2 Monday	8	9	1	9	7	1	5	5	7	5	5	10	
3 Tuesday	8	10	6	4	1	5	7	7	1	3	8	3	
4 Wednesday	4	6	6	1	10	9	9	8	5	10	6	9	
5 Thursday	10	1	2	7	9	6	6	3	4	6	4	7	
6 Friday	1	9	6	4	6	6	10	7	4	4	7	6	
7 Saturday	8	1	3	9	5	9	9	2	3	1	9	5	

B7 =RANDBETWEEN(1,10)

change the font and color from this menu, as well as some other options. Take care though; if you apply a theme now, the font of the page number will not be affected – only the shading of the circle. While you can resize the shape, you cannot move the numbers.

Now, let's put a quote on the other side of the page. Go back up to the Text group on the Insert tab and click **Text Box**, then **Insert Tiles Quote**. Click in the Quote and type your text.

With Building Blocks you can make any document look professional in just a few clicks by adding a cover page, a bibliography, a sidebar, a watermark and even an equation. Combine these design elements by applying goof-proof color themes and you look like a Word wizard.

And there's more to Building Blocks... Maybe you've come up with a color

scheme, text box or design that you're constantly copying from one document to another. You can make that element a Building Block so that it's available in all your new documents. Select the text, then click the **Insert** tab. Click **Quick Parts** in the Text group and click **Save Selection to Quick Part Gallery**.

Put the new Building Block in the Gallery it refers to – for example, if it's a Text Box, then choose Text Box from the Gallery drop-down menu. Under Options, you can choose to **Insert content in its own paragraph**. Now your element is available any time you need it from the Building Blocks Organizer.

Your wish is on your list. It's like a genie came out of the Microsoft Office button and granted you three wishes. But you were smart: for your last wish you asked that your genie would forget he'd granted you any wishes and you got three more. Here are some of the things you can cross off your wishlist for Microsoft Office Excel 2007...

Office Excel 2007
Spreadsheet capacity

If you opened a new spreadsheet and populated one cell with a dollar sign every second, it would take you more than 507 years to fill in the 16 billion cells now available in one spreadsheet in Office Excel 2007. With 16,384 columns and 1,048,576 rows, that's a lot of dollar signs. Thankfully, you can also see more cells on the screen in Office Excel 2007 using the new Zoom slide bar, which you'll find in the bottom-right corner of your spreadsheet.

Compare that to the 256 columns and 65,536 rows in previous versions, and you'll see why Office Excel 2007 is like leaving spreadsheet skid row and moving on up to a deluxe penthouse.

Click the **View** tab in an Office Excel 2007 workbook and notice that, in the

Column headings

Get rid of confusing blind spots

By indicating that your table has a header row, you'll turn on another new feature in Excel 2007, but in order to see it in action, you need to copy the data all the way down the page. Now, select the numbers in the table (no headings); hover over the bottom-right corner until your mouse pointer becomes a skinny plus sign and drag down to autofill through row 50.

Look at the top of your screen – notice the names of the months docked in the column heading row (see above). Scroll up and down the page as much as you want using your mouse wheel so you can watch the column headings dock and undock.

If you click out of the table and scroll down the page, the headings do not stay on the top row.

CAN WE FIX IT? Building Blocks enable you to quickly put a page together

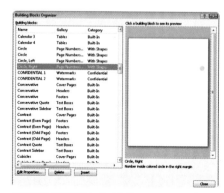

EVEN FASTER With Quick Parts you can piece together your dream document

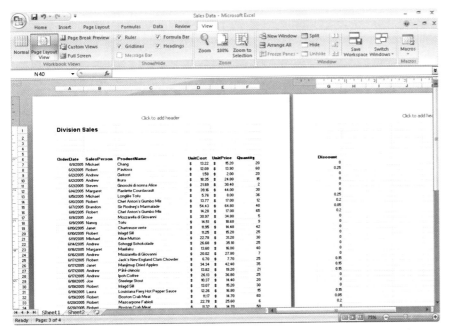

FIRST FOOTING New features in Excel 2007 make it easy to add the likes of headers and footers

Workbook Views group, Page Break Preview is still a feature. Those familiar with Excel will know that this is the fastest way to fit all the columns on a printed page. If you're a whiz with scaling, Breaks is still waiting for you on the Page Layout tab, but there's no need to manage your headers and footers from this dialog box any more.

Click **Insert** then **Header And Footer**, or click the **View** tab and **Page Layout View**. Now you can type the header and footer directly on the page like you do in Office Word 2007. Your header and footer look just the way you want them to without having to go back and forth

between Print Preview to check. When you're finished, click **Normal** on the View tab to return to the spreadsheet view.

Excel 2007 is all about formatting your spreadsheets faster so you can analyze your data better. Poor Mr ClipIt (aka, Clippy, the helpful if somewhat infuriating Microsoft Office paper clip) is animating over and over in his grave right now because he can't interrupt you to ask you what you think you are doing.

Autoformat and autofill
Open a new worksheet and type the word 'January' in cell B1. Drag the bottom-right corner (when your mouse pointer becomes a small plus sign) to autofill through September across the first row. In cell A2 type 'Monday', then autofill the days of the week through Friday down column A.

To populate the worksheet with sample data, use the =randbetween(x,y) function where 'x' is the bottom number in your range and 'y' is the top number. Then autofill across your columns and rows (more on functions later – the numbers will continue to randomly generate during this exercise).

Select the cells in your header row – just the cells, not the entire row – and

from the Home tab on the Office Fluent interface, click **Cell Styles** in the Styles group. Click **Heading 3**. Click in the blank cell next to your last column heading and type in 'October'. When you hit **Enter**, the new column heading text will automatically format to match the others but the line does not copy over. There is a way to address this. First, clear the previous changes; click **Undo** twice to delete October and remove the cell styles. Now try this approach instead...

Select cells A1 through J6. Click **Format As Table** in the Styles group of the Home Tab. Click **Table Style Medium 3 ➜ OK**. Type 'October', 'November' and 'December' to complete the header row. Notice how they format automatically? Autofill numbers into these new columns to complete the table. You may recognize this feature as Lists from Office 2003, but in addition to creating the autofilter at the top of each column, you can now take advantage of the autoformat and autofill functions of a table.

Type 'Saturday' in the first blank row under the days of the week in column A and then hit the **Tab** key. Notice that the formula automatically populated the remaining columns of data with the randbetween formula.

Try this with your own worksheets and see how converting your data to a table can help you format automatically and autofill formulas to create spreadsheets faster. With the gallery of table styles and page layout themes, you'll never have to manually draw lines around one cell at a time again.

Click the **Design** tab on the Table tools contextual command tab. Hover over the Table Styles gallery to see a Live Preview of the table styles. Click the **Page Layout** tab then **Themes**. Hover over the theme names for a preview of how the colors and fonts will affect the table.

A foray into functions
So that's the formatting dealt with. But what about the functions? What about the formulas? Fortunately, Excel 2007 ➲

CHAPTER 9 **FORMATTING**

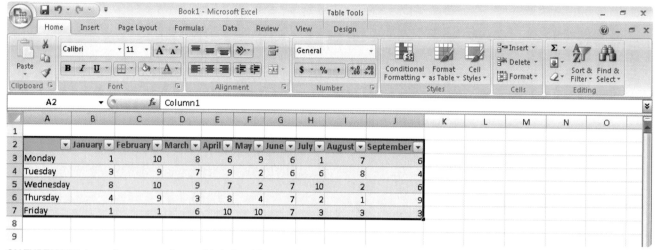

ON THE TABLE Data can be presented as a table in Excel 2007, making quantitative information easier to digest

	January	February	March	April	May	June	July	August	September
Monday	1	10	8	6	9	6	1	7	6
Tuesday	3	9	7	9	2	6	6	8	4
Wednesday	8	10	9	7	2	7	10	2	6
Thursday	4	9	3	8	4	7	2	1	9
Friday	1	1	6	10	10	7	3	3	3

also makes writing formulas a lot less scary than before.

Go back to the source data previously created and type '=co' under the January column and notice how all the functions that begin with 'co' are listed on the screen (see below). Click once on any function in the list to see its description. Double-click the function you want to use. The tip will stay with you, letting you know what values to enter to complete the function. In fact, if you click the name of the function in the tip, it will open up a Help screen with directions on how that function is used, with samples to look at. The functions can even be used to manipulate text.

For example, here's a formula in Office Excel 2007 that takes text from two columns and combines the words into one string in a new column...

In a new worksheet, name column A 'First Name' and label two new column headings 'Last Name' and 'Full Name' respectively. Complete the First Name column with Lisa, Jorge and Tonja and the Last Name column with Brown, Sanchez and Smith. Click in the blank cell under Full Name and click the **Formulas** tab on the Office Fluent interface.

In the Function Library group, click the down arrow next to Text on the Office Fluent interface and select **Concatenate**. It's pronounced kon-kat-e-nate – in case you want to start using it in everyday sentences, such as: "What we really need to do is concatenate the two teams for a more productive project."

For the Text1 field, click **Lisa**. Then, click the Text2 field and click **Brown**. Click **OK**. Now, let's put a space in between the two words. Click the cell

Better results faster

Random numbers? Copy and paste the table into a new spreadsheet. Hover over the clipboard (bottom-right) and click the down arrow. Click **Values** and **Source Formatting**

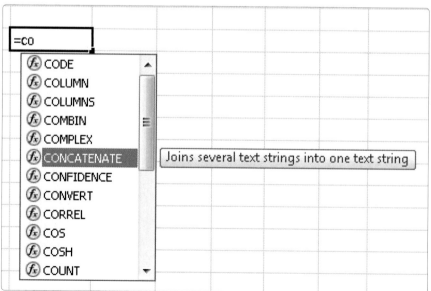

DON'T WORRY Excel 2007 can even perform functions on your text

68 EXPLORE A Real-Life Guide to Getting More Done

with the formula in it and click your mouse next to the first cell reference to get a blinking cursor. Position the cursor after the comma, and type " ", (open quote, spacebar, close quote, comma) between the two cell references, so the formula should look like this: =CONCATENATE(A2," ",B2)

What you type between the quotes is added to the field. In this case we only added a space but in the next example we add a comma and a space so it looks like Last Name, First Name. Click the blank cell next to Jose Sanchez and type '=con'. Double-click **Concatenate**, click the cell with Sanchez in it, type 'comma, open parenthesis, comma, spacebar, close parenthesis, comma' and click the cell with Jose to populate the Text3 field. The formula should look like this: =CONCATENATE(B3," ",A3)

Hit **Enter** and – wow! It's like magic.

So, now you've played with Word 2007 and Excel 2007, you'll be wanting to show off your hard work and new-found skills in a PowerPoint presentation...

Office PowerPoint 2007
Power to the people

Despite being a simple and effective presentation tool, PowerPoint 2007 is often overlooked. Many people don't consider themselves presenters; or they just don't think their meeting is important enough to create a slide show.

Well, PowerPoint is actually a real asset to the information worker, as it can be a key component in alleviating some of the fear associated with getting up and speaking in front of other people.

By having a dynamic visual aid, your colleagues won't be staring solely at you the whole time you're talking, and when they do look over they should be smiling and nodding their heads in agreement with your slides.

Admittedly, there was a time when applying styles in PowerPoint meant using the Heading 1, Heading 2 and Heading 3 styles from Word to get the best results. In Office PowerPoint 2007, you can import any Word document and PowerPoint 2007 will work at creating slides based on the layout. If you still have the Word file open that you were practicing on earlier and want to use it as an example here, you need to name it and close it, because you can't import a Word document that is currently open for editing.

To begin, open a blank presentation and click the **Home** tab on the Office Fluent interface. Click the arrow next to New Slide in the Slides group and

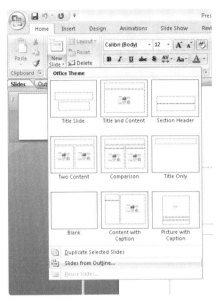

LOOKS FAMILIAR Word documents can be imported to PowerPoint and retain layout

choose **Slides From Outline** on the drop-down menu. Depending on how large a file you choose, this process may take a while. If it's a complex document with embedded images, it may not work at all. Still, PowerPoint 2007 works with most Word documents.

Now the text is in the presentation, let's get it formatted on the slides correctly. Click the **Outline** tab in the ➲

CO-ORDINATE In PowerPoint 2007 (and other Office applications) you can apply themes

upper-left corner of the thumbnail pane, just below the Office Fluent interface. Click the picture of the slide next to any body text that may have slipped in and hit **Delete**. Use your Tab key to indent titles into subheadings, and if you need to promote an item use Shift and Tab.

To change the order of bullet points, drag up or down on to another slide. Click the **Slides** tab to return to the Slides view. Delete any blank slides here. Obviously, it may look a little plain right now, but it's a start.

Once the basic formatting is complete, you can jazz up your presentation by applying a PowerPoint theme. Themes work the same way in PowerPoint 2007 as in Word 2007. Go to the Design tab to see the gallery of themes available in the Background group. Click the drop-down arrow next to Background Styles to explore more options.

If your company is running Microsoft Office SharePoint Server 2007, you can publish some or all of the slides in a presentation directly to an online Slide

Personalize PowerPoint

Get your presentation to look exactly how you want it

Sometimes you need a slide that's as unique as you are to get your point across. Creating your own custom slide layouts enables you to decide where you want slide elements such as text boxes, charts or pictures to be positioned. This takes the Slide Master concept to a whole new level...

You can place a background object, background fill, body placeholder, headers and footers, placeholder formatting, a title placeholder and a subtitle placeholder all on one slide if you like. No more Bulleted List slides you have to modify in the Master Slide screen – you've got three columns of content to make your point now. The best part is that you can reuse these custom layouts in other presentations.

To add a custom layout, click the **View** tab, then click **Slide Master** in the Presentation Views group. Scroll down to the bottom of the list and click below the last layout. Click **Insert Layout** in the Edit Master group in the Slide Master tab (see right). Delete unwanted placeholders and click the **Insert**

Placeholder arrow in the Master Layout group to choose content, text, picture, chart, table, diagram, media or clip art. When you're done, click the **Office** button, click **Save As** and select **PowerPoint Template** from the Save As Type field. Rename the file and click **Save**. This new layout is accessible any time you want to use it via the layout drop-down box.

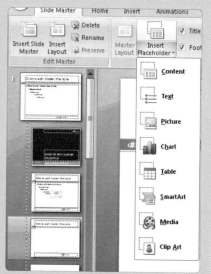

BREAK OUT Express yourself by creating your own custom-built PowerPoint slides

Library. To publish a selection of your slides to a Slide Library, click the **Office** button, then **Publish → Publish Slides**. Put checks by the slides you want to publish or click **Select All**.

Navigate your web browser to the site where you want others to access your slides. Select and copy the web address but leave off the view name from the URL (for example, /AllItems.aspx) and paste it into the Publish To: field in PowerPoint 2007. Click **Publish**.

By linking the presentation to the slides in the library you will be prompted each time you open the presentation to

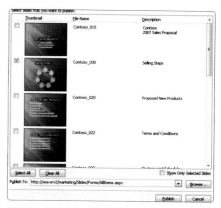

PASS IT ON With Office SharePoint Server 2007, you can share your slides online

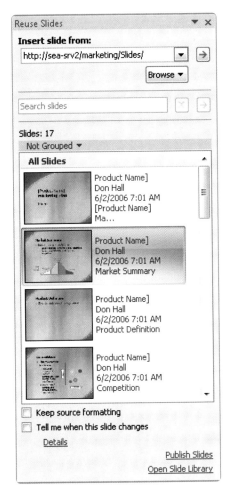

SOMETHING BORROWED You can download other people's slides for your presentation

update and synchronize any changes made online by your co-workers.

To reuse slides from a Slide Library in your own presentation, click the down arrow next to New Slide and click **Reuse Slides**. In the Reuse Slide task pane, select **Open A Slide Library** and double-click the SharePoint site where you saved the slides. You can even preview slides by hovering over the thumbnail images. Click the slide you want and – as if by magic! – it's in your presentation with the current design template applied automatically. To keep the source formatting, click the Smart Tag and select Keep Source Formatting.

After all this, congratulations are in order – you have officially taken your rightful place as the formatting superstar in your office.

Top tips

Fast formatting for the 2007 Microsoft Office system: a recap...

■ Reuse styles you like from an existing document
Click **Office** then **New → New From Existing**. Select the Word document you want to use. Now click **Create New**.

■ Save a Style Set in Word 2007
Click **Change Styles** on the Home tab of the Fluent interface, then click **Style Set → Save As Quick Style Set**. Give it an appropriate name and click **Save**.

■ Experiment with Word 2007 Building Blocks
Click on the Text Box arrow in the Text group in the Insert tab. Then click **Exposure Sidebar** (for example).

■ Apply an Office Theme to your document
Click **Page Layout** in Microsoft Word 2007. Click **Themes** and then try one out for size – Metro, for example.

■ Adjust the zoom of your spreadsheet in Excel 2007
Slide the Zoom bar anywhere between 20 and 100 per cent to get the view you want.

■ Use Excel 2007 Page Layout View
Click **View** tab and click Page Layout View in the Workbook Views group.

■ Format an Excel 2007 spreadsheet as a table
First, you need to select the data you require in a worksheet. Then click **Format As Table** in the Styles group of the Home tab. Select a

NEED MORE HELP? Go to office.microsoft. com and do a search on 'formatting'

suitable table style to create and format the table to your liking.

■ Create PowerPoint slides from a Word 2007 document
In PowerPoint 2007, click the **Home** tab. Click **New Slide → Slides from Outline**. Now double-click the Word 2007 file that you want to copy. Finally, click the **Outline** tab on the left of the screen in PowerPoint 2007 to clean up any unwanted text.

■ Create a custom PowerPoint 2007 slide layout
Click **View**, then **Slide Master** in the Presentation Views group. Scroll down and click below the last layout. Click **Insert Layout** in Edit Master group in Slide Master. Delete any unwanted placeholders; click **Insert Placeholder** arrow in the Master Layout group. Click **Office → Save As** and pick **PowerPoint Template** from the Save As Type field.

■ Reuse slides from the SharePoint library
Click the down arrow under New Slide on Home. Click **Reuse Slides** then **Open A Slide Library** in the Reuse Slides pane and double-click the SharePoint site where you originally saved the slides.

Take control of your life!

There's more to Outlook 2007 than email. With the 2007 Office release, getting your life in order is a piece of cake

You could be mistaken for thinking Microsoft Office Outlook 2007 has changed little but how wrong you'd be. The main reason for this initial impression is the fact that the Microsoft Office Fluent interface appears to be missing from Outlook 2007, but it is there – open up an email and you'll see that it magically reappears. And the more you use Outlook 2007, the more

improvements you'll see. The most obvious is the new To-Do Bar that can either sit permanently or as a pop-out bar. This handy feature lists the current calendar, appointments, messages marked for follow-up and any tasks that need your attention, all in order of priority. The minimize feature has also been added to the Navigation pane, giving you the maximum space possible.

Part of the improved reminder system includes more message flagging options, with different settings and colors. These can be applied to email and other items within Outlook 2007, helping visual scanning of messages or the calendar.

Instant searching is now available thanks to the way that Office Outlook 2007 indexes messages as they come in, enabling you to perform complex and thorough searches in next to no time.

The calendar has been updated in numerous useful ways. For starters, it's possible to email part or all of the calendar to your contacts to let them know when you're free. Internet subscriptions are also supported, enabling you to make part or all of it publicly visible. In addition, multiple calendars have been implemented, both for viewing and editing with an overlay display mode.

Email editing is enhanced thanks to the way that Outlook 2007 now uses the full Microsoft Office Word HTML rendering engine. You get improved security, the same advanced spelling and grammar checker and it's also possible to preview attachments within the email pane.

Top features

What to look Out for...

■ INDEX Indexing of emails, contacts, tasks, calendar entries and other items for speed searches
■ WORD SEARCHES Displays results as characters are typed
■ SEARCH New search and RSS feed folders
■ SUPPORT Unified messaging, SMS, voicemail and fax with Microsoft Exchange Server 2007
■ DATES Multiple calendar support with overlay editing and viewing
■ TASK To-do displays calendar, tasks and urgent messages
■ SHARE Contacts can be shared among users, via email, Exchange Server 2007 or a SharePoint site
■ PREVIEW Attachment preview allows users to view email attachments in the reading pane
■ FILTER Junk email filter/phishing and Postmark technology

Better results faster

In the calendar, go to **Edit → Automatic Formatting**. This enables you to take advantage of new color categories by applying them to predefined conditions, such as words in appointment titles

A whole raft of advanced features and services are available when Outlook 2007 is used in conjunction with Microsoft Exchange Server 2007, which is most commonly found within larger companies. There have been improvements to scheduling meetings within groups plus the advantage of having unified SMS, fax, voicemail and email delivery to Outlook 2007. So now it really is possible to organize all of the people all of the time. ⊞

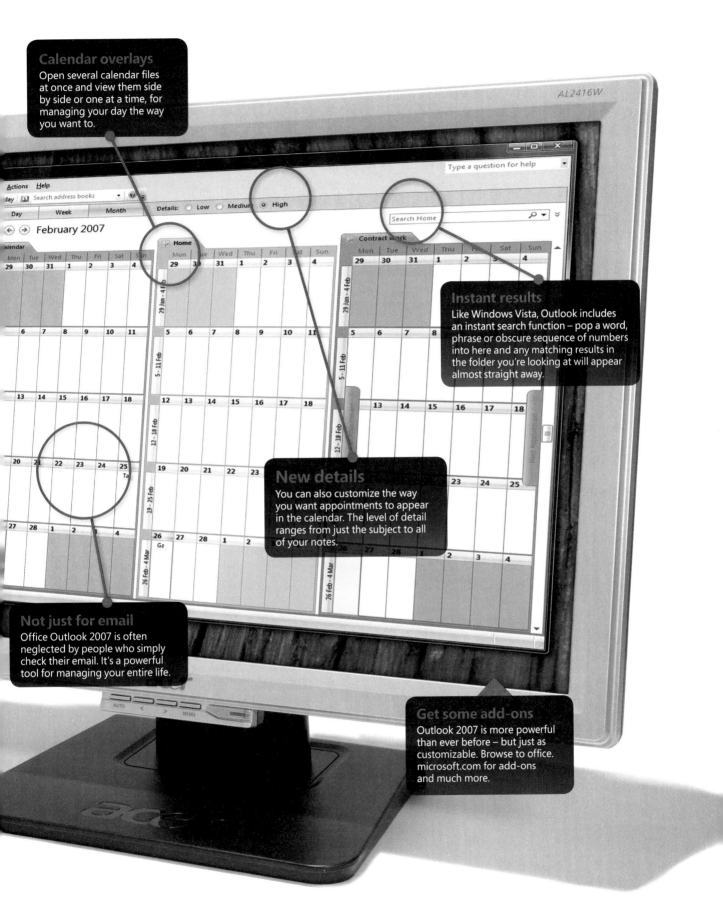

Calendar overlays
Open several calendar files at once and view them side by side or one at a time, for managing your day the way you want to.

Instant results
Like Windows Vista, Outlook includes an instant search function – pop a word, phrase or obscure sequence of numbers into here and any matching results in the folder you're looking at will appear almost straight away.

New details
You can also customize the way you want appointments to appear in the calendar. The level of detail ranges from just the subject to all of your notes.

Not just for email
Office Outlook 2007 is often neglected by people who simply check their email. It's a powerful tool for managing your entire life.

Get some add-ons
Outlook 2007 is more powerful than ever before – but just as customizable. Browse to office. microsoft.com for add-ons and much more.

Organize your days with ease

Sick of being your own secretary? Let Microsoft Office Outlook 2007 arrange your diary and emails

Microsoft Office Outlook is most commonly thought of as an email application, but you could almost think of it as an operating system in its own right. For many people, it's the first application they load when starting their PC and the last one they close before shutting it down. A large part of people's working life is centered around email,

and even the elements that aren't generally involve a what, when and almost always a who.

With Office Outlook 2007, all that stuff is available in one place – integrated into the program are day-planning, address book, to-do list and meeting organization functions, which all work out a lot neater than a jumble of sticky notes stuck to a monitor.

You can quickly switch between these core functions by using the four

permanently-visible tabs that can be found at the bottom-left corner of Office Outlook 2007: Mail, Calendar, Contacts and Tasks.

The messaging element of Office Outlook 2007 is very similar to Windows Mail, the email program included in Windows Vista (though you may be more familiar with Outlook Express, which appeared in previous versions of Windows). It's more advanced, though, because it's designed for people who receive a large number of emails, so there are many different ways to categorize messages.

While many mail programs offer instant search, the facility soon becomes redundant if you can't remember who sent you the message or what the subject line was. With Office Outlook 2007, however, you only need to remember a single excerpt from an element of an email to find it.

You can also categorize an email as soon as it arrives in your inbox with just a couple of mouse clicks. ➡

Search folders

Find those missing messages

A search folder is a continually updated archive of every message matching certain features – from a specific person, for example. There are a few folders set up – such as Unread Mail and Large Mail – but to create one right-click on **Search Folders**, then click **New Search Folder**. Choose the details you want it to look for and, from then on, clicking on its name under **Search Folders** will show everything that matches.

FILE & FIND With custom Search Folders, mails are always easy to locate

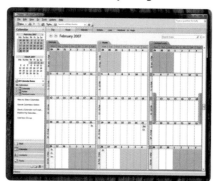

LOOK BUSY Create several calendars, then overlay them to spot any double bookings

REMINDERS Create notes on your PC or pick up scribbles made on your mobile device

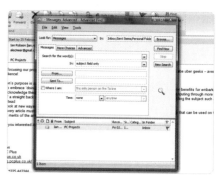

CROSS REFERENCE Advanced searches turn up messages related to the one you're looking at

Learn the secrets of perfect planning

Remember what you're doing and when you're doing it

1 TASK MASTER Not every demand on your time makes itself known in the form of an email. For that, click the **Tasks** tab at the lower-left of Outlook. Here, you can simply list everything that you need to get done.

2 MAKE A DATE Double-click on an empty line in the main part of Outlook and the **New Task** window opens. You can create a to-do entry as though it were a calendar entry. Give it a name and a start and due-by date.

3 ON TOP The job now appears in the main Tasks pane and in your Calendar. If you revisit it from either, you can amend it – update how close it is to being finished, for instance, add notes, or change the deadline.

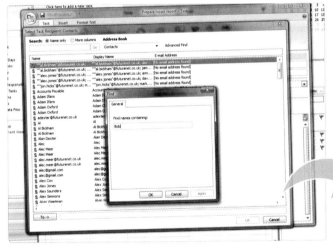

4 PHONE A FRIEND You can also involve other people in your task. Delegate to a colleague or underling by clicking **Assign Task**, then choose an email recipient. They'll get the details by email and the job then appears in their Outlook 2007 **Tasks** and **Calendar** panes.

You can delegate a task to a colleague or underling simply by clicking a button

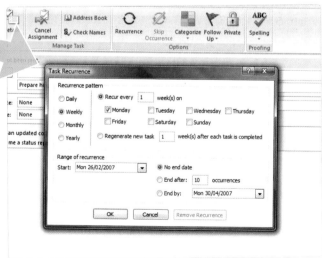

Best before dates

With Microsoft Outlook 2007 you can set expiration dates for your emails. Just click the **Message Options** arrow and, once the mail is no longer a priority, it appears with a strikethrough in the recipient's inbox.

5 PROGRESS REPORT You can send a status report to your boss when you make progress – it's a button in the **Manage Task** area of the Microsoft Office Fluent interface. If it's something you do regularly, click **Recurrence** and Outlook will remind you when it's due again.

Each category has its own search folder, so if you click on the category title from the toolbar, you'll see every email that belongs in that category. The search can also identify text that appears in the body of emails.

The integrated calendar is similarly vital in helping to sort out an otherwise disorganized life. It operates rather like a day planner, except that the appointments and tasks are infinitely editable and Office Outlook 2007 reminds you when they're looming on the horizon. It reminds other people, too; so if you're setting up a meeting, all you need to do is click **Calendar** on the bottom-left of Outlook 2007, click the day you want the meeting on, and

then double-click on the approximate starting time. A new window now opens, into which you can type a meeting name, location, time, and, optionally, the email addresses of the other attendees – Outlook 2007 then sends them an invite. If they're also using Outlook 2007, the meeting automatically appears in their calendars.

If the meeting changes at a later date, you can double-click its entry in the calendar, change the appropriate details, then click **Send update** to let everyone else know. There's also a handy **Reminder** button (a small gold bell at the top of an appointment or meeting window) which displays an alert whenever something's impending.

More dates

Never miss an appointment

You don't need to dump your entire life into one Outlook 2007 calendar; just click **New ➜ Calendar** to create an additional planner. That way, you can separate work and personal stuff, rather than having notes about visiting Auntie Flossie clogging up details of meetings. You can still check for clashes though – just click **View ➜ View in Overlay mode** and all the calendars will be visible at once, so you can quickly see if you're double-booked.

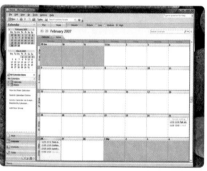

WEEK TO VIEW Arrange your calendars in daily, weekly or monthly layouts to suit you

CONNECT Windows Mobile Device Center lets you sync a Pocket PC with Outlook

DOUBLE DATE You can overlay calendar entries for specific dates to avoid clashes

Ultimate message management
Emails getting on top of you? Sort the wheat from the chaff...

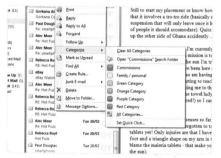

1 COLOR-COORDINATED Right-click on an email and select **Categorize** to tag it with a colored icon. There are six default colors but you can make more by clicking **All Categories**.

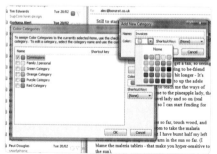

2 UNIQUE FILTERS This opens the **Color Categories** window. Click **New** to create a category, with a color from the drop-down list. Or click **Color** or **Rename** to alter an existing one.

3 QUICK CLICK If there's a category you use a lot, hit the four-squares icon and choose **Set Quick Click**. Pick a category; clicking on the square after an email then adds it to that category.

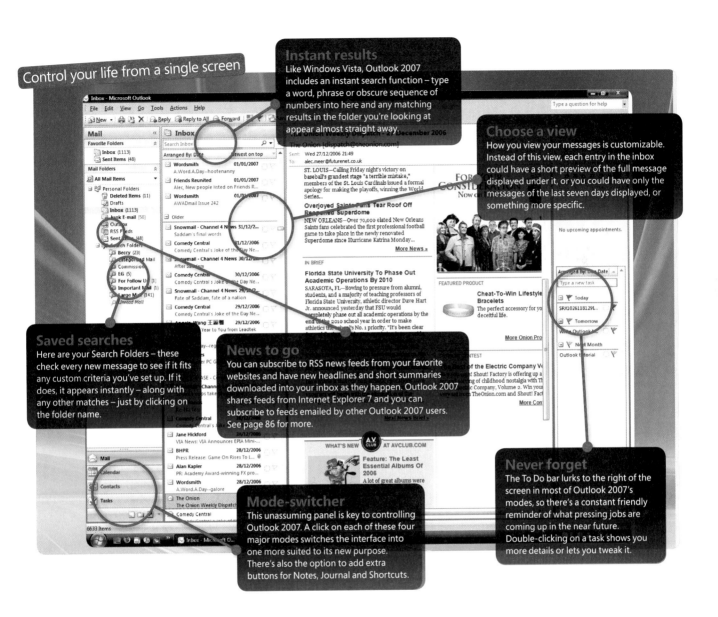

Control your life from a single screen

Instant results
Like Windows Vista, Outlook 2007 includes an instant search function – type a word, phrase or obscure sequence of numbers into here and any matching results in the folder you're looking at appear almost straight away.

Choose a view
How you view your messages is customizable. Instead of this view, each entry in the inbox could have a short preview of the full message displayed under it, or you could have only the messages of the last seven days displayed, or something more specific.

Saved searches
Here are your Search Folders – these check every new message to see if it fits any custom criteria you've set up. If it does, it appears instantly – along with any other matches – just by clicking on the folder name.

News to go
You can subscribe to RSS news feeds from your favorite websites and have new headlines and short summaries downloaded into your inbox as they happen. Outlook 2007 shares feeds from Internet Explorer 7 and you can subscribe to feeds emailed by other Outlook 2007 users. See page 86 for more.

Never forget
The To Do bar lurks to the right of the screen in most of Outlook 2007's modes, so there's a constant friendly reminder of what pressing jobs are coming up in the near future. Double-clicking on a task shows you more details or lets you tweak it.

Mode-switcher
This unassuming panel is key to controlling Outlook 2007. A click on each of these four major modes switches the interface into one more suited to its new purpose. There's also the option to add extra buttons for Notes, Journal and Shortcuts.

4 MAIL SORT To create a rule to add messages meeting certain criteria to a category, right-click on a message, click **Create rule → Advanced options**. Select the filters you want to apply.

5 FINE TUNE Click a blue underlined word to specify a requirement, such as a name. Click the bold text of 'Assigned to **category** category' to pick which category the email goes into.

6 FOLLOW UP Set a prompt to follow up emails you can't deal with right away. Right-click the message, choose **Follow Up** and say when. Click **Add reminder** and Outlook will nag you!

Keep up to date and on schedule

Having trouble keeping on top of your schedule?
Windows Calendar can keep you organized

Forget your loaf of sliced white, the calendar must serve as one of mankind's finest inventions! In the workplace, and out, we all have to make appointments – an appraisal with the boss, a routine check-up at the dentist, a date with the love of your life. While you may not forget that hot date (hopefully!), it's easy to double-book a work meeting, which is why an easy-to-use Calendar can make all the difference. Windows Calendar helps to organize your life in the form of appointments – events occurring on specific dates – and tasks, which enable you to create to-do lists, where you can

add deadlines and priority details.

When you open the program, by default one calendar is set up, but you can create different calendars for different purposes. To create another, just choose **File → New Calendar**. Tasks and appointments are then assigned to different calendars, and you can choose to view them all together or hide individual calendars by unticking them.

By default, Windows Calendar displays the current day split into hours, but you can view appointments by week, working week (Monday to Friday) or month by clicking the **View** button.

Appointments can be set to occur at a specific time, or labeled an 'all-day'

event. They can be one-off events – such as a meeting – or be set to recur at specific intervals (such as birthdays).

Create one by selecting the calendar you want it to come under and then click **New Appointment**. Fill in the Details box in the right-hand pane. To be reminded of the event up to two weeks in advance, click the **Reminder** drop-down menu and choose from the list of options.

If you have a Windows Live account, you can use the Windows Live Calendar. This enables you to access your calendar from any PC using your Windows Live account, plus you can share it with other Windows Live users, perfect for sharing events with friends and colleagues. 🟦

IT'S A DATE Forget scribbled notes in a neglected diary – this is straightforward scheduling

Take control of your life

Windows Live Calendar makes it easy to stay organized from any PC

1 **SET UP CALENDARS** Go to calendar. live.com. Two calendars are created by default; your own, plus a birthday one for your Windows Live Mail contacts. To create more, click the plus icon next to Calendar, fill in the details and click **OK**.

2 **NAVIGATE CALENDAR** Switch views by clicking **Day**, **Week** or **Month** – choosing **Agenda** enables you to see all upcoming events between two dates. Switch to a different month by clicking the arrow keys by the current month.

3 **CREATE EVENT** Select a day and then click **Add** to set up an event. Enter the basic details (such as what, where and when) and then click **OK**, or click **Add more details** to add a reminder or to make it recurring.

4 **SHARE YOUR CALENDAR** Click the **Share** button and select **Share this calendar**. You can share it with other Windows Live users with different levels of access, or create a read-only site for public or private consumption. Decide which you want and then click **Save**.

Windows Live Calendar enables you to access your calendar from any PC using your Windows Live account

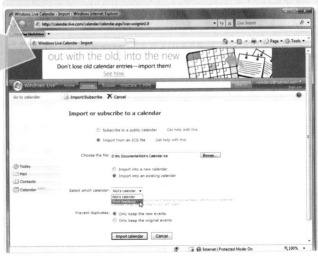

5 **IMPORT CALENDAR** Go to File → Export in Windows Calendar to save your PC-based calendar. Now open Windows Live Calendar, click **Subscribe** and choose **Import from an ICS file** to select the file and import it into a new or existing calendar.

Outlook Connector

Install this plug-in for Microsoft Office Outlook 2003 and 2007 from tinyurl.com/6rs5m2. Add your Windows Live account details when prompted and you can use your Windows Live Calendar within Outlook itself.

A noteworthy new edition

Forget handwritten scribbles cluttering your desk, start keeping research in order with OneNote 2007

Better results faster

OneNote 2007 snaps items you move to an invisible grid to make it easier to line up objects. To disable the feature, hold **Alt** while moving an object. To turn the grid off click **Edit → Snap To Grid**

If a spiral-bound notebook is a bicycle (functional, gets you from A to B), Microsoft Office OneNote 2007 is a Space Shuttle, taking you further than you thought

Top features

Look what OneNote 2007 offers

■ MORE Multiple notebooks
■ SHARING Notebooks can be shared across multiple computers
■ SEARCHES Indexed notepads with word-wheeled search
■ SYNCHRONIZATION Fully compatible with Outlook 2007
■ TABLES Support for creating and editing tables
■ TEXT SEARCH Optical character recognition is done on images so text in them can be searched
■ HYPERLINKS Links can be placed within notepad
■ BLOGGING Write up and post blog entries
■ DRAWING Tools for creating diagrams in OneNote 2007
■ CALCULATIONS Typing any arithmetical expression, followed by "=", displays the result of the calculation
■ COMPATIBILITY Send to OneNote via any application that can print to a virtual printer
■ MOBILITY OneNote Mobile for taking notes on smartphones and Pocket PC devices

possible with a note-taking application. It's a store for all your notes, research and thoughts, building on past revisions.

A big change in Office OneNote 2007 reflects the mobility needed by modern networked users. Multiple notebooks are now supported, enabling you to have different projects or parts of your life as separate notebooks within the same work file. And OneNote 2007 can work with networked notebook files.

Finding items is easier, too, thanks to the enhanced indexed search tool. Navigation is improved with a notebook list and the ability to drag pages, sections and notebooks around. You can also add hyperlinks between areas.

Note-taking itself has been made easier. If you're researching online, web content can be sent directly from Internet Explorer to OneNote, where

it can be annotated and reused. If a document is relevant to the notes you're taking, this can be embedded as well and have annotations attached.

To help create better structured notes, you can now create flexible tables with adjustable columns and rows or grab an existing table from another 2007 Office system application and drop it in. Drawing tools are welcome, too; clear diagrams can be created quickly.

OneNote 2007 integrates far more tightly with Microsoft Office Outlook 2007. Contacts, meetings, emails and tasks can be associated with notebooks.

The application also recognizes text in images that you've inserted into notes, so when a search is performed for names of people and places, OneNote 2007 displays images containing the text. Now your note-taking can really take off! ◢

TAKE NOTE Keeping all your research in one place – and in order – is easy with OneNote 2007

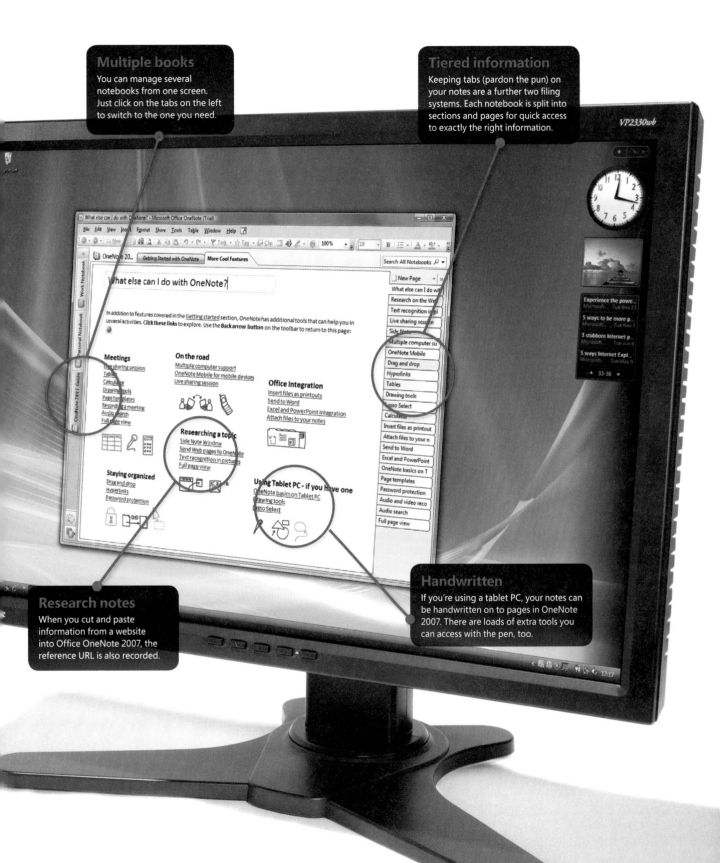

Multiple books

You can manage several notebooks from one screen. Just click on the tabs on the left to switch to the one you need.

Tiered information

Keeping tabs (pardon the pun) on your notes are a further two filing systems. Each notebook is split into sections and pages for quick access to exactly the right information.

Research notes

When you cut and paste information from a website into Office OneNote 2007, the reference URL is also recorded.

Handwritten

If you're using a tablet PC, your notes can be handwritten on to pages in OneNote 2007. There are loads of extra tools you can access with the pen, too.

Ensure you're top of the form

InfoPath 2007 takes the hard work out of data management. Now you'll always be on good form...

Gathering and processing information can be a rather repetitive and laborious task. Fortunately, InfoPath 2007 takes the sting out of it all by making it surprisingly quick and easy. It's an electronic form designer that goes beyond fancy-looking worksheets; when used in conjunction with other 2007 Office system applications it can automate parts of the collection and processing of form distribution and data management.

Designed to work in partnership with Outlook 2007, InfoPath 2007 enables you to create an email form template that can be sent to a mailing list, storing and organizing the returned information in a new Inbox folder to help you process the forms.

InfoPath 2007 forms can be merged to create a single summary for, say, a month's worth of expense forms, or the data can be collated and exported to Excel 2007 for further analysis and report generating.

With InfoPath Forms Server – available as a standalone application – you can design forms for use in web pages, too. This enables people without InfoPath 2007 to fill in forms and submit data from a compatible browser. This flexibility extends to web-based forms.

A number of new and improved views and controls have also been included in InfoPath 2007. The Read-only view, for example, is useful for creating reports, while forms can also be flagged as printable or not. The new Targeted view is handy as a quick tool to create forms for different device sizes. And there are new controls – such as the Combo Box and Multiple-Selection List Box – which add design flexibility. Horizontal repeating tables enable you to add as many columns to a table as required. Existing controls have been enhanced, too – text boxes now boast auto-advance options, allow linked images in rich text boxes and use additional date and time functions.

Top features

InfoPath 2007 has lots to offer

■ USABILITY InfoPath forms can now be used from within a browser
■ MOBILITY Mobile device support
■ EMAIL Forms can be emailed to people and filled in via Outlook
■ COMPATIBILITY Automatic conversion of forms in Word and Excel to InfoPath forms
■ INTUITIVE Improved controls
■ EXPORT Appropriate forms can be exported to Excel 2007
■ DATA PROTECTION Support for Information Rights Management
■ SHARING Publish forms to a network or SharePoint server
■ CHECKING InfoPath 2007 automatically adds data validation
■ PRINTING New Print Layout view displays forms as they'd be printed
■ OPTIMIZATION Targeted views for forms provide users with the best display possible for their browsing device
■ DESIGN Reusable Template parts

DATA DODDLE Take the faff out of form filling with Office InfoPath 2007

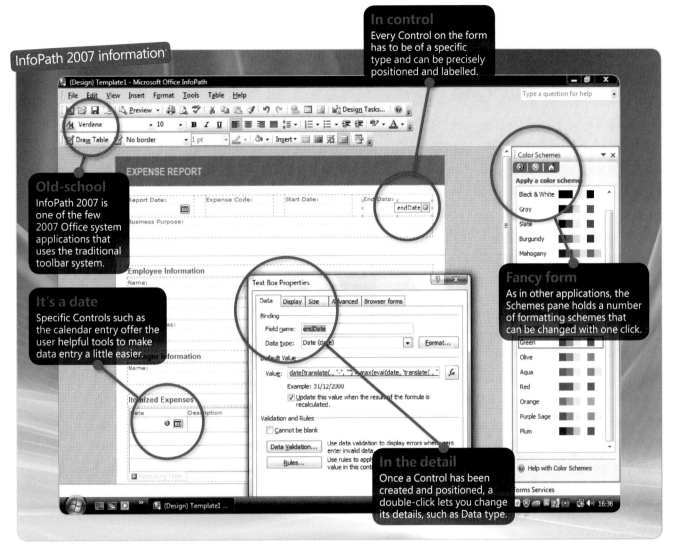

In control
Every Control on the form has to be of a specific type and can be precisely positioned and labelled.

Old-school
InfoPath 2007 is one of the few 2007 Office system applications that uses the traditional toolbar system.

It's a date
Specific Controls such as the calendar entry offer the user helpful tools to make data entry a little easier.

Fancy form
As in other applications, the Schemes pane holds a number of formatting schemes that can be changed with one click.

In the detail
Once a Control has been created and positioned, a double-click lets you change its details, such as Data type.

The immaculate conversion

Save time and trouble by converting old Word forms to InfoPath 2007

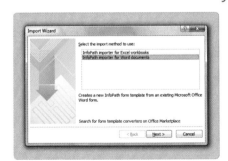

1 IMPORT WIZARD Many companies rely on Word-based documents that act as official forms. InfoPath 2007 has an Import Wizard to convert a Word document into an InfoPath 2007 form.

2 THOSE OPTIONS Open the wizard and find the Word file. There are a number of options for converting the file. For example, underlined areas can be converted to text boxes by default.

3 TIDY UP Once InfoPath 2007 has finished the conversion you're informed of any issues. These are listed in the info pane on the right. Click **Preview** to test out the converted form.

Face the future of data handling

Microsoft Office Access revolutionized databases. Now Microsoft has transformed its interface...

Better results faster

On the Format tab, in the Controls group, click **Logo**. In the Insert Picture dialog, locate the logo file and double-click it. You can now move and resize the logo to suit the form or report

The biggest change that will please long-term Microsoft Office Access users when they fire up the 2007 Microsoft Office system is the revitalized interface. With the introduction of the Office Fluent interface, Microsoft has streamlined Office Access 2007. The mess of floating windows is out and rows of neat tabbed sections are in. In addition, the new navigation pane provides quick access to database objects. If you miss the floating windows, an option is available to bring them back; which is handy for working on multiple databases.

Minor additions provide you with more information and better tools. The Fluent Gallery – constant throughout the 2007 Office system – provides a visual selection of commands, and the Mini toolbar offers handy editing tools. The Status bar at the bottom provides useful information and includes buttons for switching between views.

Form creation has had a boost. The new Layout and Report views enable you to browse and make design changes on a live form or report; and because the Layout view is WYSIWYG, you can see design changes instantly. Table creation and handling have also been improved, partly due to the new Table button in the Create tab. You can also paste tables from Office Excel 2007, and Office Access 2007 automatically recognizes data types and creates fields.

Integration with Microsoft SharePoint Server 2007 opens up whole new ways of working with Office Access 2007 and improving your organization's workflow. Migrating a database is now really easy thanks to the built-in wizard that moves keys and relationships to the server-based system. Once in place, email alerts can be set and a workflow system created to assign tasks, deadlines, protection and approval of updates. There's also support for offline updating, with Access 2007 synchronizing your changes once you are reconnected with the server.

Top features

Microsoft Office Access has plenty of new tricks up its sleeve

■ INTERFACE New streamlined Microsoft Office Fluent interface
■ FILTERS Enhanced filtering
■ GRAPHICS Support for embedded documents and images
■ DESIGN New template selection
■ CONSISTENCY Whenever a table is updated, all reports referencing the table are updated, too
■ FORMATS Rich Text can be used in memo fields
■ VIEWS New Layout/Report views
■ TABLES Improved table creation and importing
■ QUICK CHANGE Drop-down lists for a table can be modified in place
■ LOOKUPS Lookup Fields that get values by cross referencing a table now support multi-valued lookups
■ DATA SHARING Access can synchronize with Windows SharePoint Server 2007

CLEAR SCREEN The Layout in Office Access gives a What You See Is What You Get view

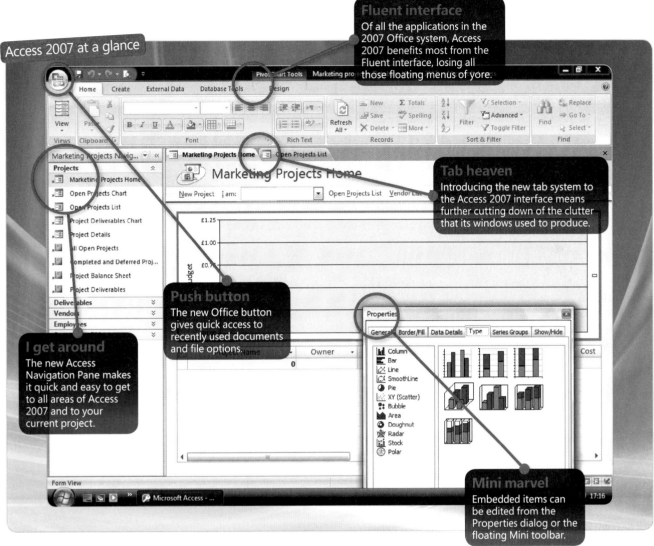

Access 2007 at a glance

Fluent interface
Of all the applications in the 2007 Office system, Access 2007 benefits most from the Fluent interface, losing all those floating menus of yore.

Tab heaven
Introducing the new tab system to the Access 2007 interface means further cutting down of the clutter that its windows used to produce.

Push button
The new Office button gives quick access to recently used documents and file options.

I get around
The new Access Navigation Pane makes it quick and easy to get to all areas of Access 2007 and to your current project.

Mini marvel
Embedded items can be edited from the Properties dialog or the floating Mini toolbar.

Databases can be cool

New features in Office Access 2007 help speed up your database creation

1 ONLINE GOODS From new templates (downloaded directly from Microsoft) to integrated online help, Access 2007 makes full use of online content, giving you the latest news and assistance.

2 INSTANT TABLES The new tools in Access 2007 enable you to 'drop in' tables in an instant. You can copy and paste from an Excel 2007 spreadsheet, creating databases with ease.

3 ATTACH THIS The new Attachment data type enables files of any type to be attached within a database. Pictures, Word documents and even multiple attachments can be applied to a record.

Heads-up on the headlines

No time to buy a newspaper? Don't worry – just get the latest stories sent to your computer...

It can be tricky to explain why RSS (Really Simple Syndication) feeds are so handy to someone who hasn't used them before but, in a nutshell, you don't go to the web, the web comes to you. Your RSS application plucks new stories as feeds from your favorite websites on a regular basis and then brings them directly to your computer screen.

The pertinent question, then, is what software to use to subscribe to and access these feeds. There's a slew of free standalone applications, and in Windows Vista there's also the Common Feeds list. This shows up your RSS headlines of choice in Internet Explorer 7 and the Windows Sidebar. In the 2007 Office

system those feeds can also appear in Microsoft Office Outlook 2007, or you can have separate feeds there if you prefer. Whichever you choose, new headlines turn up in the RSS Feeds folder as though they were emails; click on one to read a summary of the story, or click **View article** to load the entire piece in your web browser.

News views

Each website presents its RSS feeds differently – some turn up as complete stories with a picture or two, others as a single-sentence summary. With a click on the bar that appears on the top of each story when you view it, Office Outlook 2007 can download the entire article. It shows up as an attachment to

the message, so a double-click opens it without loading a browser.

If you do intend to make Office Outlook 2007 your sole source of news, it's worth adding a load of websites to begin with, and then whittling them down to the ones that present their feeds most usefully. Each feed you've subscribed to appears as a sub-folder within RSS Feeds; if you're not happy with it, a right-click enables you to either delete or rename it.

And that's it – 'really simple' indeed. See 'Deal with your desktop digests' below for how to subscribe to and manage your feeds; other than that it's simply a matter of letting Office Outlook 2007 grab headlines for you, then reading them at your leisure. ⊞

Better results faster

It's easy to share feeds with other Outlook 2007 users – just right-click on a story-message, choose **Share this feed** and it emails the subscription to a contact of your choice

Deal with your desktop digests

Subscribing to and managing your news feeds

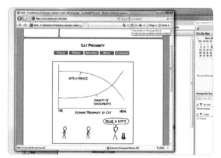

1 FEED ME There are lots of ways to add feeds. One is to visit a site in Internet Explorer 7. If the button next to the Home icon is orange, there's a feed. Click on it, then **Subscribe to this feed.**

2 SYNC IT In Outlook 2007 it appears in the RSS Feeds folder. If not, go to **Tools → Options → Other → Advanced Options** and check **Sync RSS Feeds to the Common Feed List.**

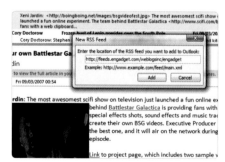

3 NEW LINK To add feeds to Outlook, right-click the RSS folder and choose **Add a new RSS feed.** You need the feed URL. Most sites have an RSS link; right-click it, pick **Copy shortcut** and paste.

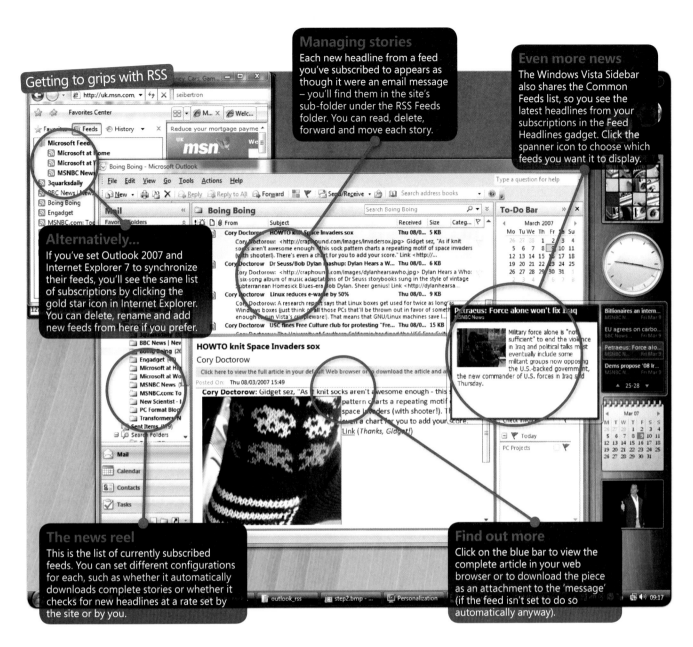

Getting to grips with RSS

Managing stories
Each new headline from a feed you've subscribed to appears as though it were an email message – you'll find them in the site's sub-folder under the RSS Feeds folder. You can read, delete, forward and move each story.

Even more news
The Windows Vista Sidebar also shares the Common Feeds list, so you see the latest headlines from your subscriptions in the Feed Headlines gadget. Click the spanner icon to choose which feeds you want it to display.

Alternatively...
If you've set Outlook 2007 and Internet Explorer 7 to synchronize their feeds, you'll see the same list of subscriptions by clicking the gold star icon in Internet Explorer. You can delete, rename and add new feeds from here if you prefer.

The news reel
This is the list of currently subscribed feeds. You can set different configurations for each, such as whether it automatically downloads complete stories or whether it checks for new headlines at a rate set by the site or by you.

Find out more
Click on the blue bar to view the complete article in your web browser or to download the piece as an attachment to the 'message' (if the feed isn't set to do so automatically anyway).

4 COMPUTER CHOICE Outlook 2007 can also recommend feeds. Click on **RSS Feeds** and the main pane displays featured and Microsoft links. Clicking one gives the option to subscribe to it.

5 ORGANIZE Each story is treated like an email. Right-click and you get the same options you would for a message, including categorizing it or marking it for a follow-up. (More on page 74.)

6 EXTRA, EXTRA To change settings, go to **Tools → Account Settings → RSS Feeds.** Choose the one you want, then click **Change.** You can tell Outlook 2007 to download extras as attachments.

Prime searching

Windows Vista is designed to never lose anything again, so how easy is it to find elusive files?

We've all experienced it: you need to find something in a hurry and while you can remember what it was about, you've no idea when you did it, what program you did it in, what you called it or where you put it. Considering we now store virtually our entire lives on our PCs, finding a document, video or photo is like looking for a needle in a haystack. Windows Vista solves the problem in style though.

The Windows Vista search engine is fast, flexible and incredibly effective, and if it can't find something, it probably doesn't exist. There are three ways to search: when you're browsing, you can use the Search box in the top right-hand corner of the window; the **Search** box in the Start Menu; or you can click **Start ➔ Search** to open the Search folder to carry out very complex searches.

When you type text in a search box, Windows Vista looks for any occurrence of that text – for example, if you typed 'john', it would look for files called 'john', documents containing the word 'john' and files created by a user called 'john'. You can specify searches a bit more by adding prefixes, such as:
Name: john This searches only for files whose name includes the word 'john'.
Modified: 2009 This searches only for files that were changed in 2009.

You can also use search operators such as AND, OR and NOT, as well as the greater than and less than symbols:
Summer AND Vacation – Windows Vista will show you files containing the word 'summer' and 'vacation'. Files containing just one of the words won't be listed.
Summer NOT Vacation – will come up with files that include the word 'summer' but don't include the word 'vacation'.
Summer OR Vacation – will show you files that contain either the word 'summer' or the word 'vacation'.
Summer Vacation – will only show

you files containing the phrase 'summer vacation'.
date: < 01/01/09 – will only show you files created before January 1 2009.
size: > 4MB – will only show you files bigger than 4MB.

You can create very complex searches, but wouldn't it be great if you could use plain English instead? You can. Open the Control Panel, click **Appearance and Personalization** and then **Folder Options**. Now, click on the **Search** tab and then tick the **Use natural language search** box. Click on **OK**, and you can now search in plain English – so, for example, you might search for 'documents by bert 2005'. ⊞

Using the search box

Get the most from those magic boxes that pop up

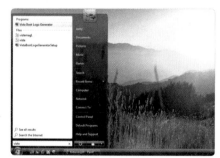

1 QUICK HITS Click **Start** menu. Type your criteria in the search box; the results appear as you type. Windows Vista searches files and browsing history, but you can carry out an internet search.

2 QUICK PICS You'll notice an extra toolbar at the top; this enables you to filter results. Click on **Document** to hide results that aren't documents, **Picture** hides files that aren't pictures.

3 BIG PIC Expand the search's scope by clicking **Advanced Search**. The options slide into view, enabling you to choose a different location and use more complex search criteria.

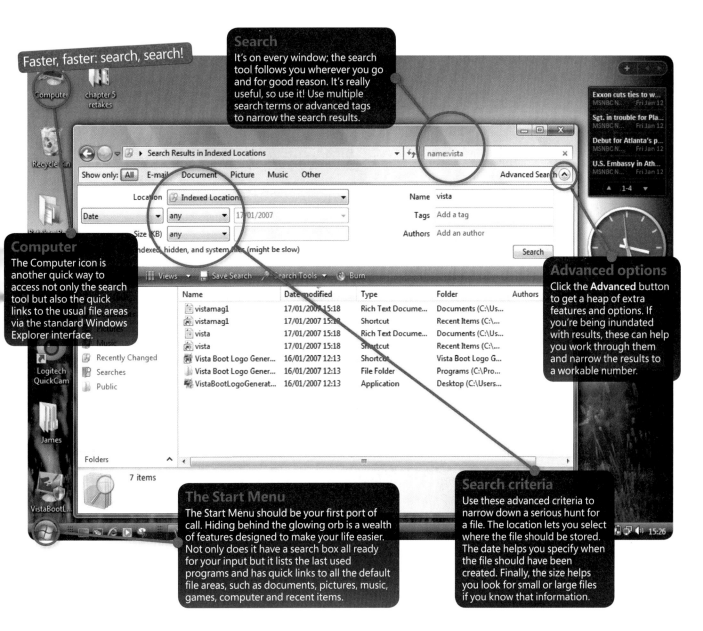

Faster, faster: search, search!

Search
It's on every window; the search tool follows you wherever you go and for good reason. It's really useful, so use it! Use multiple search terms or advanced tags to narrow the search results.

Computer
The Computer icon is another quick way to access not only the search tool but also the quick links to the usual file areas via the standard Windows Explorer interface.

Advanced options
Click the **Advanced** button to get a heap of extra features and options. If you're being inundated with results, these can help you work through them and narrow the results to a workable number.

The Start Menu
The Start Menu should be your first port of call. Hiding behind the glowing orb is a wealth of features designed to make your life easier. Not only does it have a search box all ready for your input but it lists the last used programs and has quick links to all the default file areas, such as documents, pictures, music, games, computer and recent items.

Search criteria
Use these advanced criteria to narrow down a serious hunt for a file. The location lets you select where the file should be stored. The date helps you specify when the file should have been created. Finally, the size helps you look for small or large files if you know that information.

4 SIMPLE SEARCH Open the Search folder and you get the screen shown here. Either type your search terms in the box at the top, or click the **Advanced Search** arrow to show additional options.

5 NARROW DOWN You get the same drop-down menus and fields as when you clicked **Advanced Search** in a folder – but this time, Search looks at all your files rather than a single folder.

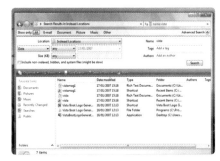

6 BURN BABY BURN The toolbar above the results includes useful features including Burn (to burn the files to CD or DVD). Save your search criteria to the Searches folder by clicking **Save Search**.

Save time by using tags

We discover the little bits of data that make searches super-smart and give you the edge

In the early days of computing, finding things was easy – not because our software was brilliant, but because our hard drives were so small that we'd run out of space after storing three text documents. Now even the humblest hardware has room for thousands of documents, photos, videos and tunes, which makes browsing for something specific time-consuming.

Tag time-savers

If it weren't for tags, we'd spend more time looking for things than looking at them. So what are tags and why are they so great? Tags are little bits of extra data that you attach to a file, and that you can search for using the Windows Vista search box. Let's say you wanted to find a photo of Uncle Fred from his birthday party – the one where he was wearing a stupid hat. Without tags, you'd wade through hundreds or even thousands of files called things such as DSC0001434. JPG. With tags, you'd search for the 'Uncle Fred', 'Birthday' and 'Stupid Hat' tags to find the right file immediately.

Tagging isn't just for photos, though. Want to find all the files – Word documents, Excel files, Visio charts and graphics – for a project? If you've tagged them all with the name of the project, you can find them again in seconds.

The big advantage of tags is that they can contain information that the file itself can't – so while Windows Vista will happily search through the content of documents, it can't see what's inside a picture or listen to a music file, and it

Find photos faster

How nested tags can make your life easier

FAMILY FILTER You can use a hierarchy of tags to hone in on what you're looking for

In Windows Photo Gallery you can organize tags like folders on your hard drive. So, for example, you might have a Family tag that contains a Children tag, a Grandparents tag and a Relatives tag, or a Holidays tag that contains tags for various destinations.

To add Family and Children tags to a picture, type 'Family/Children' in the **Add Tags** field. If the Family tag doesn't exist, Windows Vista creates it for you. You now see an arrow next to Family in the tags list; click on it to show or hide the tags it contains.

can't tell that this Word document is part of the same project as that Excel file, these photographs and this drawing of a horse. Tags add this missing data, enabling you to carry out exceptionally complicated searches using a combination of tags, filenames, document types, dates, star ratings and anything else you might want to look for.

And the good news is that tagging is very quick, because you can select lots of

files in Windows Explorer and give them all the same tags simultaneously. You'll also find a Tags field in the Save As box of most Windows Vista applications, and if you get into the habit of adding tags to everything you save, you'll have to try very hard to lose anything ever again.

It doesn't matter whether you're tagging photos, important documents or daft pictures you've found on the net; tagging is quick, simple and effective.

Let's play tag

Tagging files couldn't be easier, whether you're tagging one file or 100

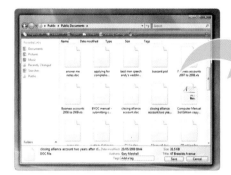  

1 NEVER TOO LATE You can add tags in many programs' **Save As** dialog boxes, but it's easy to tag files later, too. Simply find the file in Windows Explorer, make sure the Details section is visible and click on the file.

2 GET TAGGING Simply type the tags you want to add and separate them with a semicolon (;). The more tags the merrier – here, a letter to the bank has been tagged 'bank; alliance; gary; money'. Click on **Save** when finished.

3 TAG TEAM In this example, a number of files have been selected so that the tags can be added simultaneously. Highlight the files then, once again, it's just a matter of separating the tags with semicolons and then clicking **Save**.

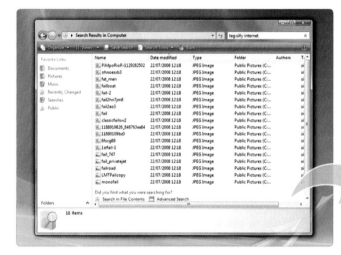

Tags enable you to carry out very complicated searches, using a combination of tags, filenames and much more

4 SPEEDY SEARCHES To look for files with a specific tag, you should use the prefix 'tag:' in the search box to see all the files you've tagged with that particular phrase. You can also search for multiple tags; simply use the 'tag:' prefix before each separate term you're searching for.

What should you tag?

It's a good idea to tag groups of things you might want to find quickly in the future, such as music – either by band or particular genre; photos of specific people, or documents from a specific job or project.

5 QUICK PICS Tagging is particularly useful for photographs, so it's great to see that the Windows Photo Gallery automatically lists the tags you've applied to your photos. Simply click on the tag in the left of the window to see all the photos with that tag.

Bluff your way in the world of blogging

Everyone's blogging, but you can turn your musings into must-read material with a little help from Microsoft Office Word 2007

Best blogs ever

1 BOING BOING A self-styled directory of wonderful things.
www.boingboing.net

2 WINDOWS VISTA Catch up with Windows Vista news.
www.windowsvistamagazine.com

3 TECHNORATI A search engine for blogs and feeds.
www.technorati.com

4 BLUE'S NEWS Games blog with a definitive style; lots of links.
www.bluesnews.com

Traditionally, blogs have been completely online – you read them online, and you write them online. There's an administration panel hidden behind the scenes, menus for categories, date information and a large void in which you write your post. You type the words. You click **OK**.

No mess, no fuss.

However, blog for more than a few days and you begin to see the problems. A web browser's primary function is displaying content; receiving it is a bonus. Take too long typing a post and it disappears when you submit it, taking your deepest thoughts with it, as the site you're using admits it signed you out of your account half an hour ago. Use

Office Word 2007 to pen your entries and that's a thing of the past. It doesn't even connect to your blogging site until you're ready to post, and it keeps a backup of everything you write in case anything goes wrong (so long as you saved it). And you never need to worry about typing 'teh' instead of 'the'. Ah, the joys of AutoCorrect...

We are talking about using Word 2007 as a text editor here, though, not as a word processor. There's a difference: unlike a standard document, fonts, paper size and images are handled by the website itself, using the rules of your blogging engine's theme. Headers, italics and bold text are the only major exception to this – what you see is *not* what you get. ⊞

Spread the word

Get yourself heard on the internet in six easy steps

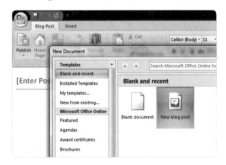

1 READY, SET, BLOG To create a blog post, click **New** and pick **New blog post** from the list. If you've already set everything up, go straight to the editor – if not, you need to enter some settings.

2 UP AND ATOM Several prominent blogging tools are coded in. If the one you're using isn't included on the list, you need to find out whether it supports either Atom or MetaWeblog.

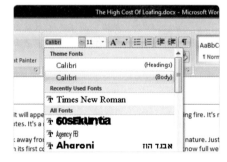

3 NOT MY TYPE In the editing window, the Fluent interface gets shorter. The default font is Calibri. Don't worry about the font choice for now though; the blog sorts out the font after posting.

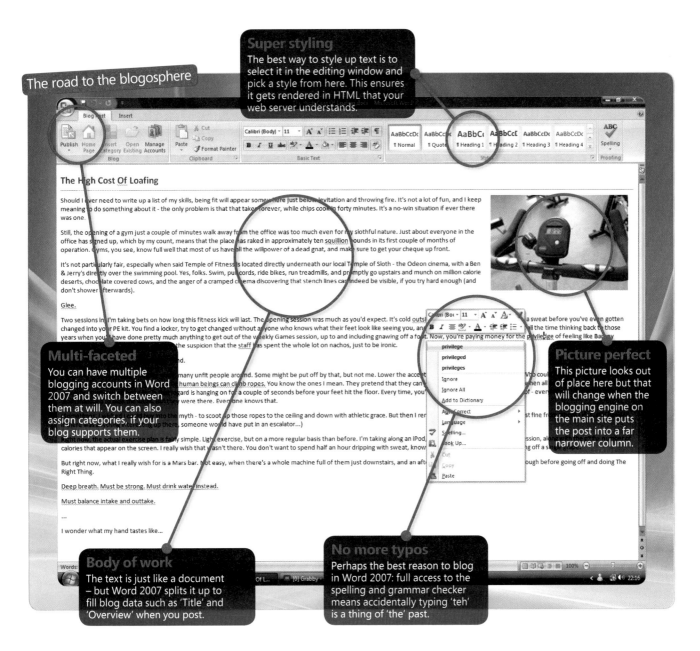

The road to the blogosphere

Super styling
The best way to style up text is to select it in the editing window and pick a style from here. This ensures it gets rendered in HTML that your web server understands.

The High Cost Of Loafing

Should I ever need to write up a list of my skills, being fit will appear somewhere just below levitation and throwing fire. It's not a lot of fun, and I keep meaning to do something about it - the only problem is that that takes forever, while chips cook in forty minutes. It's a no-win situation if ever there was one.

Still, the opening of a gym just a couple of minutes walk away from the office was too much even for my slothful nature. Just about everyone in the office has signed up, which by my count, means that the place has raked in approximately ten squillion pounds in its first couple of months of operation. Gyms, you see, know full well that most of us have all the willpower of a dead gnat, and make sure to get your cheque up front.

It's not particularly fair, especially when said Temple of Fitness is located directly underneath our local Temple of Sloth - the Odeon cinema, with a Ben & Jerry's directly over the swimming pool. Yes, folks. Swim, pull cords, ride bikes, run treadmills, and promptly go upstairs and munch on million calorie deserts, chocolate covered cows, and the anger of a cramped cinema discovering that stench lines can indeed be visible, if you try hard enough (and don't shower afterwards).

Glee.

Two sessions in, I'm taking bets on how long this fitness kick will last. The opening session was much as you'd expect. It's cold outside, so you work up a sweat before you've even gotten changed into your PE kit. You find a locker, try to get changed without anyone who knows what their feet look like seeing you, and all the time thinking back to those years when you'd have done pretty much anything to get out of the weekly Games session, up to and including gnawing off a foot. Now, you're paying money for the privilege of feeling like Bambi... the suspicion that the staff has spent the whole lot on nachos, just to be ironic.

Multi-faceted
You can have multiple blogging accounts in Word 2007 and switch between them at will. You can also assign categories, if your blog supports them.

Picture perfect
This picture looks out of place here but that will change when the blogging engine on the main site puts the post into a far narrower column.

But right now, what I really wish for is a Mars bar. Not easy, when there's a whole machine full of them just downstairs, and an aft... ough before going off and doing The Right Thing.

Deep breath. Must be strong. Must drink water instead.

Must balance intake and outtake.

...

I wonder what my hand tastes like...

Body of work
The text is just like a document – but Word 2007 splits it up to fill blog data such as 'Title' and 'Overview' when you post.

No more typos
Perhaps the best reason to blog in Word 2007: full access to the spelling and grammar checker means accidentally typing 'teh' is a thing of 'the' past.

4 IN STYLE Begin typing. Use the style window, top-right, to add headers, bold text and italics. Don't worry about making it look pretty – complicated styling is lost when you post.

5 ARCHIVE IT To save a post, click **Save**. Word 2007 remembers it's a blog and adjusts the Fluent interface, so you can open posts and make changes without visiting your blog's admin panel.

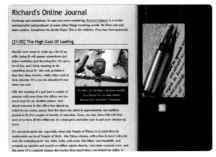

6 FAME AT LAST When finished, click **Publish**. Word 2007 automatically puts pictures in the right place, but if you want images to go elsewhere, you need to set up a log-in for an FTP directory.

Make your writing come alive the easy way

Don't let technology block your inspiration. Now you can publish what you're passionate about without the pain

If you're interested in venting your angst or appreciating the finer things in life without necessarily getting into a two-way conversation, you'll be pleased to find that Windows Live Writer can make publishing a blog post incredibly easy.

If you're new to the art of blog posting, you can do the whole thing through Windows Live Writer. Alternatively, if you're already up and running you can automatically configure your blog to publish to most major blog services, including Windows Live Spaces, SharePoint, WordPress and many more.

Because blog posting is not just about the written word, Windows Live Writer has been designed to make the inclusion of different media a truly simple process for even the most inexperienced of online diarists. You can insert photos, maps, emoticons and other rich media. And you don't have to worry about being an online designer – type up your post, insert your media, and you can continually preview how your post looks as you compile it.

If there is a website that you enjoy visiting, you can easily share it with the readers of your blog by adding a link to it. With Windows Live Writer, adding a link to a website is as simple as clicking a button and entering the address. Once you've added the link, your readers simply need to click on it with their mouse and they will be taken straight there. Linking to useful or interesting websites is a good way of providing a service to your readers, and will encourage them to check out your blog on a regular basis. ▮

Live and kicking

Ensure your blog is always box-fresh

Editing tools
You can set up links to previous posts and other web pages, and insert and edit tables. And run a spell check to avoid any typos.

Gallery garnish
With plug-ins from Windows Live Gallery, you can add music feeds, emoticons and quotes of the day.

Omni-online presence
Windows Live Writer lets you post to multiple blogs, and it can detect specific themes for each one.

Scheduled scribbling
You can set a blog to post on a certain date so you can maintain your online presence even when you're not online. And you can compose blog entries offline, then publish them when you're back on.

BLOG OUT You can write blog entries when you're offline, then publish them later

Use Windows Live Writer to say anything

Publishing your thoughts worldwide has never been easier

1 NEW BLOG When you use Windows Live Writer for the first time it asks if you have a blog. If you haven't signed up with Windows Live Space, select **Create a new Windows Live Space for me**. It also works with other blogging sites.

2 NAME IT Enter your Windows Live ID and Live Writer connects to the internet and downloads the necessary settings from Windows Live Spaces. Once it's finished – it only takes a few seconds – you're asked to give your blog a name.

3 WRITE AWAY Windows Live Writer looks like a word processor – which is essentially what it is. To create a new post, type it in the main editing window. You can add other items such as pictures or maps with the links on the right.

4 LINK UP You can add links to websites – just click on **Insert Hyperlink...** and type in the address of the site you want. If your friends have blogs, or there is a blog that you like, linking to them may encourage them to link back to your blog, which is a great way to get more readers.

5 ON OR OFF You can use Windows Live Writer to write your blog while you're not online. When you've finished expressing yourself, make sure that it will be displayed the way you want by previewing it. Click **View** then select **Web Preview**.

Blogging made easy

Plenty of websites – such as Windows Live Spaces (spaces.live.com) – will house your writing free of charge. Used with Windows Live Writer, writing and publishing for the whole world to see is really simple.

6 MAKE IT PUBLIC Click **Publish** to upload your post to your Windows Live Space. If you'd rather not share your thoughts with the entire planet, click on **Options** and then **Permissions** to limit who can read your blog.

Keeping your system safe and secure online

Windows Vista offers the most protected Windows platform yet, giving you the ultimate in PC peace of mind

Security might not seem as sexy as the Aero Glass interface or the Windows Vista cool multimedia tools, but it's one of the most important reasons for upgrading.

When Windows XP was designed, most of us didn't have always-on broadband connections – and then when we got them, assorted net nasties were quick to go on the attack. Websites attempted to install malicious software, spammers created avalanches of infected emails, and if you connected an unprotected PC to the internet, it would be full of damaging infections in a matter of minutes.

Microsoft did its best to thwart the attacks, but no sooner did it fix one problem than another one popped up in its place. The answer was clear; instead of patching Windows, Microsoft needed to completely rethink the way Windows worked. And with Windows Vista, that's exactly what happened.

Self-protection

Not all the problems came from outside, though. If you're a fan of gory PC gaming, you'll be vividly aware that some games aren't suitable for young children. And, as anyone who uses the internet knows, offensive and utterly unsuitable content is only ever a few clicks away. As more and more of us have moved our PCs from a small study room to the main front room, the need for parental controls has grown. In Windows Vista there are six key tools that keep your system safe and secure: Windows Security Center, which enables you to control security options; User Account Control (UAC), which stops software (and other users) from doing things without your permission; Parental Controls, which keep the kids safe and keep the system safe from your kids; Windows Defender, which hunts and kills malicious software; Windows Firewall, which is designed to stop anything dodgy getting on your system in the first place; and last but not least, BitLocker, which keeps your private files private. Together they offer rock-solid security and peace of mind. Over the next few pages you'll discover how to use them to keep you – and your system – safe. ⧉

ON YOUR SIDE Windows Vista comes with built-in defenses against outside influences

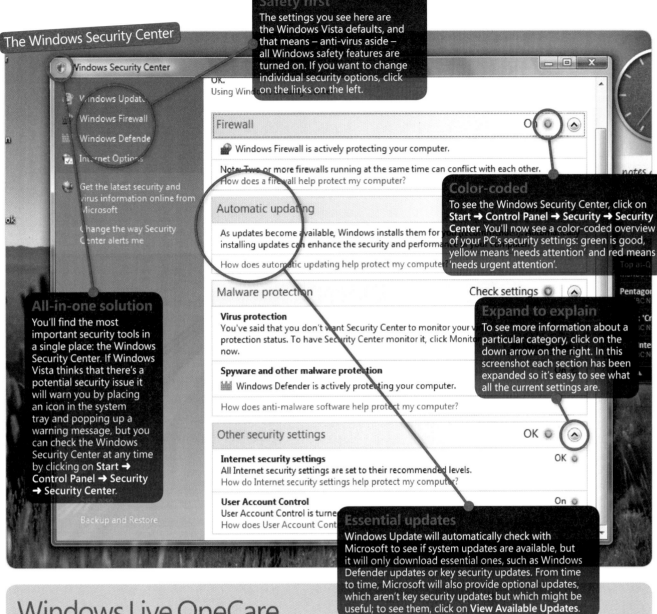

The Windows Security Center

Safety first
The settings you see here are the Windows Vista defaults, and that means – anti-virus aside – all Windows safety features are turned on. If you want to change individual security options, click on the links on the left.

Color-coded
To see the Windows Security Center, click on **Start → Control Panel → Security → Security Center**. You'll now see a color-coded overview of your PC's security settings: green is good, yellow means 'needs attention' and red means 'needs urgent attention'.

All-in-one solution
You'll find the most important security tools in a single place: the Windows Security Center. If Windows Vista thinks that there's a potential security issue it will warn you by placing an icon in the system tray and popping up a warning message, but you can check the Windows Security Center at any time by clicking on **Start → Control Panel → Security → Security Center**.

Expand to explain
To see more information about a particular category, click on the down arrow on the right. In this screenshot each section has been expanded so it's easy to see what all the current settings are.

Essential updates
Windows Update will automatically check with Microsoft to see if system updates are available, but it will only download essential ones, such as Windows Defender updates or key security updates. From time to time, Microsoft will also provide optional updates, which aren't key security updates but which might be useful; to see them, click on **View Available Updates**.

Windows Live OneCare

For hassle-free, continuous PC protection, go to onecare.live.com

There's no doubt that Windows Vista is the most secure version of Windows so far, but there is still more you can do to protect yourself, your children and your data – both on and offline.

Working quietly in the background on your computer, Microsoft Windows Live OneCare is an always-on PC-care service that protects against viruses, spyware, hackers, and other unwanted intruders. This online service is ever-evolving and features such as multi-PC management, printer sharing support, and centralized backup of up to three PCs covered under the same OneCare subscription are already available.

Providing all-in-one protection in a single convenient package, Windows Live OneCare offers anti-virus and anti-spyware scanners, a two-way firewall and anti-phishing technology, which together offer protection from viruses, worms, Trojans, hackers, phishing and other threats. These run continuously and can be automatically updated, too.

With additional performance management to keep your PC in tip-top condition – along with Backup and Restore plus Instant Help features – it's an invaluable package.

Stop spyware with Windows Defender

Protect your PC from unwanted programs and malware with the help of this vigilant tool

In some ways owning a PC is like owning a pet – it takes a lot of looking after. If left to its own devices it could get into all sorts of trouble. This is where a guiding hand comes in useful and, as part of Windows Vista, you get Windows Defender, a program that will help you and your PC defend against malicious or unwanted programs.

You've probably heard of spyware and adware, which are programs that sneak on to your system and snoop on your personal data, blast you with adverts and generally fill your PC with nonsense. They're often hard to detect and difficult to remove, which is why Windows Defender is so handy. It does two important things – it gets rid of

unwanted programs from your PC, and it stops them getting into your system in the first place. You can launch the program by clicking on **Windows Defender** in Windows Security Center.

Fully integrated

Windows Defender works with Internet Explorer to help you decide whether new software should or should not be installed; it provides always-on protection that monitors key system locations and watches for changes that signal the presence of spyware.

It works by combining a number of useful and very clever strategies. Superior scanning and removal technologies use up-to-date spyware definitions created by Microsoft, with

help from Windows Defender users who submit reports of potential new spyware.

At all stages, Windows Defender is simple to use and comes with preconfigured settings to help you set up a stable platform and then continue to stay secure. An improved user interface gives you more control over your software. Common tasks such as scanning, blocking and removing unwanted software are easier than ever, and a Software Explorer helps you understand which software and services are running on your computer and stops or disables 'rogue' software. Windows Defender automatically handles many common tasks and interrupts or alerts you only in the case of serious issues that require immediate action.

Windows Defender

Secure your system against spyware and other internet nasties

1 LAST SCAN When you launch Windows Defender, it tells you when it last scanned your system. If you want Windows Defender to scan automatically, click **Tools** in the toolbar.

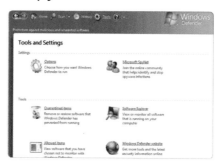

2 OPTIONS The Tools and Settings screen enables you to see what software's running and what files are quarantined. Want to check the scanning settings? Click on **Options**.

3 SELF-DEFENSE Windows Defender will check for updates then scan your system at 2am every day. If you want to change the time, use the fields for **Frequency** and **Approximate Time**.

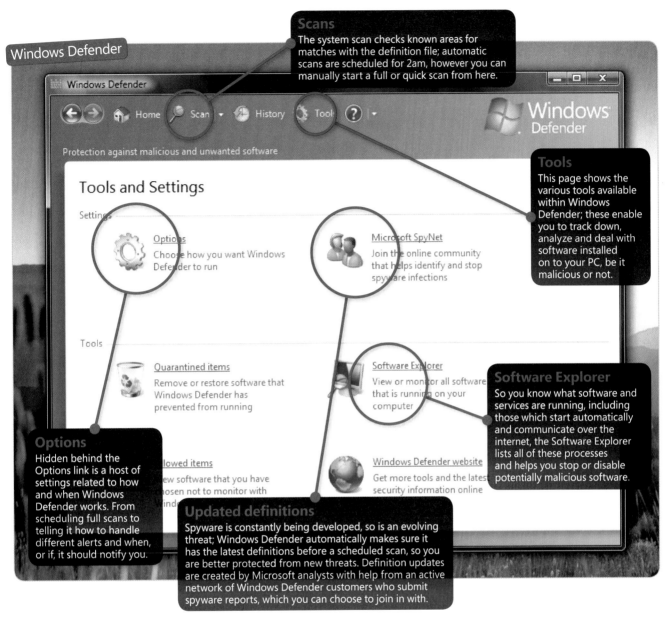

Windows Defender

Scans
The system scan checks known areas for matches with the definition file; automatic scans are scheduled for 2am, however you can manually start a full or quick scan from here.

Tools
This page shows the various tools available within Windows Defender; these enable you to track down, analyze and deal with software installed on to your PC, be it malicious or not.

Windows Defender

← → 🏠 Home 🔍 Scan ▾ 🕐 History 🔧 Tools ❓ ▾

🪟 Windows Defender

Protection against malicious and unwanted software

Tools and Settings

Settings

Options
Choose how you want Windows Defender to run

Microsoft SpyNet
Join the online community that helps identify and stop spyware infections

Tools

Quarantined items
Remove or restore software that Windows Defender has prevented from running

Software Explorer
View or monitor all software that is running on your computer

Software Explorer
So you know what software and services are running, including those which start automatically and communicate over the internet, the Software Explorer lists all of these processes and helps you stop or disable potentially malicious software.

Allowed items
View software that you have chosen not to monitor with Windows

Windows Defender website
Get more tools and the latest security information online

Options
Hidden behind the Options link is a host of settings related to how and when Windows Defender works. From scheduling full scans to telling it how to handle different alerts and when, or if, it should notify you.

Updated definitions
Spyware is constantly being developed, so is an evolving threat; Windows Defender automatically makes sure it has the latest definitions before a scheduled scan, so you are better protected from new threats. Definition updates are created by Microsoft analysts with help from an active network of Windows Defender customers who submit spyware reports, which you can choose to join in with.

4 MORE POWER Real-Time Protection (on by default) checks on crucial elements of Windows and warns of attempts to change them: only disable if using another anti-spyware package.

5 ON-DEMAND Scan at any time by clicking **Scan** in the toolbar. The process takes a few minutes because it peers into every corner of your PC to make sure you're spyware-free.

6 THE NEWS Once the scan has completed, Windows Defender will tell you the results. If your PC is free from nasties, you'll see the 'Your computer is running normally' message.

Prevent hackers with Windows Firewall

Keep hackers at bay and arm yourself against online attacks with this simple but thorough defense system

The news is always rife with how another hacker has attacked some computer system in the world. It's not as though these hackers are physically attacking systems; they're attempting to gain access via the internet. To stop this sort of malicious attack, the Windows Firewall is a critical first line of defense.

You might be wondering how it's possible for someone to gain access to a computer over the internet. In order to communicate with other computers, PCs have various ports – so, for example, chat software might use one port, file sharing software another, network printing yet another, and so on. Ports are a bit like real-world doors – if you don't

keep them locked, there's always the possibility that an unwanted intruder will sneak in. Windows Firewall addresses the problem by locking any ports you're not using, and by doing so it can prevent some of the nastier kinds of online attacks from affecting your PC. It's switched on by default and you can see its settings by clicking on **Windows Firewall** in Windows Security Center

Properly configured, the Windows Firewall can stop many kinds of malware before they can infect your computer or other computers on your network. Windows Firewall, which comes with Windows Vista, is turned on by default and begins protecting your computer as soon as Windows starts. The Windows Firewall Control Panel is designed to be

easy to use, with several configuration options and a simple interface.

Clever is the word

More advanced than the Windows Firewall in previous versions of Windows, the firewall in Windows Vista helps protect by restricting other operating system resources if they behave in unexpected ways – a common indicator of the presence of malware. For example, if a component of Windows that is designed to send network messages over one port on your PC tries to send messages by way of a different port due to an attack, Windows Firewall can stop that message leaving your computer, thereby preventing the malware from spreading to other users. ⊞

In real life... Protect your ports

**Adam Ifans,
Editor,
*Windows Vista:
The Official Magazine***

Generally, Windows Firewall will work quietly in the background protecting your computer system. However, there may be the odd occasion when it highlights a problem that needs fixing or program limits that need adjusting. To investigate examples like these, take a look at the **Exceptions** tab, which will show you a list of network services – such as File and Printer Sharing – plus other programs that have been given access through the Windows Firewall.

If you are experiencing problems with a single program or service, it's possible that Windows Firewall is blocking it. So if Remote Desktop, for example, doesn't seem to be working, it's worth checking to see whether it has been given the seal of approval. Scan the list of tick boxes and the name of the feature you're having problems with; if the service/program is unchecked, tick the box and see whether it instantly fixes the problem. Alternatively, the **Add program** button makes it possible to add individual programs; you can restrict access for these to the local network or even individual IP addresses.

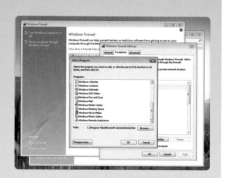

EXTRA PROGRAMS You can add programs yourself, as well as configuring individual ports and restricting access to the local network or specific IP addresses

Slamming the internet front door

"If your name's not down, you're not getting in!"

1 **LOCKED** Windows Firewall blocks incoming connections. If a program attempts a connection, Firewall will ask whether it should be allowed. If yes, Firewall can remember your answer; if no, the program will remain blocked.

2 **STRONG SECURITY** Click **Change Settings** to see more options. If you're in a potentially insecure environment such as an airport or other public place, the **Block all** option is worth using for maximum security.

3 **GUEST LIST** Unless you've selected **Block all**, Windows Firewall blocks connections from programs you haven't added to exceptions. Check **Notify me...** in the Exceptions tab so that you can override any decisions you want to.

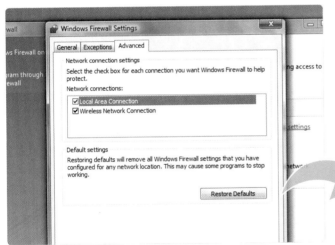

4 **DIFFERENT STROKES** Windows Firewall can have different settings for different connections. In this screen it's keeping an eye on our local network, but if we installed a wireless networking card we'd be able to set different rules for our wireless network – without changing our local network settings.

The Windows Firewall blocks certain connections; check Notify me so that you can override any decisions

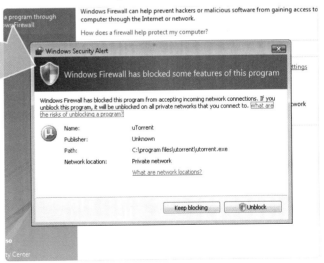

Those different settings...

The ability to vary settings in Windows Firewall is handy if you use your PC in different locations: Windows Firewall will detect which network connection you're using and use the appropriate settings to protect.

5 **IN ACTION** When it comes to general use, you'll probably hear nothing from Firewall – it'll just happily monitor things. If you run a new program that tries to access the internet in an unusual way, that's when an alert will be generated and you'll need to decide if the program should have access.

Set up your PC so it's safe for all the family

It's great that children are so computer literate, but you still need to keep tabs on what they're up to...

So you've secured your system against malicious online attacks, it's time to think about the children. There very well might be content on your computer that you don't want them to see, such as details of the family finances or important work documents. You might enjoy the odd game of Doom 3 but be less keen for your seven-year-old to play it.

Even if you're not sharing a system you probably want to make sure your children don't stumble on to any unsuitable internet sites. The good news is that the Parental Control features in Windows Vista cover all of these issues, and they couldn't be easier to use.

The real worry for parents, though, is what their children use the computer for. It's bad enough that they've already borrowed 'Soldier Trainer: Attack, Attack' from the cool kid in the playground, and are now learning marksmanship behind your back, without the added worry of what websites they're visiting and who they're talking to online.

Safe to surf

There's no substitute for sitting with your kids and teaching them to use a computer responsibly but, in the longer term, when you can't always be in the room with them, Windows Vista will let you breathe a bit more easily.

In the Home Basic, Home Premium and Ultimate editions you can set up monitored accounts for every youngster in your family from the Control Panel, using the Parental Controls button. From here you can create User Accounts, within which your child can fully personalize their desktop and settings. However, what they can view, read and play is controlled by filters for games and web content that you set up (**Start ➜ Control Panel ➜ User Accounts and Family Safety ➜ Parental Controls**).

The Web Filter option is particularly useful for very young children, because you can make an exclusive access list of suitable sites, and limit your child's browsing to these.

Try a dedicated kids' TV website as a starting point; many of them have a section for grown-ups, with helpful guidelines about how to give your kids computing time responsibly – and it'll be an entertaining start for your child's first foray into PC use. ⊞

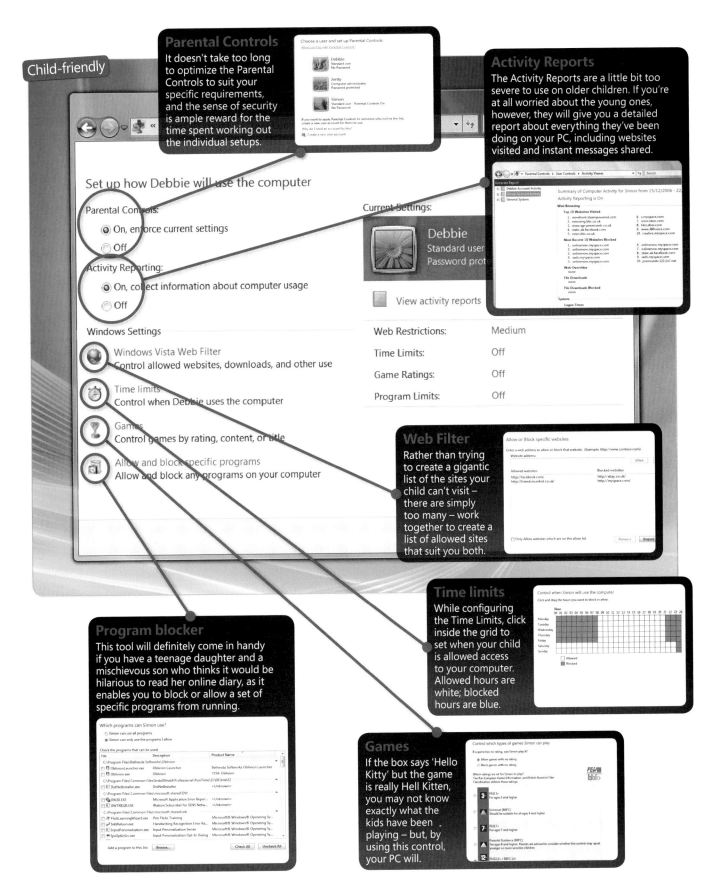

Child-friendly

Parental Controls
It doesn't take too long to optimize the Parental Controls to suit your specific requirements, and the sense of security is ample reward for the time spent working out the individual setups.

Choose a user and set up Parental Controls
What can I do with Parental Controls?

Debbie
Standard user
No Password

Jonty
Computer administrator
Password protected

Simon
Standard user - Parental Controls On
No Password

If you want to apply Parental Controls to someone who isn't in this list, create a new user account for them to use.
Why do I need an account for this?
Create a new account

Activity Reports
The Activity Reports are a little bit too severe to use on older children. If you're at all worried about the young ones, however, they will give you a detailed report about everything they've been doing on your PC, including websites visited and instant messages shared.

Set up how Debbie will use the computer

Parental Controls:
- On, enforce current settings
- Off

Activity Reporting:
- On, collect information about computer usage
- Off

Current Settings:

Debbie
Standard user
Password prote

View activity reports

Windows Settings

Windows Vista Web Filter
Control allowed websites, downloads, and other use

Time limits
Control when Debbie uses the computer

Games
Control games by rating, content, or title

Allow and block specific programs
Allow and block any programs on your computer

Web Restrictions:	Medium
Time Limits:	Off
Game Ratings:	Off
Program Limits:	Off

Web Filter
Rather than trying to create a gigantic list of the sites your child can't visit – there are simply too many – work together to create a list of allowed sites that suit you both.

Allow or Block specific websites
Enter a web address to allow or block that website. (Example: http://www.contoso.com)
Website address:
Allow
Allowed websites:
http://facebook.com/
http://friendsreunited.co.uk/
Blocked websites:
http://ebay.co.uk/
http://myspace.com/
Only Allow websites which are on the allow list
Remove   Import

Program blocker
This tool will definitely come in handy if you have a teenage daughter and a mischievous son who thinks it would be hilarious to read her online diary, as it enables you to block or allow a set of specific programs from running.

Which programs can Simon use?
Simon can use all programs
Simon can only use the programs I allow
Check the programs that can be used:

File	Description	Product Name
C:\Program Files\Bethesda Softworks\Oblivion		
OblivionLauncher.exe	Oblivion Launcher	Bethesda Softworks Oblivion Launcher
Oblivion.exe	Oblivion	TES4: Oblivion
C:\Program Files\Common Files\InstallShield\Professional\RunTime\11\00\Intel32		
DotNetInstaller.exe	DotNetInstaller	<Unknown>
C:\Program Files\Common Files\microsoft shared\DW		
DW20.EXE	Microsoft Application Error Repor...	<Unknown>
DWTRIG20.EXE	Watson Subscriber for SENS Netw...	<Unknown>
C:\Program Files\Common Files\microsoft shared\ink		
FlickLearningWizard.exe	Pen Flicks Training	Microsoft® Windows® Operating Sy...
InkWatson.exe	Handwriting Recognition Error Re...	Microsoft® Windows® Operating Sy...
InputPersonalization.exe	Input Personalization Server	Microsoft® Windows® Operating Sy...
IpsOptInSrv.exe	Input Personalization Opt-In Dialog	Microsoft® Windows® Operating Sy...

Add a program to this list: Browse...   Check All   Uncheck All

Time limits
While configuring the Time Limits, click inside the grid to set when your child is allowed access to your computer. Allowed hours are white; blocked hours are blue.

Control when Simon will use the computer
Click and drag the hours you want to block or allow.
Hour
00 01 02 03 04 05 06 07 08 09 10 11 12 13 14 15 16 17 18 19 20 21 22 23 24
Monday
Tuesday
Wednesday
Thursday
Friday
Saturday
Sunday
Allowed
Blocked

Games
If the box says 'Hello Kitty' but the game is really Hell Kitten, you may not know exactly what the kids have been playing – but, by using this control, your PC will.

Control which types of games Simon can play
If a game has no rating, can Simon play it?
Allow games with no rating
Block games with no rating

Which ratings are ok for Simon to play?
The Pan European Game Information, and British Board of Film Classification defines those ratings.

3   PEGI 3+
    For ages 3 and higher

    Universal (BBFC)
    Should be suitable for all ages 4 and higher

7   PEGI 7+
    For ages 7 and higher

    Parental Guidance (BBFC)
    For ages 8 and higher. Parents are advised to consider whether the content may upset younger or more sensitive children

12 PEGI 12+ / BBFC 12+

Never lose a file or photo again

Windows Vista makes backing up easier than ever, so now there's no excuse not to protect your files from corruption or deletion

In the past, data backup was difficult and costly, but Windows Vista features a built-in back-up tool that's simple to set up, supports a wide range of back-up media (including CD and DVD) and can be scheduled to run automatically at set intervals.

You can back up to CD or DVD, although you're restricted by capacities – 650MB for individual CDs; 4.7GB (or 8.4GB if you have a dual-layer drive and compatible discs) for DVDs. The Windows Vista Backup and Restore tool splits the backup so it can be spanned across many discs, but this isn't practical if you're updating it regularly.

You can also back up to another location on your network, such as a shared folder or a Network Attached Storage device. The device needs to be switched on when your backup runs, and performance depends on the speed of your network connection.

The easiest option is to use an external hard drive, attached via a USB or Firewire port. Some PCs also come with eSATA ports – these external ports work with a limited number of drives but offer superior performance to USB or Firewire.

A fourth option – not supported by Backup and Restore in Windows Vista – is to back up online. Various service providers offer space, as do some security programs.

The Windows Vista Backup and Restore tool backs up important files but it doesn't record system and program preferences, like desktop or Microsoft Office settings. If you're running Windows Vista Business, Enterprise or Ultimate edition, you'll notice a **Back up computer** option. This launches the Windows Complete Backup tool, which backs up key files and settings that will enable you to get Windows Vista back up should your PC fail – your programs and preferences are preserved, making it a more convenient option than reinstalling Windows Vista from scratch.

For many other backup programs you're able to pick folders, but these may not store program or Windows settings. If you don't have access to the Windows Complete Backup Tool, you need a third-party solution that can create an entire image of your hard drive.

Backing up your files

Three steps to help safeguard precious documents, photos and videos

1 SCHEDULE BACKUP Type 'backup' into the Start Menu Search box and select **Backup and Restore Center**. Now click **Back up Files**. Select whether to save to CD, DVD or external hard drive.

2 FILE TYPES Decide which types of files you want to include in the backup, such as TV shows, emails and so on. Hovering over each category reveals more details about what is included.

3 SELECT A FREQUENCY Choose how frequently you want to perform the backup. Obviously, the frequency depends on how often you add to or change files on your hard drive.

Shadow Copy in action

Accidentally overwritten or erased a file? Windows Vista can retrieve it

If you're running Windows Vista Business, Enterprise or Ultimate edition, you can take advantage of Shadow Copy; a regularly backed up copy of files that you can open, copy to another folder or restore over current versions.

Shadow Copies work in conjunction with System Protection (**Control Panel → System and Maintenance → System** and clicking on **System Protection**). Incremental changes to files are stored along with backups taken by the Backup

and Restore tool as you work. To restore a previous version of a file, right-click it and choose **Restore previous versions**. You can open a file to check the version, make a copy of it in another folder or drive, or restore it to the desired version.

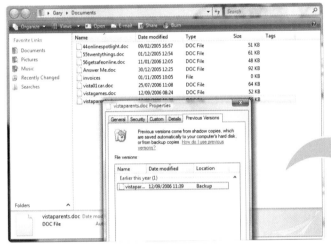

1 **TIME TRAVEL** Restoring a file is easy – right-click on the file to recover, choose **Properties** and go to the Previous Versions tab. A list of previous versions appears. Click on the version you want and click on **Restore**.

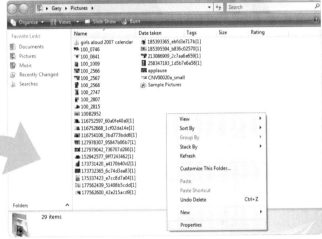

2 **UNDO DELETE** You can also use Shadow Copy to restore deleted files. Simply find the folder that originally contained the file, right-click (making sure you're not right-clicking on a file), and choose **Properties → Previous Versions**.

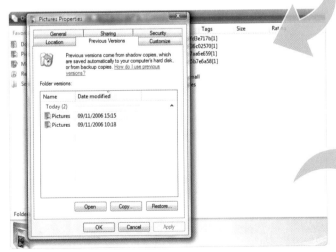

3 **BACK AGAIN** Choose the version that you want to restore and then click on the **Restore** button. This replaces the entire folder with an earlier version – restoring deleted files, but also removing any files added afterwards.

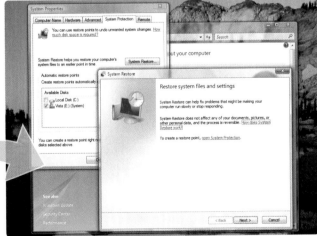

4 **SORT IT** In contrast, System Restore can take your entire system back in time, but documents and other files remain unaffected because System Restore only covers the Windows system files, not personal ones.

Taking your PC out and about

The whole world's going mobile and Windows Vista is the way to get the best out of your laptop

"Wow"
On in an instant
Windows Vista takes advantage of new hardware based low-power modes. This means that when you 'shut down' a PC it's actually in a low-power state, so it can spring back to life in seconds

There was a time when if you wanted sheer power you'd buy a desktop, and if you wanted portability – and had a great deal of money to spare – you'd buy a laptop. However, in recent years that has all changed. Laptop prices have plummeted while at the same time their power has increased so, as a result, many people are now buying laptops as desktop replacements. In fact, by late 2006, laptops were outselling desktops by a significant margin.

Performance v portability
These days, there are two main kinds of laptop buyer. Those who want a laptop solely for home or office use don't need to worry about battery life because their machines will generally be plugged into a wall socket. To these guys, it's performance that matters. Mobile users, on the other hand, need to squeeze as much life out of their batteries as they possibly can – a tough challenge when they too need their PCs to perform at a high standard, often while using power-draining wireless networking.

Versatile Windows Vista
With Windows Vista, Microsoft needed to provide features for both kinds of laptop user. But that's not all. Home and office users occasionally take their laptops out and about, while mobile users often use their laptops at home or in the office, so Windows Vista needs to be flexible enough to deliver maximum performance when a laptop's plugged in and still provide maximum portability when it's on the move. As if that wasn't challenging enough, tablet PCs complicate things even further. Twist a tablet's screen this way and it's a standard laptop; twist it that way and it's a touch-sensitive screen that uses handwriting recognition instead of a keyboard, and a stylus instead of a mouse. Then there's the Pocket PC, which ditches the keyboard altogether, shrinks a tablet PC to the size of a hardback book and is as likely to be used on a sofa as in a roadside café.

Windows Vista has to satisfy all of these demands – and here you'll discover that it does so very well indeed.

Introducing the Windows Mobility Center
Memorize this shortcut, because it's your new best friend...

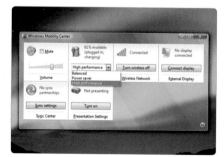

1 INSTANT INFO Press the **Windows** key and **X** and the Windows Mobility Center pops up. It's a dashboard for various mobile system settings. Here, the battery's charging and Wi-Fi is on.

2 QUICK CHANGE The Battery section enables you to switch between power management schemes – handy if you've been running in power-saving mode but need a quick burst of power.

3 MISSION CONTROL Click specific icons to go to the relevant Control Panel section. Here the battery icon is selected, by going to **Control Panel → Hardware and Sound → Power Options**.

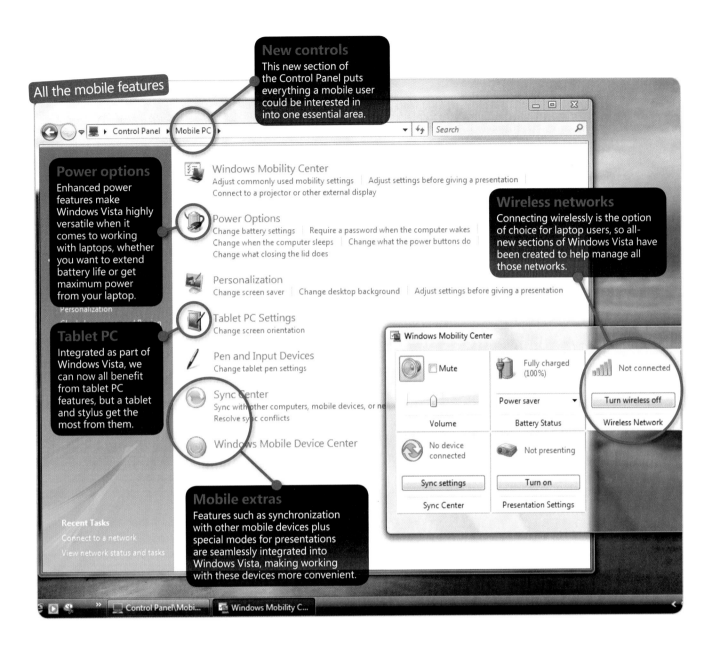

All the mobile features

New controls
This new section of the Control Panel puts everything a mobile user could be interested in into one essential area.

▸ Control Panel ▸ Mobile PC ▸   ▾ | ⁺⁴⁹ | Search

Power options
Enhanced power features make Windows Vista highly versatile when it comes to working with laptops, whether you want to extend battery life or get maximum power from your laptop.

Windows Mobility Center
Adjust commonly used mobility settings | Adjust settings before giving a presentation
Connect to a projector or other external display

Power Options
Change battery settings | Require a password when the computer wakes
Change when the computer sleeps | Change what the power buttons do
Change what closing the lid does

Personalization
Change screen saver | Change desktop background | Adjust settings before giving a presentation

Wireless networks
Connecting wirelessly is the option of choice for laptop users, so all-new sections of Windows Vista have been created to help manage all those networks.

Tablet PC
Integrated as part of Windows Vista, we can now all benefit from tablet PC features, but a tablet and stylus get the most from them.

Tablet PC Settings
Change screen orientation

Pen and Input Devices
Change tablet pen settings

Sync Center
Sync with other computers, mobile devices, or ne
Resolve sync conflicts

Windows Mobile Device Center

Windows Mobility Center
☐ Mute | Fully charged (100%) | Not connected
Volume | Power saver ▾ | Turn wireless off
| Battery Status | Wireless Network
No device connected | Not presenting
Sync settings | Turn on
Sync Center | Presentation Settings

Recent Tasks
Connect to a network
View network status and tasks

Mobile extras
Features such as synchronization with other mobile devices plus special modes for presentations are seamlessly integrated into Windows Vista, making working with these devices more convenient.

Control Panel\Mobi... | Windows Mobility C...

4 WHICH WIRELESS? Clicking on the wireless network icon opens the **Connect to a Network** dialog box, which displays any wireless networks nearby that you could connect to.

5 MONITOR MONITORS The display icon launches the **Display Settings** dialog box, which enables you to control any external displays that you have connected to your computer.

6 PERFECT PRESENTATION **Presentation Settings** gives you options such as turning off the screen saver so it won't cut in mid-slide, and turning the volume down or off.

Save time on the move

Windows Mobile Device Center can help organize your life and save you valuable time. We show you how to make it happen

 Today our lives are jam-packed with work, family and social commitments. Everyone's looking for ways to speed up mundane tasks, and a great way to do this is with a Windows Mobile device, keeping information and files to hand while away from your computer. However, so much time can be wasted trying to synchronize the information held on your PC with a mobile device, that the chore of doing it can often outweigh the benefits.

The whole point of Windows Vista is to make life easier, and a new feature called Windows Mobile Device Center has been included so you can update your mobile device in less time than it takes to make a cup of coffee.

To get started, simply plug your Windows Mobile device into your PC's USB port – or if you've got a Bluetooth connection for your PC, you can synchronize the devices wirelessly. Once connected, Windows Mobile Device Center automatically appears and shows a picture of your device. You're then presented with two options...

If you're connecting to a computer that you want to be synchronizing files with on a daily basis, select **Set up your device** because this makes a permanent

The whole point of Windows Vista is to make life easier

pairing between your PC and that specific device. However, if this is a one-off pairing, click **Connect without setting up your device**.

You're then given a list of the types of data that can be automatically synchronized with your device. If you use Microsoft Office Outlook, you can set it to automatically synchronize your inbox, contacts, appointments and calendar, so wherever you are, you're never without that vital information.

Tweak to fit

These synchronization settings can be changed at any time by plugging in your device as usual and going to **Mobile Device Settings → Change content sync setting**. Check or uncheck each type of information to control whether it will be updated when the sync is complete. Most options also have a **Sync Settings** menu where elements can be tweaked.

With Windows Vista your devices don't have to be for work. Windows Mobile Device Center seamlessly links into Windows Media Player where it's easy to add music, pictures and videos to devices. Just drag and drop files into the sync pane on the right, click **Start Sync** and let Windows Vista do the rest. All that's left now is to enjoy that coffee – and your extra bit of free time.

Introducing Windows SideShow

Check out the tiny screens that have some very big ideas

When your PC's powered up it's capable of almost anything, but sometimes you don't need all that power – and booting your laptop just so you can look up a phone number or play an MP3 file seems like overkill. Enter Windows SideShow, which combines Windows Vista and PC hardware to make your computer even more useful.

SideShow-enabled devices have a second, external screen that runs Gadgets – little applications that get information from Windows Vista. For example, you could use SideShow to look up addresses from your laptop without switching it on, or to check your email for new messages, or just to listen to some of your music. It's very clever and it isn't limited to computers, either; SideShow has also been designed to work on mobile phones and other portable devices. There aren't very many about at the moment, but we'll see a number of SideShow-friendly devices – and in particular, lots of laptops – appearing in the near future.

ON THE SIDE SideShow enables you to gain instant access to the data on your device

Setting up your mobile device
How to create the perfect partnership

1 CONNECT Plug in your device via USB (or use Bluetooth to connect wirelessly) and Windows Mobile Device Center should recognize it and start up automatically. If it doesn't load, search for it in Start Search and open it manually.

2 PAIR UP When you first plug in your device you can choose whether or not to start a permanent partnership. If this is your main PC, choose **Set up your device** to save effort next time. You can delete the partnership later if you wish.

3 START SYNCING You will see a list of media types to synchronize. The items you choose will be updated each time you sync. If you want to use email, contacts and calendar synchronization, you need Office Outlook.

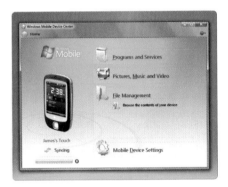

4 EXPLORE You can use Windows Mobile Device Center to peruse all the data on your phone. This enables you to add files manually to the device, or copy data from the phone to your hard drive using Windows Explorer.

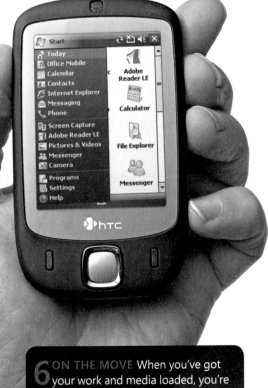

5 MULTIMEDIA Setting up your mobile device doesn't have to be about emails and appointments. Mobile Device Center lets you set up pictures, music and video clips which you can easily export. Go to **Pictures, Music and Video → Add media from Windows Media Player**.

6 ON THE MOVE When you've got your work and media loaded, you're ready to go out and start reaping the full rewards of Windows Mobile.

Mobile media

When is a phone not a phone? When it's a Windows Mobile handset your cell phone can be so much more...

Everyone loves a gadget, and there's one way to make sure that yours is bang up-to-date – check that it runs Windows Mobile. From smartphones to portable media centers, pocket PCs to in-car facilities, Windows Mobile can now be found at the heart of such products, ensuring your mobile device offers the most useful features.

Take a look at a smartphone... With Windows Mobile, you are furnished with essential applications, communication abilities and fun media tools in a true next-generation gadget. It puts the capabilities of a Windows PC, and all of your important information, into the palm of your hand. Plug a Windows Mobile smartphone into your PC and it'll synchronize with Outlook email, contacts, calendars, notes and tasks. And you can take documents on the move – and edit them no matter where you are with Microsoft Office for Mobile.

HAVE PHONE, WILL TRAVEL With a Windows Mobile smartphone your options are always open

Not just a pretty phone

It's not all about work... you can stay entertained on the move with the integrated Windows Media Player. Play high-quality music and video – wherever you are. It's easy to manage and enjoy all of your media, from PC to smartphone. And, as Windows Media Player supports the most widely used and owned music and video media formats, such as MP3, Mpeg-4 and Windows Media, you can be sure that you can take your PC collection on the move.

Windows Mobile will also unleash the full power of your camera phone, as it offers control over your photo collection and provides a mobile photo studio so you can organize and upload images, and use them to personalize the phone. With access to automatic face recognition, panoramic modes and more you can be assured of a perfect photo, which you can then easily synchronize with your PC or email direct to friends.

Having fun with your phone is easy, too. Fast processors, large displays, outstanding mobile graphics and hard button controls are perfect for enjoying the latest mobile games. Quick to download and fun to play, you can enjoy big-name games like Guitar Hero 3, Call of Duty 5 and over 500 other games.

Last but by no means least, Windows Mobile's communication features are obviously second to none, which is good as we're still primarily talking about a phone! Excelling at all text and voice communications, a Windows Mobile smartphone will keep you and your contacts in constant communication, via voice, email, instant messenger or text message, and you can work directly with your existing email accounts and many of your instant messenger services, so you won't even have to change your habits or update any contact details. Windows Mobile combines facility with simplicity very nicely indeed.

In real life...
Mobile magic

James Stables, Section Editor, Windows Vista: The Official Magazine

I always used to wish I had important files and email on the move, which is why Windows Mobile is so handy. My Windows Mobile device is sync'd with my PC, so I have all my documents and messages to hand wherever I am. In Windows Vista, the Windows Mobile Device Center syncs data automatically, so I just connect my phone to my PC and let the technology work its magic.

What to look for in a Windows Mobile Device

1 **Does it have a hard keyboard?**
Many people find typing difficult on a touchscreen keyboard that lacks key response; with a real, hard keyboard there's a familiar feel to typing. Phones can offer either slide-out full-length keyboards or fixed full-width keyboards.

2 **Is the memory expandable and how?**
While smartphones come with built-in memory for storing applications and information, this quicklys fill up. Many phones offer flash memory expansion slots, so you can easily add up to 32GB of extra storage, enabling you to carry around music and movie collections alongside contacts and emails.

3 **What type of screen does it use?**
Screen resolutions will vary depending on the shape and size. Square-like screens start at 320x240 but will go as high as 480x640, for pin-sharp pics and text. Models with longer, landscape style screens can provide resolutions of 240x400 and tend to offer more touch-based applications.

4 **Ask about wireless connections**
It's important to check which mobile bands the phone supports. If you travel abroad ask for a quad-band device for maximum foreign coverage. Secondly, a 3G phone supports maximum data speeds. In addition, support for Wi-Fi can help save money accessing the internet over a free broadband connection at work, home or in a café. The latest devices also offer GPS navigation.

5 **How much talk time will it offer?**
As with all mobile devices, the amount of battery life you get from the device is crucial. Check both the talk time and the standby time. Standby time will be measured in days – 14 days is typical. Obviously, the battery gets most use during talk time – expect at least four hours' talk time.

Talk to the hand (held device)

And listen and view and edit...

1 **STAY IN CONTACT** With 3G technology, you can stay in touch by voice or text. Use Smart Dial to quickly ring important contacts or Click-to-Call to dial a number in a message or web page. Emails are to hand; integrating with existing accounts and formatted for the device. For instant messaging fans, threaded text messages produce a conversation style format.

2 **ENJOY YOUR MEDIA** As Windows Mobile includes Windows Media Player, it supports common media formats. Synchronizing with the desktop version of Windows Media Player, select your music and video to turn your smartphone into a portable entertainment center.

3 **DOCUMENT CONTROL** Microsoft Office for Mobile provides seamless compatibility between your desktop Office documents and your Windows Mobile Device.

4 **ORGANIZE YOUR LIFE** A powerful calendar lets you keep track of appointments and, as it syncs with Outlook, it's always up to date. Alongside this, are task lists and note-taking features.

5 **THE WEB, ANYWHERE!** With Windows Mobile and Internet Explorer Mobile, you have the worldwide web at your fingertips. Search direct from your device for information, keep track of share prices, or simply catch up on world events.

What's in a name?
A whole lot of technology, that's what

3G Refers to the ability to connect with third generation mobile networks. 3G phones have access to a high-speed digital network, which usually includes access to the internet.

ACTIVESYNC Synchronizes information between smartphone and Windows PC. Maintains consistency between desktop and smartphone emails, contacts, calendar and photos.

GSM (Global System for Mobile communications) is the most widely used communication system for mobile phones. If you travel a lot, opt for a quad-band phone.

BLUETOOTH Wireless technology; Bluetooth provides internet access with a mobile digital data contract.

MICROSD Small size; big storage

HSDPA HSDPA (High Speed Downlink Pocket Access) is the technology behind 3G phones. If you see this listed in the supported bands, you know it's a 3G phone.

FLASH MEMORY The storage of data on thin, small cards. A number of memory card types exist, but MicroSD is the most commonly used format within mobile smartphones. ⊞

The wonder of wireless

With the latest wireless technologies built in to laptops, there's no limit to where you can get online

After years of hype, we're finally getting to the stage where computing really is ubiquitous. It doesn't matter where you are or what you're working from, Windows can find a way of getting you online and working on documents, emails or even sharing holiday photographs that you took literally seconds ago.

The technology of getting connected has progressed from the often difficult task of finding a Wi-Fi hotspot… Over the last 12 to 18 months, most major cell phone networks have launched reasonably priced data packages, usually offering access through a simple USB modem, which looks identical to a memory stick. The chances are, though,

that you may not even need one of those to get online wherever you are.

For a start, an increasing number of laptops have 3G modems built in – all you need to do is install a SIM card, in the same way you would a cell phone. But why go to the trouble? If you have a Windows Mobile phone or, indeed, almost any smartphone with Bluetooth, the Windows Vista Mobility Center can connect you to the internet using the modem built into your handset.

Online organization

And what will you do once you're online? Well, just as accessing your email through a service like Hotmail is almost identical to using a desktop application, there are hundreds of online tools for

keeping your data in sync across a variety of devices. Windows Live (home. live.com), for example, is an all-in-one portal for your email and IM contacts, as well as SkyDrive (see below).

Away from your laptop, you can chat to friends using tools like Windows Live Messenger on any web-enabled device. If you're part of a larger organization, though, you may have access to the full power of the unified communications services that are an integral part of the Microsoft Office system. Syncing your local applications with Microsoft Office Communications Server, you can access all of your documents wherever you are, and be in touch with all your contacts, all of the time, while retaining control over the way they can get hold of you.

"Wow" On the go

You can work on Office Word and Excel documents on your Windows-powered phone – the Windows Mobile Device Center converts Office 2007 files to ones best suited for handsets

Drive in the sky

Take your data online with Windows Live SkyDrive

1 PORTABLE STORAGE If you regularly take your laptop away with you, you probably have a USB hard drive for carrying files such as photos that you want to access from more than one PC.

2 TRAVEL LIGHTER You don't need it any more! With a Windows Live ID – the same as your login for Messenger or Hotmail – you have access to SkyDrive. This gives you 25GB of free web storage.

3 IN THE CLOUDS SkyDrive storage exists in 'the cloud' – held securely on web servers – and backups are kept automatically. Upload files that you need to access anywhere or share with others.

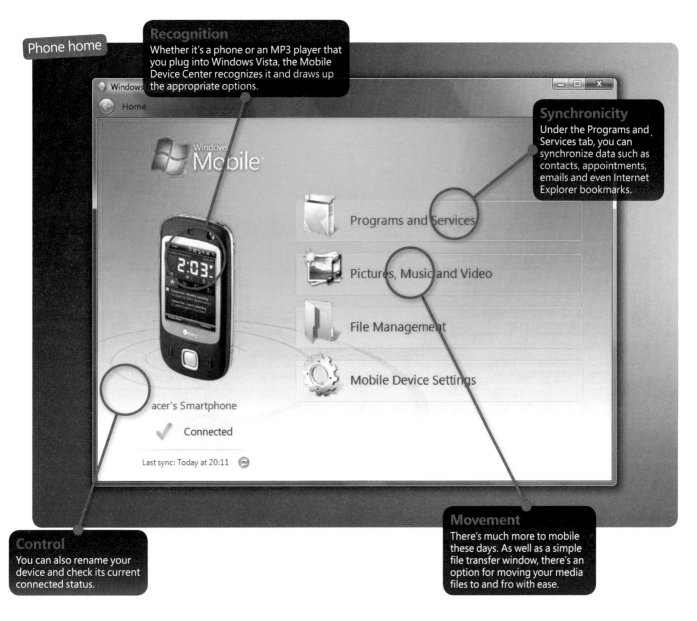

Phone home

Recognition
Whether it's a phone or an MP3 player that you plug into Windows Vista, the Mobile Device Center recognizes it and draws up the appropriate options.

Synchronicity
Under the Programs and Services tab, you can synchronize data such as contacts, appointments, emails and even Internet Explorer bookmarks.

Programs and Services

Pictures, Music and Video

File Management

Mobile Device Settings

acer's Smartphone

✓ Connected

Last sync: Today at 20:11

Control
You can also rename your device and check its current connected status.

Movement
There's much more to mobile these days. As well as a simple file transfer window, there's an option for moving your media files to and fro with ease.

4 FILE EXPLORER To log in to SkyDrive, point your browser at home.live.com and sign in. The first page you see looks a little like File Explorer – it has a tiered folder structure to organize your data.

5 QUICK AND SIMPLE Getting data on and off your SkyDrive is simple. Click on the folder you want to access and you're presented with a large area that you can drag and drop files on to.

6 FRIENDS' ACTIVITY You can also see what your friends have been up to lately, and whether they've uploaded any public files, such as photos, that they'd like to share with you.

Connect, share and update

"Wow"
Media Extender

When it comes to sharing media, Windows Vista is ready to rock. It can detect and share media with all manner of devices, including the Xbox 360, and other Window Vista PCs

If you've more than one PC it's time to get connected; Windows Vista makes it easier than ever

Networking multiple computers has many advantages: it enables different users to share files and applications, as well as share a single internet account.

Setting up a network can be as simple as plugging in a few cables and, once

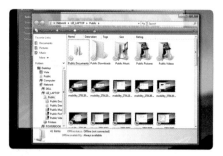

RESTRICT ENTRY If you don't want users on your network to edit your files, limit access

done, you're soon able to gain the benefits of sharing files and resources.

There is, quite rightly, a certain level of paranoia associated with networks and the internet in general. The trick with networking is to take a less-is-more approach and limit access to the bare minimum required. For example, if people only need to view the files in your Public folder but don't need the ability to edit them, it makes sense to limit their access accordingly, so you should use the Network and Sharing Center to give read-only access rather than full access.

Conversely, you're not limited to just sharing the Public folder and nothing else if you don't want to be. If **File Sharing** is switched on in the Network and Sharing Center you can share any

folder by right-clicking on it in Windows Explorer and clicking **Share**. Don't worry about rendering your system vulnerable, even with this level of access it's still possible to add passwords to specific folders to limit availability.

Working together

Windows Vista also offers ways to make sharing files easier with its new Sync Center. This handy feature enables you to work on files while you're away from a network or while the shared PC is powered down; any changes made can then be synchronized once the shared files are available again.

Follow the 'Connecting to another PC' walkthrough on the opposite page to see how this can be activated and how you can take full advantage of it. 🏁

Share and invite with Live Mesh

Share and synchronize your files across multiple computers

While Live Mesh is currently a preview version, it already enables you to share and synchronize files, access those files on the internet, and also provides remote access to your PC. Not only does this work with Windows XP and Windows Vista, it also works with web-enabled mobile phones, PDAs, and Apple Macintosh computers.

With Live Mesh you can simply choose a folder on your computer and give others access and

synchronization capabilities from Windows Explorer. They can see the files or, if you choose, change or add files themselves. The Live Mesh preview has a 5GB online store, making files – including ones that have not been synchronized – accessible via a Remote Desktop. Should you be using a machine away from home, you can log on and access one of your devices that is online. From here a web page opens and you get control of your PC.

Go to www.mesh.com and sign in

OWN DEVICES Whether it's another PC or a mobile phone, it's easy to add a device

with your Windows Live ID, then click on **Add Device** and **Install**. Once you've installed the Live Mesh software, you're good to go.

Connecting to another PC

Access other PCs and synchronize amended files

1 HELLO Click **View Full Map**: you should see something like this. In addition to the internet connection, the desktop PC can see the laptop. Right-click the other computer and click **Open**.

2 EASY EXPLORE Here, you're looking at the laptop, or at least the bits that the laptop's owner has given permission to look at. In this example, you can browse the Public and Printers folders.

3 SEE FILES Double-click **Public**. If you've got read-only access you'll be able to open and copy files; if you've got full access you can edit or delete files or copy files from your hard disk.

4 WAIT A BIT You can ensure these files are always available, even when you're not connected. To do this, go back one step, right-click on **Public** and click **Always available offline.**

5 SIMPLE SYNC Open Sync Center from **Control Panel → Network and Internet → Sync Center.** You'll see that there's an entry already in there – Offline Files. Double-click the icon to see more.

6 OFFLINE BROWSING You should now see the folder you wanted available at all times – in this case the Public folder on the laptop. Click on **Browse** to see the contents of that folder.

7 CHANGES The laptop is no longer connected but the files are available. By using the local copy of the laptop files, changes will be applied to the originals when the files are synchronized.

8 UPDATE Return to Sync Center. Above Offline Files you'll see **Sync**, which synchronizes files immediately, and **Schedule**, which enables you to sync files at specified times.

9 OPTIONS The Network and Sharing Center provides additional options. Under Public Folder Sharing you can limit access to your Public folders, or you can password-protect shared files.

Move files from your PC to your pocket device

Portable computers are getting smaller, as Pocket PCs and smartphones displace the laptop – Windows Vista is well prepared

With Windows Vista you can transfer files from your computer to your mobile device manually, but a far better option is to use the built-in Sync Center to automatically update your device whenever you connect it to your PC.

If you're using the 2007 Microsoft Office system, this can synchronize all manner of documents and data between the two devices, enabling you to take your emails, to-do list, notes, calendar, contacts and much more with you wherever you go. You can then make changes to them on your device and have the updates synchronized back with the originals, for when you're back at your desktop computer.

Pocket PCs have been around for some time and are a perfect way to take your documents, email and even media out and about with you, in a device that's a fraction of the size and weight of even the smallest laptop. With Windows XP it used to be necessary to install an additional application to synchronize data between your desktop PC and the Pocket PC, but the good news is that this functionality is built into Windows Vista, which makes working with your portable devices even easier.

Building upon the Pocket PC technology are smartphones. These are mobile phones that boast all the functionality of a full-blown Pocket PC but happen to be mobile phones as well, making for incredibly useful devices.

CONNECT 4 Your mobile device can talk to your PC with Windows Mobile Device Center

Installing a Pocket PC

It's as easy as 1, 2, 3...

1 INSTALL THE DRIVERS Connect your Pocket PC or Windows Mobile device with the supplied cable and switch it on. After a few seconds you'll see this message as your PC spots the device.

2 DECIDE THE DEFAULT AutoPlay asks if you know what you want Windows Vista to do when you connect – for example, you may want your PC to automatically transfer music.

3 SIMPLE SYNC Go to **Control Panel →Network and Internet**. You can specify whether your device should connect via USB or Bluetooth, while Sync Center enables you to transfer files.

Using Sync Center

Moving files on to your mobile device is easy with Sync Center

1 **NO MOBILE** When you first open Sync Center it shows you a list of partnerships – because there aren't any set up yet, the list is blank. Click on **Set Up New Sync Partnerships** to introduce Sync Center to your mobile device.

2 **HELLO THERE** This example shows a Windows Mobile PDA/smartphone with a storage card. Sync Center spots it and confirms it can synchronize media files. Click on **Storage Card** and then **Set Up** to finish creating the partnership.

3 **SUFFICIENT SPACE** Sync Center opens Media Player and, if you've got a fairly small storage card, you see this warning saying you don't have enough space. Don't worry about it – you don't have to synchronize your entire media collection.

There are some types of file that Sync Center won't send; the good news is, manual transfers are easy

4 **MANUAL MOVING** There are some types of file, such as Word documents, that Sync Center won't send to your mobile device. The good news is: manual transfers are easy. Just click on **Start ➜ Computer** and you'll see your device at the bottom of the list of drives and devices.

Media on the move

As the power of mobile devices increases, you can do even more with them. Most are more than capable of handling video playback, meaning that not only can you take your phone with you, but your media as well.

5 **TRADITIONAL TRANSFER** Double-click on your portable device to see the available storage options. In this case there are two – the Pocket PC's internal storage and its storage card. Copying files to either location is simply a matter of dragging and dropping over the icons.

Meet up with Windows Meeting Space

Share your desktop and invite others to meetings you can chair without leaving your PC

For many, especially those in business, the most important networking feature of Windows Vista is Windows Meeting Space; the replacement for the NetMeeting program in Windows XP, enabling you to share your screen with someone else on your network (either an individual or an entire group). You can share a single file, an application or your entire system, which means you can use Windows Meeting Space to deliver presentations or even training sessions.

Everything you do on screen is mirrored on the other person's screen in real time, and you can even give them remote control over your PC, so they can not only be shown how to do things, but try things out, too. If you combine it with internal phone calls or Windows Live Messenger's voice chat features, the potential is mind-boggling. Despite its power, it's easy to set up and use, and you can use Windows Meeting Space in any edition of Windows Vista (if you're running the Home Basic edition, you can join other meetings, but can't create meetings of your own).

You can leave the meeting at any time, but that doesn't mean the meeting will close as soon as the person who called it goes away; a meeting continues until everyone leaves.

In real life...
Keep it secure

**Neil Mohr,
Contributor,
Windows Vista: The
Official Magazine**

If you're opening handouts created by others, they might contain a virus, so keep your security software on. There are low-tech risks, too... For example, you might share the wrong file as a handout; avoid this by sharing a single file rather than an entire application.

Meeting and greeting
Invite your colleagues to a virtual conference

1 PEOPLE POWERED Enable a feature called People Near Me, which enables you to see whether there are any people near you on the network. Go to **Control Panel ➔ Network and Internet** and click on **People Near Me**.

2 SIGN IN You now have to go through the very simple signing in process, which begins with another dialog box. Just select the **Sign In** tab and click on **Sign in to people near me**, then click on **OK** to continue.

3 MEET AND GREET Before you can set up a meeting, you need to ensure that People Near Me is also set up on the PC(s) you want to communicate with. The process is identical to the one outlined in the previous steps.

4 START IT UP On your own PC, click on **Start a new meeting** and give it a password. Without this, people won't be able to join you – that's good, because it keeps out unwelcome attendees. Click the green arrow when you're done.

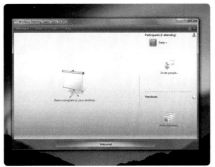

5 NO ONE HOME The Meeting Space screen is divided into three; the big section on the left shares a program, the top-right section shows who's in the meeting, and the bottom-right section enables you to provide handouts.

6 COME TOGETHER Invite People displays potential attendees. To invite a person, click their name then click **Send Invitations**. Tick **Require participants to type the meeting password** if you want a password-protected meeting.

7 JOIN THE PARTY In this example, the invite has appeared on the recipient's PC with a warning – you're not a trusted contact in their address book. However, the invitee knows you're trustworthy, so they click the **Accept** button.

8 MAKE AN ENTRANCE In this case the invitee does know the password, so they need to enter it and click on the green arrow. They'll see a progress bar for a few seconds as Windows Meeting Space joins the meeting.

9 SHOW OFF Back on your PC, it's time to show what Windows Meeting Space can do. Click on the **Share** icon and a security warning pops up, saying that if you share your desktop other people will be able to see it.

10 PICK A PROGRAM You can select a program to share by clicking on it and clicking **Share**, or you can click on **Browse** to launch and share a file that isn't already open. For now, though, select **Desktop** and then click **Share**.

11 SCREEN SHARING This is what attendees see – your desktop, in real time. You'll see that Windows Vista has changed the graphics slightly. Sharing uses Aero Basic instead of Aero Glass, as there's no need for fancy visuals.

12 TALK IS CHEAP In addition to sharing your desktop, you can also send notes to other people in the meeting. To do this, right-click over their name and choose **Send A Note**. Type your text and click **Send**.

Stress-free teamwork

A number of colleagues working on the same document? Try group work without the gremlins...

Better results faster

The best way to share documents between authors in the 2007 Office system is to use Groove 2007 and shared workspaces. No more clogging inboxes with documents going to and fro

Many people have to produce documents that require extensive review processes; it's slow, frustrating and often ends up with a piece of work full of mistakes. Thankfully, technology has caught up...

If you're given the job of collating the final version of a document after three people have made changes to it, it used to be the case that you'd have to have several documents open at once as you inched through them word by word trying to spot each change.

Now, however, the tri-pane review panel means it's easy to compare and combine two versions of an Office Word 2007 document. Not only does this system highlight the smallest differences between two documents, it also marks all deleted, inserted and moved text. You can also activate Synchronous Scrolling so that both documents roll up and down at once. The Reviewing Pane displays the number (and type) of changes that have been made, while Track Changes outlines what's been altered, how it's been altered and who made the amendment – and you can set how you want the amends to appear.

Once you've checked through everything, it's easy to combine the documents into one. If you've got copies from several sources, you can merge them two at a time until you're left with one final document, and with Document Inspector you can make sure that none of your changes (or anyone else's) are seen, as the tool removes any unwanted comments or hidden text.

Once you've got your master copy, you can use the Reading Mode, which puts the entire document into full screen, making it easier to proof. You can also use the Contextual Spelling Checker to make sure no spelling mistakes have crept in.

Business documents often require disclaimers and other predefined content that have to be copied and pasted from previous documents. Building Blocks let you do this without hassle, and you can choose from a predefined gallery or create your own. The only thing you have to worry about is explaining to your boss why you have so much free time...

Two become one

Merging two documents is now a headache-free process

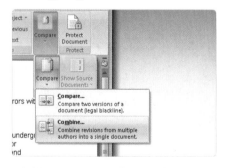

1 COMBINE Your colleagues have made changes to a document and you need to amend the original. Go to Review, select **Compare ➜ Combine** (combine revisions from multiple authors...).

2 FIRST VERSION A new dialog appears. Under Original document, click on the name of the document into which you wish to combine the changes. If you can't find it, try Browse for original.

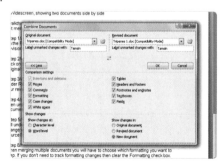

3 COPY CAT Now look under Revised document and browse for the document that has the changes from your colleagues. When you've found it, click on the **More** button.

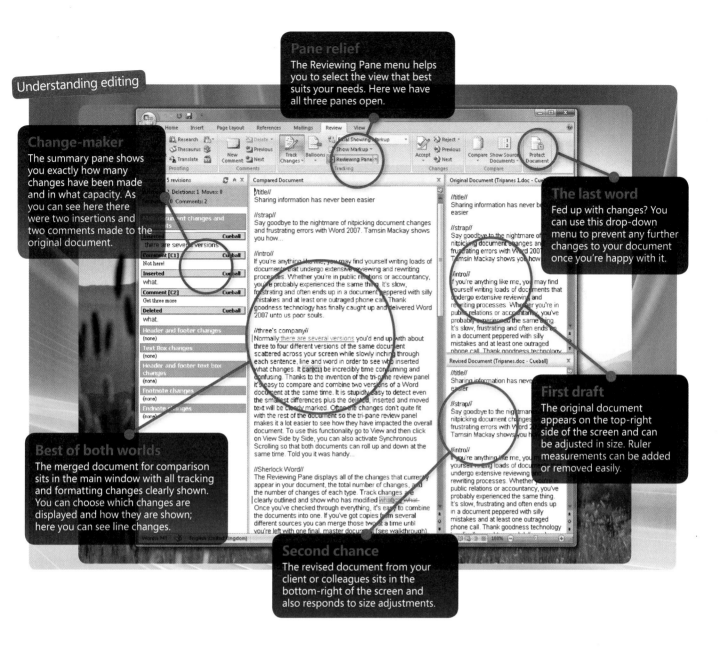

Pane relief
The Reviewing Pane menu helps you to select the view that best suits your needs. Here we have all three panes open.

Change-maker
The summary pane shows you exactly how many changes have been made and in what capacity. As you can see here there were two insertions and two comments made to the original document.

The last word
Fed up with changes? You can use this drop-down menu to prevent any further changes to your document once you're happy with it.

First draft
The original document appears on the top-right side of the screen and can be adjusted in size. Ruler measurements can be added or removed easily.

Best of both worlds
The merged document for comparison sits in the main window with all tracking and formatting changes clearly shown. You can choose which changes are displayed and how they are shown; here you can see line changes.

Second chance
The revised document from your client or colleagues sits in the bottom-right of the screen and also responds to size adjustments.

4 COMPARE You'll be presented with a range of options of what Word 2007 can compare. Under Comparison settings you can say which of these comparisons you'd like Word to run.

5 SEEING DOUBLE Under Show changes in, click on **Original document** and then **OK**. If you want to change documents, choose between Hide Source Documents or Show Source Documents.

6 CONSISTENCY When merging multiple documents you have to choose which formatting to keep (if altered). If you don't need to track formatting changes, clear the check box.

Be a project manager...

Things can get disorganized on a group project, but with Office OneNote 2007 they are far more manageable

You may begin a group project with real direction and enthusiasm, only to become swamped with research notes, as well as amendments and comments from various colleagues. With OneNote 2007, though, you'll find that you have a helpful project manager to hand. You can add data in a variety of ways, and you can share all your notes with others really easily.

Before you begin, open a new notebook in OneNote 2007 and give it a memorable title, such as 'The Biography of Franklin D Roosevelt'. Then collate all the ideas your staff or colleagues have come up with. Now create tables for each of the categories you might need

(look at the walkthrough opposite for a guide). These help you arrange all the incoming information to suit your needs and make it easy for anyone else to understand. You can even create sections for each element, such as President, Great Depression and Biography. These can be broken down even further so that everyone in your group knows exactly what tasks have been allocated to them.

If you are using internet research, you can send the content of these web pages directly across to your notebook, including screen clippings, so that you have a visual display of all the information you need. It may start to look a little cluttered as you're copying different elements across but once it's

all stored inside your notebook, it is easy to search through, share with others and annotate.

OneNote 2007 lets you share your notebook with anyone else online and, if someone doesn't have the program, you can email entire pages or sections with just one click. This makes gathering and sharing your data extremely easy.

You can also create a table of contents that hyperlinks to the relevant information by right-clicking anywhere in your notes, which makes navigating your workbook a pleasure. So say goodbye to hundreds of email hours trying to keep everybody in the loop – let them see all the information they need in one place and reply with one definitive answer. ⊞

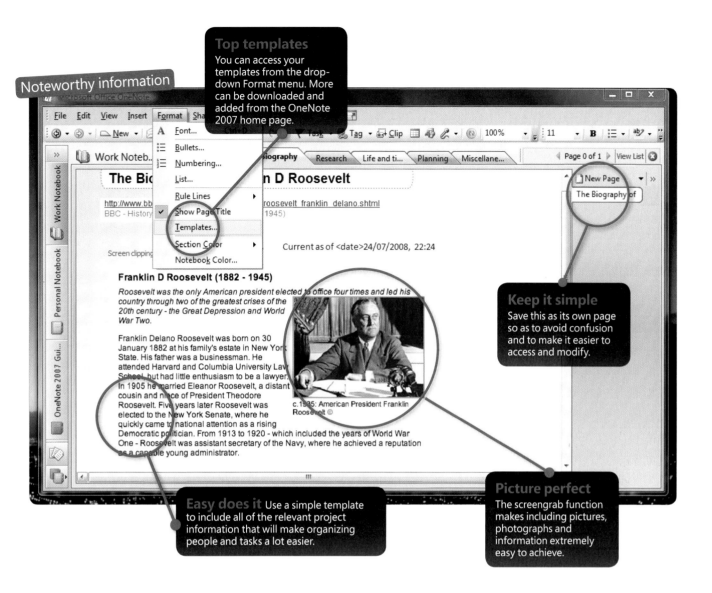

Top templates
You can access your templates from the drop-down Format menu. More can be downloaded and added from the OneNote 2007 home page.

Keep it simple
Save this as its own page so as to avoid confusion and to make it easier to access and modify.

Easy does it Use a simple template to include all of the relevant project information that will make organizing people and tasks a lot easier.

Picture perfect
The screengrab function makes including pictures, photographs and information extremely easy to achieve.

Perfect projects

Keeping on top of a group assignment is easy

1 **TABLE BUILDING** To create a table, go to **Table → Insert Table**. A pop-up menu asks how many columns you need, so enter the number of columns and rows required.

2 **UP TO DATE** Keep a sentence at the top of the page that reads 'Current as of <date>' and use **Alt**, **Shift** and **D** to insert the current date. This is great for keeping track of changes.

3 **FIND ANYTHING** If other people work on your notebook, you may need to track their entries. To find any information in OneNote, press **Ctrl** and **F**, and insert the relevant keywords.

Arm yourself with free online help and updates

With the 2007 Microsoft Office system, there's plenty of free help, updates, templates and tutorials waiting online

When you buy and install the 2007 Microsoft Office system, not only are you getting a useful and powerful suite of applications, but you're also gaining access to a raft of online extras.

To find out more, go to **www.office. microsoft.com** and get a taste of all the free resources and features that are available to help improve your computing experience.

You'll be able to make sure your programs are always up-to-date and

BE INSPIRED There are hundreds of templates to get you started or give you inspiration

completely secure by getting the latest updates; the Office Update tool found on the download page automates the

update process so you'll never have to think about it – just set it, then forget it!

Alternatively, the Microsoft central download site – at **www.microsoft.com/ downloads** – enables you to search for and download any required updates.

And there's more...

But the Microsoft Office system website isn't just about such serious stuff... The site will also help you get the most from all the Office 2007 programs, no matter whether that's through templates, tutorials, training or tips.

If you've ever searched for a template when using one of the Microsoft Office system applications, you may have noticed that there's an online search; this uses the same database of templates that's on the Microsoft Office Online website. Click on the **Template** link and you'll find a handy search tool, but beyond this is a further selection of extra resources. Community help, suggestions and submissions are all available and provide a brilliant way to exchange ideas and grow your template-creating talents.

If you're struggling to master all the ins and outs of some of these powerful applications, again the Microsoft Office Online site will come to your rescue. Just click on the **Help and How-to** link and you'll find a host of searchable tutorials and helpful articles, though again there's more here than first meets the eye. Links on the left open up gateways to comprehensive training packages. You'll be amazed at the range of answers to hand, from the simplest useful nugget to full-blown complex how-to guides.

UP TO SPEED The Office Online website is packed with helpful links, downloads and templates

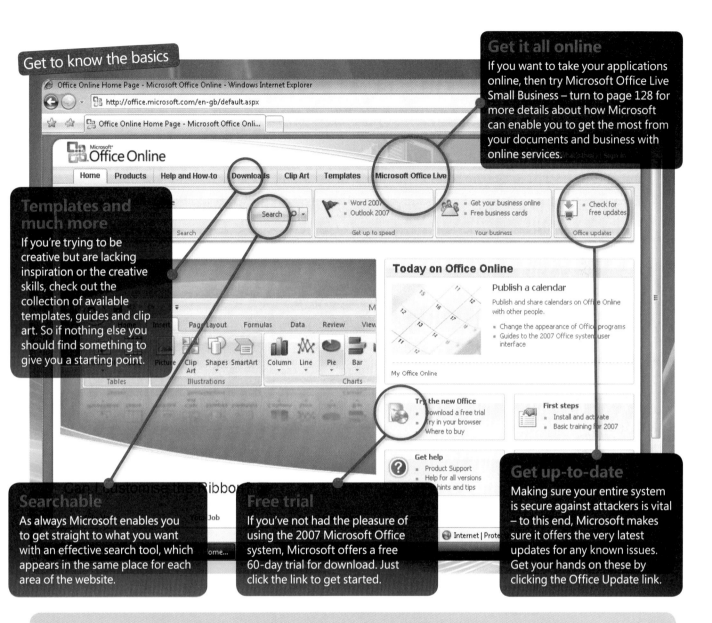

Get to know the basics

Get it all online

If you want to take your applications online, then try Microsoft Office Live Small Business – turn to page 128 for more details about how Microsoft can enable you to get the most from your documents and business with online services.

Templates and much more

If you're trying to be creative but are lacking inspiration or the creative skills, check out the collection of available templates, guides and clip art. So if nothing else you should find something to give you a starting point.

Searchable

As always Microsoft enables you to get straight to what you want with an effective search tool, which appears in the same place for each area of the website.

Free trial

If you've not had the pleasure of using the 2007 Microsoft Office system, Microsoft offers a free 60-day trial for download. Just click the link to get started.

Get up-to-date

Making sure your entire system is secure against attackers is vital – to this end, Microsoft makes sure it offers the very latest updates for any known issues. Get your hands on these by clicking the Office Update link.

A world of help

There are more than just templates and updates waiting for you online

We're better together – that's never truer when you're looking for help. Trying to figure out a dilemma, whether it's a type of formatting in Word 2007 or an equation in Excel 2007, can be frustrating on your own. That's why Microsoft provides a place where you can share ideas, ask questions and get help. It's called Microsoft Discussion Groups and there's a huge section dedicated to all things Microsoft Office. Browse to www.microsoft.com/office/ community/en-us/default.mspx.

You're able to search the entire site or pick a section. It's also possible to access these groups using a Newsgroup reader such as Microsoft Outlook Express or newer versions of Microsoft Outlook. You'll need to add a 'News' account and use the address msnews.microsoft.com.

CALL ALL Real help from real people online

Work on documents wherever you are

Microsoft Office Live Workspace enables you to access your work from anywhere, plus edit and share it with colleagues

 If you've ever been left without a vital document, or wished you could work on a report or project plans with a colleague, there is an answer. Microsoft Office Live Workspace means you can save your documents to the web and share them with a group.

Obviously, there are plenty of online services, such as Windows Live SkyDrive, which enable you to upload and share files. What makes Office Live Workspace different is that it allows seamless saving and uploading between Microsoft Office and the internet.

Like the Windows Live suite, Office Live Workspace works with your Windows Live ID. To get started go to workspace.officelive.com and register

your Windows Live ID with the service. You can then download the Office Live Workspace Connector, which enables Microsoft Office to communicate with your Office Live Workspace.

Saving online

The connector software adds a new **Save As** button to the menu. This works just like the one that saves to your hard drive, but your work is saved online. Now you can save and load documents directly from Microsoft Office, without having to resave files on to online spaces.

While online storage is one of the best features, your Office Live Workspace provides much more than a simple drive service. You can set up workgroups, share documents and create workspaces,

where people can log in and leave comments on documents. This is great for group exercises, and all changes to documents are tracked so you can see who made the last amendments.

Microsoft SharedView, which enables you to offer users remote access to your PC, has also been included.

Compatibility is another great feature of Office Live Workspace, because the service doesn't just work with the 2007 Microsoft Office system, it also works with the old 2003 version, too. This means that colleagues with older software aren't left out of the loop, and you can use the service on a work PC. Even if you're not allowed to install the connector software, you can still use the workspace over the web.

Set up media sharing in five minutes

Share your music and videos with other people on the network

1 SIGN UP Register your Windows Live ID at workspace.officelive.com. If you haven't got a Live ID, register here (for free), then use it to take advantage of the whole range of Windows Live services.

2 INSTALL When you log in, you can install the Office Live Update. This adds functionality to Microsoft Office, so documents can be saved or loaded from the web, without going via a browser.

3 SAVE AND LOAD In Office Word 2007 the new option is in the main Office menu (in Office 2003 the options are on a toolbar). You are prompted to enter your password if not logged in.

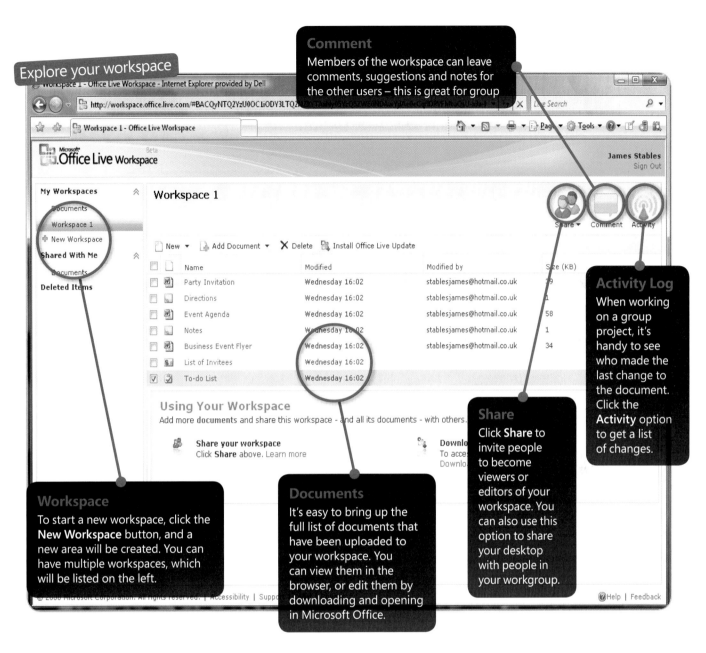

Explore your workspace

Comment
Members of the workspace can leave comments, suggestions and notes for the other users – this is great for group

Activity Log
When working on a group project, it's handy to see who made the last change to the document. Click the **Activity** option to get a list of changes.

Share
Click **Share** to invite people to become viewers or editors of your workspace. You can also use this option to share your desktop with people in your workgroup.

Documents
It's easy to bring up the full list of documents that have been uploaded to your workspace. You can view them in the browser, or edit them by downloading and opening in Microsoft Office.

Workspace
To start a new workspace, click the **New Workspace** button, and a new area will be created. You can have multiple workspaces, which will be listed on the left.

4 CREATE A WORKSPACE You can create a public workspace for your workgroup, so people can access the same documents, make changes, resave and make comments in a panel.

5 SHARE WORKSPACE To invite other parties into your workspace, click on **Share** and **Share workspace**. You can choose whether each person is allowed to edit or just view the documents.

6 SHARE SCREEN In the Share option there is a function to share a screen with a member of your party, so that you can work on a document simultaneously using Microsoft SharedView.

CHAPTER 17 **ONLINE**

Get the web working for you

Microsoft's Office Live Small Business lets you play with tools previously reserved for the big boys...

You can't get something for nothing, especially when it comes to business services. Or can you? As it happens, you can get a lot of free tools and applications when you sign up for Microsoft's Office Live Small Business at smallbusiness.officelive.com.

You can think of Office Live Small Business as an outsourcing service for all the technical stuff that makes big business more efficient. It's a hosting service that gives you an online presence as well as the tools to manage your website. But there's more. You also get a free domain name and up to 100 email addresses, with 5GB of storage each.

Then there's a suite of online collaboration tools for sharing customer information and documents with colleagues – all safe in the knowledge that your private network is secure. In addition, security threats are constantly being monitored – and responded to – on your behalf by the industry-leading Microsoft Security Response Center.

You can also optionally subscribe to an Email Marketing tool or purchase online advertising on networks such as MSN and Live. For now, though, you may just be interested in establishing your first online presence and reaching new consumers through targeted keywords in Live Search.

Whatever the size of your company, Office Live Small Business can help. ♣

Better results faster

In some organizations, you can share workspaces with colleagues on the road and access email through the Outlook interface wherever you are

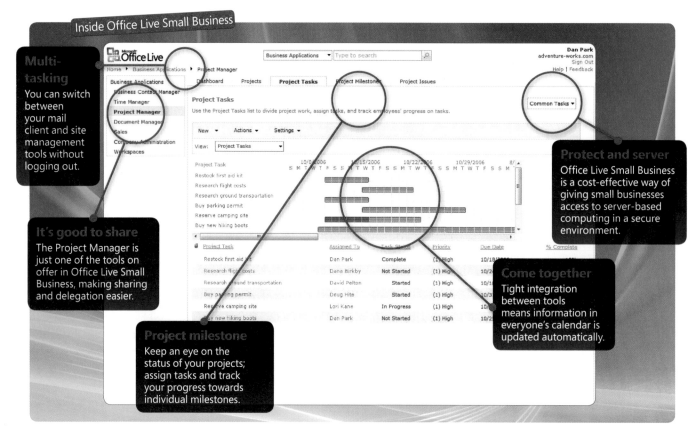

Inside Office Live Small Business

Multi-tasking
You can switch between your mail client and site management tools without logging out.

It's good to share
The Project Manager is just one of the tools on offer in Office Live Small Business, making sharing and delegation easier.

Project milestone
Keep an eye on the status of your projects; assign tasks and track your progress towards individual milestones.

Protect and server
Office Live Small Business is a cost-effective way of giving small businesses access to server-based computing in a secure environment.

Come together
Tight integration between tools means information in everyone's calendar is updated automatically.

Get yourself online

Office Live Small Business makes it easy to have an online presence

1 YOU ARE HERE
Every Live subscriber gets their own web space, domain name and email addresses; a company-based email creates a professional edge.

2 KEEP CURRENT
The more data you have about customers, the more you can offer. In Office Live Small Business you can access an up-to-date contact database.

3 EXCHANGE NUMBERS
Using protected workspaces, you can share info with colleagues. Images, documents and project timelines can be stored and edited.

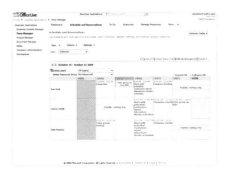

4 GET TOGETHER
The sharing facilities don't just apply to swapping documents. You can set reminders and appointments with anyone who has a Windows Live ID.

What do I get with Office Live Small Business?

Sign up for your favorite service at smallbusiness.officelive.com

Feature	What that means for you...	Included free	Add-on feature
Domain name registration	Choose your website address and get a free .com domain name registration for the first two years. Alternatively, you can register a .org, .net or .eu address free for the first year	✓	
Domain branded email	Obtain up to 100 email accounts with your domain name in the address	✓ [1]	
Website hosting	Include plenty of pictures, logos and documents on your website with 500MB of website space	✓	
Website design tools	Design your site using easy-to-use tools with your browser; no software or web design skills necessary	✓	
Site reports	Find out how many people are visiting your site, how they're using it, and more	✓	
Contact Manager	Keep track of your customer interactions and opportunities online	✓	
Workspaces	Share documents with others on your own password-protected site	✓	
Project Manager	Plan projects, assign tasks and monitor progress – all online	✓	
Support	Get around-the-clock help when you need it	✓	
Resource Center	Access articles, tips and advice from experts or share with the community	✓	
Search word advertising	Get noticed by advertising with keywords that people search with to find businesses like yours	✓	✓ [2]
Email marketing	Keep your customers up-to-date with promotions and newsletters		✓ [3]
Additional storage	Add more website or business-application storage if you use up your free 500MB		✓
Additional domain names	Add more domain names that will lead people to your website		✓

1 Requires signup for custom domain name registration: com domains are free for the first two years. Alternatively, .com, .org, .net, .or .eu domains are free for the first year only.
2 AdManager offers properties in the Microsoft AdCenter, which includes MSN.com and Live.com.
3 Email Marketing beta is free for up to 200 email messages per month while the service is in beta.

Power up Internet Explorer 8

Internet Explorer 8 makes browsing faster, safer and easier than ever, but you can make it even better...

Internet Explorer is designed to make web browsing easier, and it's packed with useful features such as easy web searching, one-click access to Windows Live services, and Web Slices to keep on top of your favorite sites. But it's capable of even more. There's a huge range of accelerators, add-ons and toolbars that make Internet Explorer 8 even more useful. From social networking to shopping, document handling to downloading, these 10 add-ons mean much better browsing. They're free, and you'll find all 10 – and many more – at www.ieaddons.com.

1 RESEARCH & SHOP FOR PRODUCTS

You know that shopping online can save you a packet, but how do you find the best deals – and make sure the product you're looking at is worth the cash? The Shop and Save with Live Search Products accelerator gives you instant product prices, cashback offers,

VACATION BOOKING TripAdvisor enables you to read other people's reviews of resorts

product reviews and other relevant information, and helps you save when shopping online.

2 XMARKS

Formerly known as Foxmarks, Xmarks is an add-on that stores your Favorites on the internet, so you can access them from any internet-enabled PC that you install Xmarks on. It's particularly useful if you use shared

computers – if you have multiple PCs at home, for example, or if you'd like to use the same Favorites at home and at work.

3 BUGMENOT

One of the more annoying things on the internet is when sites demand you register just so you can read an article or forum post. BugMeNot can provide user names and passwords that should let you in.

4 ONERIOT

You can use Web Slices to stay up to date with your Facebook friends' status updates, but the OneRiot toolbar takes it further by adding notification buttons below the Address Bar. These enable you to visit the various bits of Facebook (Home, Profile, Friends and so on) but they also enable you to see when somebody's sent you a friend request, whether you have new messages or if anybody's tagged you in a photo. There's a version for MySpace, too.

5 YOONO

If, like us, you're on loads of social networks, Yoono can save you a great deal of time and effort. In much the same way that multi-chat software enables you to connect to different instant messaging services, Yoono can connect you to Facebook, MySpace, Twitter, Flickr and FriendFeed, as well as AOL Instant Messenger, Google Talk, MSN Messenger and Yahoo. You can also share content with other Yoono users, for example by tagging web pages with 'like' or 'hate'.

In real life... Accelerate to navigate

Matt Hanson, Writer, *Windows Vista: The Official Magazine*

I'm rubbish with directions so I always need to consult websites such as Live Search Maps (http://maps.live.com/) when visiting unfamiliar territory. In earlier versions of Internet Explorer this

would involve a process of copying the ZIP code, opening up the website, pasting in the code and searching for the location. Thanks to the Accelerators tool in IE8 I can now accomplish this task in just one click, without even leaving the web page! All I need to do is highlight an address or ZIP, right-click and select Map with Live Maps.

SEARCH SHOP Keep up with the latest in bids and bargains with eBay's search plug-in

6 TRIPADVISOR
Booking a holiday? Save time, money and heartbreak by using this accelerator to look up resort or hotel names on TripAdvisor, where travellers tell the truth about the places they've stayed – good and bad.

7 DEFINE ACRONYM
If you've ever encountered an acronym and wondered what it meant, this will make your online life much more comprehensible. Highlight the acronym, select the accelerator and see definitions from the fields of science, government, IT, business, even slang.

8 COOLIRIS
Ever wished the internet looked more like it does in Hollywood

WHO YOU KNOW Addicted to social networks? Yoono puts your favorites inside your browser

movies? With Cooliris, it does. Once you've installed the browser add-on, it's just a matter of carrying out a web search at www.cooliris.com, but instead of text links, you see a wall of images you can sweep through, zoom in and generally muck about with. It's fascinating, gorgeous and makes you feel that we're all living in the future.

9 WEATHER CHANNEL TOOLBAR
Want to know when it's going to rain, and whether to take a scarf with you or not? Get this handy toolbar, which sits in browser window and keeps you constantly in the know with frequent weather updates where you live. It also provides links so that you can check the weather for the next 10 days and see the top weather reports in video. If you do a lot of travelling, this feature works well in conjunction with TripAdvisor.

10 EBAY VISUAL SEARCH
If you're a shopping addict on a tight budget, eBay's search plug-in will be right up your street. Simply click the arrow in the Search box (located at the top right-hand corner of the browser), select eBay, type the kind of item you're looking for and you'll see stacks of results including pictures and prices. It's a simple and very useful tool, so expect lot of other retailers to offer similar search tools for their own shops in the near future. As if it wasn't easy enough to spend on internet purchases, now online splurges are even easier!

VISUAL WEB Cooliris is guaranteed to wow you. It turns web searching into a wall of images

Do things quicker in Windows Vista

Are you using your PC to its full potential? Here are 11 ways to optimize the way you use Windows Vista

1 Schedule

If your PC is left on when not in use, you can schedule common tasks to occur. Go to the Start Search menu, type in 'Task Scheduler' and hit **Enter**. Once the Scheduler is open, select **Tasks** and edit the time they occur and how long they last, along with other options. The tasks you'll probably want to run most often are Defrag and System Restore.

2 Integration

You can save time on reading emails and news by integrating them into your email program. Do this by downloading Windows Live Mail from get.live.com. From here you can add different mail accounts, send instant messages and get RSS feeds delivered.

ALL IN ONE Save time and stress by combining all your emails and feeds in one program

3 Streamline

To make it quicker to open programs or folders that you use on a regular basis, you need them to be easy to access. The desktop is the most obvious place, although desktop icons require

NAME DROPPING Add tags to your files to make them quicker and easier to find in future

a double-click. An even faster way is to put them on the quick launch toolbar at the bottom of the screen or, if space is tight, you can put them in the Start Menu. Simply left-click on a folder or program and drag it to wherever you would like it to go.

4 Synchronize devices

If you're constantly adding new songs, pictures or videos to your PC, and you want them on your MP3 or portable media player as well, then you want to set up a sync partnership. When your device is plugged in and set up, Sync Center will detect whether new files have

PERFECT HARMONY Set up a partnership to ensure your MP3 player is always in sync

been added to your PC and add them to your device. To do this, go to **Start → All Programs → Accessories → Sync Center**.

5 Tag your files

If you've got a lot of photos or music stored on your PC, you'll want to be able to find them quickly and easily. You can tag files by left-clicking them and adding or changing the text in the bottom of the window they're open in. You can also tag multiple files by selecting them all, right-clicking one of the highlighted files, clicking on **Properties** in the drop-down menu, and selecting the Details tab.

6 Start up in seconds

When you shut down your PC it can take a few minutes to power down – and then even more time to start up again. You can avoid this process by using the Sleep function. Just open the Start Menu and click on the power button. This will save your current session and put your PC into a low-power state. All you need to do to start it back up is click the power button on your computer's case.

7 Use the Start search

To really save time using your PC, you need to master Start search. When you've got a lot of files, programs or emails to sift through, you can find them quickly by opening the Start search menu and typing into the box. The less you type, the more options you get (for example, type 'cal' and you'll get calculator, calendar, and so on). You can also save your searches, so you can find things again in a hurry.

8 Renaming files

When you've got a huge number of files you'd like to rename, instead of altering them one by one, you can rename them all in just a few clicks. Hold **Ctrl** and left-click each file, or left-click and drag to select all the files. Then press **F2**, type in a common name to use for all the files, press **Enter** and all the files will be given the same name, with the exception of a number at the end.

9 Disable UAC

User Account Control (UAC) is the in-built security prompt designed to safeguard against potentially damaging changes. It's a great feature, but it slows you down a bit. If you'd prefer not to have it popping up, turn it off by typing **User Accounts** into the Start menu search, and clicking on **Turn User Account Control on or off**. Of course, this is not recommended, but it is there.

10 Change users

When you've got a whole family using just one computer, you'll probably have set up individual accounts. To swap between these accounts, just press **Ctrl**, **Alt** and **Delete** on your keyboard, and select **Switch user** to change.

CTRL, ALT + DEL A quick way to lock your PC while you're away or to switch between users

11 Add gadgets

You don't have to open Internet Explorer each time you want to check on the weather or look at your eBay account. Instead, use Windows Sidebar gadgets by right-clicking on the Sidebar and selecting **Add gadgets**. To get more gadgets, go to gallery.live.com to download and install what you want.

10 keyboard shortcuts

Control your computer at the touch of a button or two

Quit application
One of the most useful shortcuts you'll ever know. To quickly close a window, you can use this command to close them without using the mouse. When you're on the desktop, it even opens the box to enable you to shut down or restart your PC.

Copy and paste
To copy and paste text from one file to another, just highlight the text, press **Ctrl** and **C**, then open the second file and press **Ctrl** and **V**.

Rename
When you've selected an item, pressing **F2** enables you to rename it without having to left-click it twice with a gap in between (which avoids accidental opening of the file).

Auto web address
Instead of typing a whole website address (such as www.google.com) just type the middle bit and hold down **Ctrl** and **Enter** for the 'www.' and '.com' to be filled in for you.

Cycle through windows
If you've got Windows Vista Home Premium or Ultimate, holding the Windows key and pressing **Tab** repeatedly cycles through all open windows in Flip 3D. Taking your finger off the Windows key opens the window highlighted.

New window
If you're in Internet Explorer or a program such as Microsoft Office Word, you can create a new window by using this shortcut.

Show desktop
To get to the desktop quickly, you don't have to click on the show desktop icon. Just hold the Windows key and press **M**.

Page refresh
Press this every time you want to refresh a page – ideal if you're waiting for an eBay auction to end.

Select all
When you've opened a folder brimming with all sorts of files, but want to quickly delete them all or move them somewhere else, hold **Ctrl** and press **A** to select all the files in the folder.

Quick print
Whenever you need to print – be it an internet site or an open email – just hold **Ctrl** and press **P** to quickly open the print box.

And don't forget...
Start Menu
Just press the Windows key to open the Start Menu, and if you want to search for something, type it into the Start Menu search box.

24 shortcuts that make using your PC a breeze

Speeding up your computer isn't all about upgrading hardware. By using shortcuts, you – and your PC – will work faster than ever

Many people feel that their PC is slowing them down, but do you ever feel that the opposite is true? You may be going the long way round to accomplish tasks, but by learning some shortcuts, you'll be using Windows Vista faster than ever – leaving your PC to catch up with you.

1 Use keyboard shortcuts

Get into the habit of using keyboard shortcuts for any task you do regularly, and the time you save will soon add up.

Ctrl and C Copy the selected item
Ctrl and X Cut the selected item
Ctrl and V Paste the selected item
Ctrl and Z Undo
Ctrl and Y Redo
Ctrl and A Select everything

QUICK ACCESS Get access to your Computer and Documents folders from your desktop

2 Access Computer or Documents quickly

Do you often need to access your Computer, Documents or Network folder? To add their icons to your desktop, right-click the desktop, select **Personalize**, then click on **Change**

desktop icons, and select which icons you want. By right-clicking on them you can navigate to their advanced features.

4 Use the Windows key to open up programs

When the **Windows** key is used with a number you open up the corresponding program in your Quick Launch menu. For example, if Internet Explorer is the third icon in the Quick Launch area, press **Windows** key and **3** to open it up.

5 Skip to the end

When working on a document, you can send your cursor to the end of the line using the **End** button. **Ctrl** and **End** take you to the end of the document. If you are viewing a website, pressing the **End** key takes you to the bottom.

6 Bringing it back home

In a text document, pressing the **Home** button takes you to the beginning of the line, while **Ctrl** and **Home** takes you to the top of the doc.

7 System info in a flash

Pressing the **Windows** key and holding down **Pause** brings up the System Properties of your computer.

8O Task Manager, where art thou?

In previous versions of Windows, holding **Ctrl**, **Alt** and **Delete** opened up the Task Manager. In Windows Vista that takes you to a different screen, so if you want to go to the Task Manager, hold down **Ctrl**, **Shift** and **Esc**.

3 Get familiar with the Windows key

The Windows key can be used with others to quickly access applications

Windows key and D	Display the desktop
Windows key and E	Open Windows Explorer
Windows key and F	Open a search window
Windows key and G	Scroll through the gadgets on your Sidebar
Windows key and L	Lock your computer
Windows key and R	Open the Run dialog box
Windows key and T	Scroll through the applications on your taskbar
Windows key and U	Open the Ease of Access Center
Windows key and X	Open the Windows Mobility Center
Windows key and Tab	Bring up Flip 3D
Ctrl and Windows key and Tab	Make Flip 3D remain on the desktop, so you can switch between apps using arrow keys or mouse

9 Create a shortcut

To create a shortcut, find the program, right-click it and select **Send to ➜ Desktop (create shortcut)**.

10 Check network connection status

To quickly check your net connection, go to **Start ➜ Control Panel ➜ Network and Internet ➜ Network and Sharing Center ➜ Manage network connections**. Right-click on the connection and select **Create Shortcut**.

11 Know Internet Explorer shortcuts

The following shortcuts will help you browse the web faster than ever:

Ctrl and F Find something on a page
Alt and Home Go to home page
Alt and Left cursor Go back
Alt and Right cursor Go forward
Ctrl and D Add page to Favorites
Ctrl and H Open History
Middle mouse button or Ctrl and Left mouse button Open link in new tab
Ctrl and W Close tab
Ctrl and T Open new tab
Alt and D Select Address bar
Ctrl and Enter Add http://www. to the start of text in the Address bar and .com to the end

12 Lock your PC

If you want to lock your PC quickly, make a shortcut. Create a shortcut, and type in '%windir%\system 32\rundll32.exe user32.dll, LockWorkStation' as the location. Give the shortcut a name and click **Finish**.

13 Assign hotkeys

To make using shortcuts even faster, right-click on a shortcut, select **Properties** and in **Shortcut key** hold down the keys you want to use. Now press those keys to launch the shortcut.

14 Pin frequently used programs

Pin programs to the Start menu so they are always within easy reach: hold **Shift**

15 Send an email from your desktop

Make a new shortcut and type in 'mailto:' followed by your recipient's email, for example 'mailto:windowsvista@futurenet.com'. Click **Next**, give the shortcut a meaningful name and then click **Finish**. Double-clicking the shortcut will open up a blank email with the address already filled in.

EASY EMAIL You can send an email to a contact direct from your desktop

while right-clicking the file or program and select **Pin to Start menu**. With a registry tweak you can enable this for folders: be careful as incorrectly editing the registry can cause problems. Type regedit into **Start Search** and press **Enter**. Navigate to **HKEY_CLASSES_ROOT\Folder\shellex\ContextMenu Handlers**. Right-click **ContextMenu Handlers** and select **New ➜ Key** and name it {a2a9545d-a0c2-42b4-9708-a0b2badd77c8}

16 Assign Start programs

If you have a program you open as soon as you turn on your PC, get it to start automatically. Create a shortcut to the program and move it to **Start ➜ All Programs ➜ Startup**. Right-click, select **Open** and paste the shortcut here.

17 Quick email attachments

You can quickly add attachments to an email by clicking the file and dragging it to the body of the email.

18 Create shortcuts to favorite websites

You can save time by having shortcuts to frequently visited websites on your desktop. Browse to the page that you want and then drag and drop the small icon in the address bar to your desktop.

19 App Launcher gadget

The App Launcher gadget (available from gallery.live.com) grants fast access to files and folders by clicking on an icon that launches them.

20 Get breaking news with RSS feeds

If you check a number of news websites regularly, save time by subscribing to their news feed (by clicking on the orange RSS icon).

21 Put files in their place with Send To

Add applications you use to open files to the **Send To** menu. You can also add folders to the **Send To** list. Open up Windows Explorer and in the Address bar type '%APPDATA%\Microsoft\Windows\SendTo' and add shortcuts.

22 Start Search

Use the Start Search to quickly launch programs. Below are handy phrases to bring up applications:

CMD Command prompt
DEV Device Manager
SYS System Restore
NETW Connect to Network Projector
UPD Windows Update
PROG Default Programs
EVE Event viewer

23 Dragging and dropping

To copy a file while using drag and drop hold down the **Ctrl** key, to move a file hold down **Shift** and to create a shortcut hold down the **Alt** key.

24 Launch programs from the Taskbar

Add toolbars to help access programs. Right-click the taskbar, go to **Toolbars ➜ Address** to add an address bar.

Do More

If you're ready to put Windows Vista and the 2007 Microsoft Office system to good use, try these projects

Get your inbox under control

Is your inbox overflowing? Are you tearing your hair out trying to find important emails? Here's how to get into a few good habits

An inbox that isn't properly maintained can quickly become unmanageable, and keeping track of your emails can turn into a nightmare. If you find that your inbox is regularly flooded by unnecessary emails, then one of your first tasks should be to cut down on the new messages you receive.

Send any email you don't wish to receive to your Junk folder by right-clicking and selecting **Junk E-mail ➔ Add Sender to Blocked Senders List**. This will also prevent any future emails from the sender going into your inbox.

Using the subject line correctly will help your recipients organize and keep track of emails, and will hopefully encourage them to do the same. The subject should relate to the email and should be succinct; avoid vague titles such as 'hello' because neither you nor your recipient will know what the message is about, which will hinder subsequent searches.

Most email programs come with tools that enable you to create folders and automatically filter emails into the correct folder, and using these will help you categorize and keep track of emails as soon as they are delivered to you.

There is also a number of programs available that integrate with your email application and make organizing your emails easier than ever. Xobni works as

an add-on to Office Outlook, so you can use it without having to exit the program – and it's free, too (download it from www.xobni.com). Its features include super-fast searching – as soon as you start typing a word, name or email address the search begins. Also included are in-depth contact details and threaded conversations, where you can see all emails sent between you in chronological order. Another plug-in for Office Outlook is SpeedFiler ($24,95-$39.95, snipurl.com/27cd9) which concentrates more on organizing your emails. It has advanced filing and folder-management features, keeping your inbox clean and manageable as well as giving you the ability to file messages you've already sent to folders.

In real life...
My mail

James Stables, Section editor, *Windows Vista: The Official Magazine*

When it comes to email, I love Microsoft Office Outlook 2007 and the amount of control it places in the hands of the user. I get in excess of 100 emails a day but, thanks to all the search options, filtering and spam control, my inbox is capable of sorting much of it out without me getting involved – the only thing Office Outlook 2007 can't do is reply for me! Apart from email, the integration with the calendar and RSS feeds means that keeping in touch – and keeping informed – couldn't be more simple.

MESSAGE MANAGEMENT Keep your emails in order and you'll find messages at your fingertips

Six ways to beat email overload
It's never too late to get organized – make your life easier today!

1 CREATE FOLDERS By using folders to store your emails, you can keep your inbox free from clutter while still knowing where to find a certain email. If your inbox is filling up with emails telling you what your friends are up to on Facebook, you might want to create a 'Social websites' folder. To create a new folder, right-click on an existing folder, such as Inbox, and then select **New folder…**

2 SET FILTER RULES To create filtering rules in Windows Mail, go to **Tools → Message Rules → Mail**. Next, set the conditions of the filter; for example, the sender of the email. Then choose the action your inbox should take when the conditions are met; for example moving the email to a specific folder. Now you can leave your inbox to organize your emails while you work on something else.

3 GET RID OF SPAM You can configure your spam filtering by going to **Tools → Junk E-Mail Options**. Windows Mail scans emails for words, phrases or addresses that may indicate spam. By choosing the **High** level of protection, fewer emails will get through. Some legitimate emails may be classed as spam, however, so glance through your Junk E-Mail folder regularly.

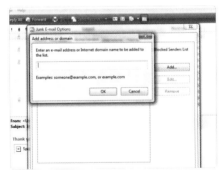

4 BLOCK LISTS If you receive spam from only a few sources, you can block the specific address or domain they're coming from to prevent any more junk messages getting through to your inbox. From **Junk E-Mail Options**, click on the **Blocked Senders** tab and then select **Add**. Enter the email address you want to block; if you get emails from different addresses but they originate from the same domain, enter the '@' sign, and then type in the domain name, for example '@spam.com'.

5 SEARCH WITH XOBNI If you're having trouble hunting down certain emails in your Microsoft Office Outlook inbox, then you might want to consider downloading the free add-on, Xobni, from www.xobni.com and use its advanced search tool to locate stray attachments, contacts and emails. This is more thorough than most mail program search tools, and as soon as you start typing the search will begin – enabling you to find what you're looking for quickly and efficiently.

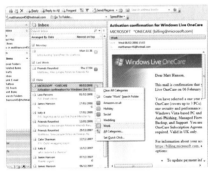

6 USE SPEEDFILER The SpeedFiler add-on for Office Outlook enables you to categorize your emails in just a few clicks. Right-click on the empty **Category** square by the subject line and select **All Categories**. Rename the categories then exit, right-click on the square again and select the category you want to assign to the email. You can create a search folder that contains all emails of a category by clicking the **Categorize** button, then selecting **Open 'Category Name' Search Folder**.

Download management

Downloading over the internet can tie up valuable PC time. Use Task Scheduler to time it right

How come when you download movies or software over the internet, your PC never seems to manage it at the speed promoted by your broadband provider? There are a number of possible reasons – large files can take time, or there may be a lot of traffic when you're trying to download.

Thankfully, there are many ways you can reduce the amount of time it takes for downloads to arrive on your PC. The first of these is to download the files overnight, when there are fewer people online.

By using Task Scheduler, you can schedule your PC to run your downloads while you sleep! Just create a new task, set when you want the download manager to open (and start downloading), then create another task telling the PC when to shut down. If you schedule your downloads to start during the night, your internet connection is freed up in the day, and your downloads will be faster, too, as they'll be running during off-peak hours. There are lots of other things Task Scheduler can do; it can run Disk Defragmenter when you're asleep, back up files during dinner, or send emails while you're at work.

Another method of speeding up downloads, especially if they're of the larger variety in file size, is to use a download manager designed for the job. One such example is Free Download Manager (www. freedownloadmanager.org), which increases the speed of downloads by splitting each file into sections. The other advantage of using a download manager is that if a large download fails part-way through, the manager will remember where it stopped and resume the rest of the download again. It's also worth checking with your broadband provider to see if they offer a premium speed service, such as Comcast's PowerBoost. ⊞

"Wow" Meter reading

If you want to get an idea of how long a download might take, go to snipurl.com/2a9jf and try the BitMeter II freeware, which includes a handy download time calculator

How to schedule your downloads

1 FEEL SLEEPY To get your PC to go to sleep after a period of inactivity. Type **Power Options** into **Start Search** and in the window that opens, click on **Change when the computer sleeps**.

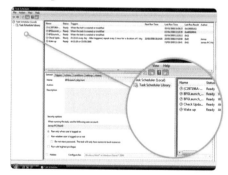

2 SCHEDULE SET- UP Now you need to type **Task Scheduler** into **Start Search** and open up the program. Click on the **Task Scheduler Library** folder in the left-hand menu.

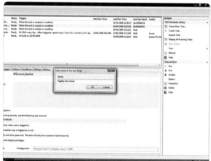

3 GOOD NIGHT In the right-hand **Actions** menu, click on **New Folder** and enter the name you want to call it. Pick something appropriate – in this case, we've called it Nightly Download.

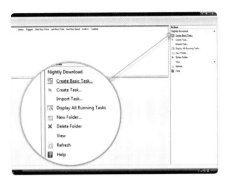

4 SET A TASK This new folder will now appear in the Task Scheduler Library menu. Click on it and, in the right-hand Actions menu, click on **Create basic task**.

5 TIME IT Give it a name and select when you want it to open, then click **Next**. We want to do a disk defragment every other day, so it is set to recur every two days at 00:00am.

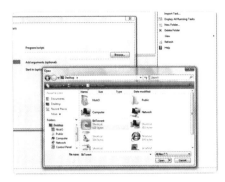

6 PROGRAM Click on **Next** and choose **Start a program**. Then click on **Next → Browse** and look for the program you want to open – we're clicking on BitTorrent.exe in this example.

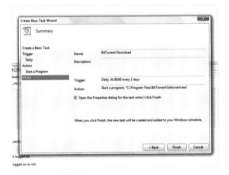

7 PROPERTIES Once you've found and opened the relevant program, check the tick box **Open the Properties dialog for this task when I click Finish** and then click on **Finish**.

8 CONDITIONS In the window that now opens, you need to click on the **Conditions** tab and under the Power heading, check the tick box **Wake the computer to run this task**.

9 LIMIT YOURSELF So you don't breach your limit/overrun night hours, turn the PC off after it's been downloading for, say, one to six hours, by scheduling another task in the same folder.

10 SET AGAIN Click on **Create basic task** again. Now set this new task to start on the same day as the BitTorrent downloading task you have just set up, but a few hours later.

11 SHUTDOWN Choose **Start a program → Next**, browse to the Shutdown file (in C:\Windows\System32\shutdown.exe), and in the box that says **Add arguments**, type **-s**.

12 FINISH Click on **Finish**, close Task Scheduler and your tasks will all be ready to begin running at the times that you've set, helping to save you both time and money.

Create an online magazine for free

Can't afford to publish a paper-based magazine? It's easy to create a glossy publication that people can read online without paying a penny

 If you manage a local baseball team, for example, or run a small business, you can really benefit from creating a monthly newsletter of events or a catalog to show off all your products.

By doing this, you'll not only be keeping people in the loop, but you'll also be able to keep them updated about current or future happenings. You could do this already with a simple website, but an even better way is to create an online document that can

be either read on screen or printed out, using the free service available at www.yudu.com.

Get creative

You can convert anything you want, from a simple text-only newsletter to a highly professional-looking catalog that you've created in Microsoft Office Publisher or Adobe InDesign. Once you're done, you can then choose where to advertise it.

You can then link to your document from your existing website, send it to people by email or, if you like to be a little more interactive with your public announcements, you can put the whole thing into a blog. The great thing is, no matter how large the magazine, because

it's just a link that you're providing, people don't have to download anything if they'd rather not look at it.

Don't forget – it's also completely free of charge to create an online magazine, and you'll be doing your bit for the environment, too, because you're not using up valuable ink or paper.

If you follow the steps on the opposite page, you can discover how to create an online publication in your tea break. First things first, though – you'll need to create a really good magazine or newsletter before you can put it online. One of the easiest ways to do this is to use a template from office.microsoft.com and, using Office Publisher, simply edit all the elements, adding your own pictures and words.

In real life...
Perfect publicity

 **Jo Membery
Operations editor,
Windows Vista: The
Official Magazine**

I've recently been helping out with a community project and we wanted to publicize what we were doing. However, we're all committing to it in our spare time, so we needed something simple to use, and we're all doing it voluntarily, so wanted something affordable, too. Office Publisher 2007 has proved invaluable in helping us create a polished look for small programs, leaflets and newsletters. Then, uploading our creations to online sites is a doddle and sending to digital print is far less of a nightmare than we anticipated – and doesn't cost a cent!

GET IN PRINT Create online or printed magazines with ease, thanks to Office Publisher 2007

Get your mag online in nine easy stages

Putting your publication out there for all to read is easier than you think

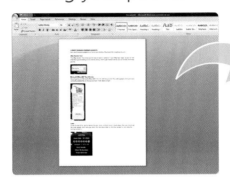

1 CREATION First you need a piece to publish. It can be a simple text file from Word 2007 or a graphic-rich masterpiece from Publisher 2007.

2 CONVERSION You need to turn your document into a PDF. Go to www. freepdfconvert.com, choose the file, add your email address and click **Convert**.

3 SAVE TO YOUR PC You're emailed the converted PDF as a compressed ZIP file. Save it to your hard disk and double-click on it to extract the PDF.

4 UPLOAD PDF Now you can publish it. Go to www.yudu.com and click on **Browse** to upload your PDF. Find it and click on **OK**, then enter your email.

5 ALL THE INFO Click on **Publish**. Now you need to enter some more details. Choose a title and category, and enter some keywords to help people to find it.

6 PUBLISH IT Now you're ready to publish. Click on **Publish** again and you're sent an email telling you where the publication is available to see online.

7 TELL THE WORLD After you published the document, you'll have been sent an email with some attachments. Right-click the html text file and save it to your hard drive.

8 BLOG IT Open this file and highlight the text you need. Copy it by right-clicking and selecting **Copy**. Now go to your blog website. Create a new post and paste the text in.

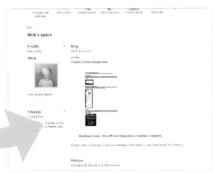

9 READY TO GO Now, when you look at your blog, you'll see that a link pointing to your online publication has been created, along with an image of the magazine.

Control your PC with your voice

The Windows Speech Recognition makes Windows Vista one of the most accessible operating systems there is. Find out how it works

Working with a PC when you can't use a keyboard and mouse can be a struggle. Tasks that you usually take for granted, such as opening a program, can become cumbersome and time-consuming.

This needn't be the case, though, because Windows Vista comes with a host of tools that enable you to interact with your PC through alternative methods. Windows Speech Recognition is one of those tools, and allows you to control your PC using just your voice.

Through Windows Speech Recognition, you can use voice commands to open and close programs, and navigate the internet. You can also use it to type out words into documents and emails as you say them, which could help you work faster.

Speak up

The advanced technology behind Windows Speech Recognition allows it to configure itself to your speech patterns with the minimum of fuss while you talk, so the more you use Windows Speech Recognition, the more accurate it becomes. If you go to **Start ➜ All Programs ➜ Accessories ➜ Ease Of Access ➜ Windows Speech Recognition**, you can start the voice recognition tutorial. This shows you how to use Windows Speech Recognition through voice commands, and the best thing about it is that while you are learning the commands, and learning how to dictate and correct text, Windows Speech Recognition is configuring itself in the background.

To open programs using your voice, you just need to talk through each stage. For example, to open a program you just say "Start", then "All Programs", "Accessories" and then the name of the program. Most mainstream programs and websites work with the 'say what you see' commands of Windows Speech Recognition, where you read out the name of the button or tool you want to use, and it's selected.

Take this down

Using Windows Speech Recognition for dictating documents and emails in applications such as Microsoft Word is

Take the tutorial

Learn the basics of controlling your PC with your voice

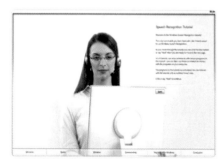

1 GET STARTED To start, you need to complete a tutorial. This not only helps you learn the commands but also configures Windows Speech Recognition to understand your voice.

2 BASIC COMMANDS The tutorial explains how to begin by saying "start listening". The text feedback is also explained, where you are told whether the PC has understood you.

3 DICTATE NOTES Then you are taken through the process of dictating to a word processor or email program. You're shown how to add punctuation and correct mistakes, and given tips.

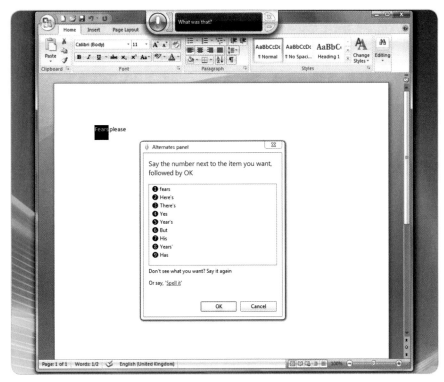

I BEG YOUR PARDON? Inevitably some words are misheard, but it's simple to correct any mistakes

easy, too. Say what you want typed and the words appear. You can speak quite quickly, but pause between sentences to make sure your speech is understood.

Punctuation is added by saying its name, while starting a new line is just a matter of saying "new line". To correct mistakes, say "correct" then the word you want to replace and you are given a selection of choices; if it is not there, all you need to do is say "spell it" to spell out the word.

COMMON COMMANDS	
Start voice recognition	Say "start listening"
Stop voice recognition	Say "stop listening"
Display a list of voice commands	Say "what can I say?"
Click an item by name	Say the item's name, for example "start" for the Start menu
Double-click an item	Say "double-click" then the name of the item, for example "double-click Recycle Bin"
Switch between open programs	Say "switch to" and then the name of the program, for example "switch to Paint"
Scroll in a window	Say "scroll" and then the direction, for example "scroll down"

DICTATION COMMANDS	
Select a word in a document	Say "select" and then the word you want, for example "select want"
Select a number of words in a document	Say "select", then the first word you want to select, "through", and then the last word. For example, "select then through last"
Correct a misheard word	Say "correct" and then the word you want to correct
Delete a word	Say "delete" and then the word you want to delete
Insert a new line	Say "new line"
Start a new paragraph	Say "new paragraph"
Insert punctuation	Say the name of the punctuation mark, for example "comma"
Insert the word for a command	If you want to dictate a word that is also a command, to save confusion say "literal" and then the word. For example, to write "comma" rather than inserting one as a punctuation mark, say "literal comma"
Insert a number as a symbol	When dictating, if you say a number it spells it out. If you want the numeral symbol, for example 6, say "numeral six"
Place the cursor before a word	Say "go to" and then the word
Place the cursor after a word	Say "go after" and then the word
Capitalize the first letter of a word	Say "caps" and then the word
Capitalize all letters in a word	Say "all caps" and then the word

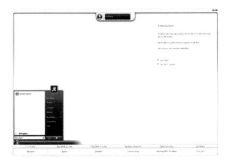

4 READY TO LAUNCH Next you're shown how to open and work with programs. All you need to do is say the name of the tool or menu command of the program to use it.

5 WORKING WITH WINDOWS Finally you are taught about controlling windows. This covers everything from scrolling through and closing windows to switching between open programs.

Make a home security webcam

A simple webcam can be used to monitor your home from wherever you are in the world – for free

When you're away from home, complete peace of mind is something that normally only money can buy. And rather a lot of money at that. The problem is that if you're unfortunate enough to have your home broken into and burgled, it's possible that your much-loved possessions won't ever be recovered and the perpetrators won't be caught.

Face value

The best way to make sure this doesn't happen is to have some method of capturing the faces of any would-be burglars. There are plenty of products on the market that alert you to any disturbances and enable you to log in from the internet to view your home, but in most cases these are very expensive. For a cheaper alternative, check out the many free download options that enable you to transform your existing webcam into a sophisticated motion-sensing camera.

This has proved to be a successful security trick, and there has been a spate of cases where thieves have been arrested and property recovered with the use of a webcam security device. The most famous example was of a British man who was alerted to a break-in, despite being in Australia. He called the police and the thieves were caught while he watched from abroad!

Of course, security isn't the only use for a webcam. You can use yours to see what your pets get up to while you're out, or set up a cheap baby video monitor that can be accessed from a laptop downstairs. Baby video monitors retail for about $150 and usually feature pretty poor-quality video, so using your existing webcam can prove a better option.

One of the best free tools to do this with is HomeCamera (www.homecamera.com), a web-based application that offers most of the features needed for a decent home-monitoring system. Many applications offer the same service, but few offer free motion detection, plus email and phone alerts. Most IP cameras on the market require a complicated FTP or HTTP upload service to view captures online, but HomeCamera makes all of this easy and, above all, manageable.

The way the service works is split into two elements. The first is by using client software to monitor your webcams and look for any motion picked up by them. The second is an online element, which recognizes any cameras you have attached to the clients you have installed. From your area on the HomeCamera website, you can view your camera as a still image or even a live video stream.

Camera tricks

The benefit of using HomeCamera is that it recognises any webcam and synchronizes automatically when it's plugged in. Just run the client software, which can be downloaded from the website, and it will take feeds from any USB camera.

HomeCamera can also send photographs taken from the motion sensor to your mobile phone, which are sent using credits. Every photo sent to a mobile costs one credit, and while you only get five when you sign up, you can always buy more from the website when you need them, at the cost of $10.50 for 100.

BE VIGILANT We can't always be at home, but now we can still keep an eye on our property

Secure your home in minutes

Turn your webcam into a motion-detector with HomeCamera

1 SET UP Register on the HomeCamera website, then download and install the client software. Connect your USB webcam and let Windows Vista find the drivers. Run the HomeCamera program and, in the console, click **Add Camera**.

2 LABEL A feed from the camera should appear in the window, and there are fields to enter the name of the camera, a description and picture quality. Label the feed something memorable as you may want to add other cameras later.

3 WORLD IN MOTION Once you've set up your camera, you can add motion detection to turn your simple webcam into a crime-busting system. Go to the Setup Camera icon, and in the Motion Detection tab, click **Enable**.

Successful security: thieves have been arrested and property recovered with the use of a webcam

4 ALERT You can set up times for motion detection to be on automatically, and adjust the sensitivity from the Motion Detection tab. When you press **OK** any motion detected by HomeCamera via your webcam will be noted. You will then be sent an email to the address that you used to set up your account, with a still image of what has been detected, enabling you to take appropriate action if required.

5 LOGIN When you want to view your feed, just log on to www.homecamera.com and sign in. All your webcams should show the main screen, where you can choose to view still images, a feed of stills (which is good for slower internet connections) or a live video feed.

Home library

The words 'database design' can strike fear but using Microsoft Office Access is easier than you'd think

Do you think databases are dull? Then think again. Databases are the defining application of the computer age. Without the ability to store huge tables of simple information and cross reference it all, there would be no internet, there would be no video games, there would be no ATM machines, there would be no space flight, there would be no...

You get the picture?

Nearly everything in computing is database driven – whether it's a Microsoft Outlook contacts list or a store of object details in a virtual world, the ability to create recordable entries in a bespoke multi-field database and search quickly using a number of variables is what makes computers work.

Describing the background process is confusing; because the database is such an important type of software, a lot of work has gone into adding powerful new abilities over the years that – ultimately – makes them harder to understand.

Data details

Luckily, you don't have to register at the Harvard Business School to use or even build a database. Using a database like Microsoft Office Access 2007 is very simple. You create a template record and populate it with information, which can be anything from customer contact details to information about books you own. Then you create a simple front end that makes it easy to enter the data, and then – if you need – you add the back end reporting tools that use the entries you've created to perform another operation. That might be populating invoice details, recommending a reading list or matching DNA samples – there is little a database can't do.

At its heart, a database is simply a very large spreadsheet, like the ones created by Microsoft Excel. You might,

for example, use a simple Excel table for keeping track of stock, jobs done or DVDs purchased. The time to switch to using a more powerful databasing tool such as Access is when you find yourself repeatedly entering the same information – such as a customer's address – over and over again. Because databases can cross reference separately stored pieces of information like invoice numbers and customer details, they are simply a more efficient way of working.

The key, though, is not to be scared. Follow the walkthrough and you'll have mastered the basics of databases in six steps – by the end you'll be addicted, and databasing everything you own!

"Wow" Extra tables

Once you've set up your database, don't forget you can carry on making changes and adding new reporting functions. You'll find loads of advice at **tinyurl. com/clyjq3**

You don't have to go Dewey

To create a database of your home library with Office Access 2007

1 BOOK LOOK A database can be just as useful at home as it is at work. If you've built up a decent library, it can be difficult to find a particular book if you need to refer to something.

2 INFO TO GO For most people's home library, only a few bits of information are needed, but forward planning can identify which bits of data will repeat a lot and may need their own database.

3 AUTHOR'S NOTE If there are books by the same author, create two lists, one for books and one for writers, then cross reference them. Double click **Add New Field** and type in the writer's name.

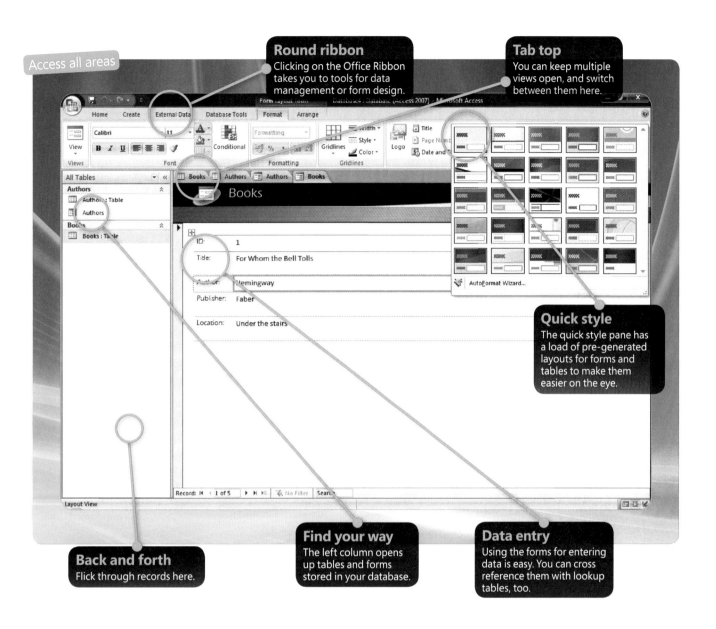

Round ribbon
Clicking on the Office Ribbon takes you to tools for data management or form design.

Tab top
You can keep multiple views open, and switch between them here.

Quick style
The quick style pane has a load of pre-generated layouts for forms and tables to make them easier on the eye.

Back and forth
Flick through records here.

Find your way
The left column opens up tables and forms stored in your database.

Data entry
Using the forms for entering data is easy. You can cross reference them with lookup tables, too.

4 MAKE A FORM It's worth creating a form interface for adding data. Save the form as 'Authors', go to **Create** and select **Form**. Change the colors using the **AutoFormat** options under **Format**.

5 ENTERING DATA Close the form and reopen it from the column on the left. Enter the name of your first author, and select the table on the left and click **Refresh** – the data you entered appears.

6 TABLE TWO Start a table for books. For the Authors column, right-click on **Add New Field** and select **Lookup Column**; a wizard turns this into a search field that looks in the Authors table.

Publish your first blog in Windows Live Space

Writing an online blog is a great way to share your thoughts and interests without needing to know about web programming

A decade ago, the only way to document your thoughts on the internet was to create your own website in HTML and manually upload it. Whenever you wanted to add any news, you had to change the entire site and then re-upload. Thankfully, things are now far easier. A number of different blogging platforms exist, providing you with an empty slate upon which to scrawl, type, upload images and share links without the need to know anything more than how to use a word processor.

Blogs can be about anything. Don't be afraid to wax lyrical about whatever appeals. If you're passionate about a subject it will come through... If you're a keen gardener, share stories on how your vegetables are doing each month. NFL fan? Write about this year's season and

LIVE VIEW Windows Live Writer enables you to see how your page will appear when online

speculate on next year's. Anything from snowboarding to stamp collecting is fair game, and because of the wide-reaching nature of the internet, even the most niche subjects attract like-minded

readers. What's important is that you do have something original to write about; a blog with no purpose except to link to hilarious YouTube videos will do nothing to establish your voice. Likewise, mundane diaries are likely to be ignored by most; no one is particularly interested in how long you had to wait in the supermarket, or whether you're feeling giggly or cautious this morning. People will only read your blog if there's useful and interesting information in it.

Keep it snappy

Once you've decided on your subject matter, you can let rip. But remember, a blog shouldn't be an unedited stream of consciousness; a 700-word, single-paragraph ramble is not for online consumption. Think about how you read content on the internet. Generally, your attention span will be shorter than if reading a story in a newspaper. Keeping your posts short and snappy will ensure that your readers read them in their entirety. Try to keep each post under 250 words, and if you need to summarize, use bullet points; they're easier on the eye, and as a result more enticing.

While appealing to a human audience is paramount, it's the internet's non-human readers that wield the power to propel your blog into the mainstream... Search engine 'web crawlers' will swarm over your blog posts, looking for keywords and links with which to classify you. The more relevant and accessible the information in your blog is, the more chance you have of appearing in the first few pages of search engine results.

Tie your style to your content

Once you've come up with the words, you need to think about the look

While it's what you write that matters most, a unique look will draw readers in. Windows Live Space provides various set themes designed to complement what you're writing about, such as 'movie buff', 'photo enthusiast' and 'bookworm'.

For a truly personal approach, you can edit the various colors, images and typefaces. If you're writing about a relaxing subject such as gardening, pastel greens may be appropriate; an

exciting topic such as IndyCar racing might warrant bolder colors such as blue and red. Windows Live Space also enables you to set a background image, but don't go for something too complex or it will detract from your post. You can also change the layout of your blog and add 'gadgets' (similar to those found in Windows Sidebar) which can pull in content such as your latest Flickr photos or Amazon book reviews.

Write, illustrate and publish a blog
How to write a great blog post with Windows Live Writer

1 CREATE LIVE SPACE Once you've installed Windows Live Writer, you need to configure your blog. By default, the program will create a Live Space, although you can blog to other platforms such as WordPress and Blogger.

2 CUSTOMIZE You can use the **Customize** menu to set your blog's style, then choose **View → Edit using theme**. This will apply any visual changes you've made in Windows Live Writer. Pressing **F12** will show you a preview.

3 CHOOSE HEADLINE Choose a meaningful, non-cryptic headline that summarizes your post. Now you can write! Type as if you were working on a document in a word processor. Use keywords and keep things concise.

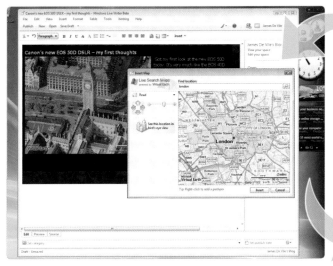

4 ADD IMAGES Adding a picture will add interest and provide your readers with a visual cue to the content of your post. Text wrapping is switched off by default, so change **Text wrapping** to left or right. You might also want to add a margin.

5 AERIAL SHOT If you can't find a picture to illustrate your blog, you can use Live Search Maps to add an aerial shot of a relevant location. Click **Insert Map**, search for the location you want, then click **See this location in bird's eye view**.

Essential download

If you haven't already signed up for Windows Live, you might want to investigate Windows Live Essentials. The free download includes Windows Live Writer, Mail, Messenger, Movie Maker, Photo Gallery and more.

6 PUBLISH IT Check your post, then click **Publish**. Your blog will be uploaded to the web for the world to read. Most blogs allow readers to comment and link; the more comments and links, the higher your blog will appear in search rankings.

Finance is easy

Get on top of your finances; grab the know-how and the strategies to stay ahead of the game

Time is money – we're all becoming increasingly aware of the significance of this adage, but the world of finance can be full of complex calculations and strange terminology. Admittedly, there's a lot to learn and track if you want to keep on top of savings, investments, mortgages, loans, etc, but once you get into the swing, it needn't be stressful.

First things first – get a budget! Whether it's commercial or domestic, a budget is essential and the benefits extensive. If you don't have a personal budget, go to http://office.microsoft. com, go to Templates and grab yourself a Personal Budget Spreadsheet. This template offers a simple tool for sorting finances. With a solid spend strategy, you will almost certainly end up with disposable income each month – instead of worrying about how far over your

overdraft you've gone... And, while you may hate the idea of a budget, you're bound to love the idea of a holiday!

If you do manage to save, you may want to consider investing your money. If so, it's a good idea to get your head around the terms used in financial circles, especially if you're thinking of booking an appointment with a financial advisor. A site like MindPicnic (www.mindpicnic. com/tag/finance/) offers free courses in learning about essential factors, such as how to 'translate' a financial report and understanding equity derivatives.

Staying on top

Now it's time to set up Windows Vista to maximize your time and results. Go to the website, RSS Specifications (www. rss-specifications.com/rss-directory.htm), where you'll find feeds for anything from bank rate changes, mortgage rates, currencies to industry news and more.

SaneBull, an online financial website (www.sanebull.com/) has great gadgets with live stock quotes and investment news. The RSS feeds and gadgets will ensure you have the latest figures at your fingertips. And there are other tricks, too... Many leading financial publications have a web presence, such as the Financial Times (www.ft.com). These offer extra features like podcasts, blogs and cell phone alerts, so you're not just privy to the figures, you're also aware of trends, too. There's no need to lose valuable time searching for important financial information when you can have it delivered to your door.

"Wow" Excellent!

If you consolidate your formulas in Excel 2007, you can create pie charts and graphs to display your data. Go to **Insert → Charts** and select a pie chart and your data will be displayed perfectly

Control your statements

Use Excel to manage your bank statements and finances

1 OPEN UP Open a spreadsheet and add headings, such as 'income', 'expenses' and 'balance'; to lock the headings in place click under the column and select **Freeze Panes** under View. Call the sheet 'Current Account'.

2 FORMULA Enter the figures, and the balance. For the second line fill in the amounts, then enter the formula '=E2+B3-C3'. E = balance amount in line above; B = income, C = expenses. The balance will adjust automatically.

3 VALUE Repeat the formula for each line but adjust the values for E, B and C accordingly (ie, for line four the formula will read '=E3+B4-C4'). Adjust the column widths by simply dragging them as far along as you want.

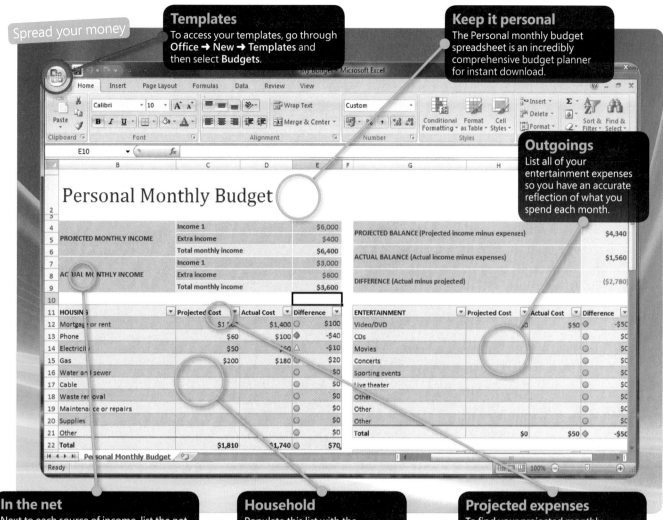

Templates
To access your templates, go through
Office → New → Templates and
then select Budgets.

Keep it personal
The Personal monthly budget
spreadsheet is an incredibly
comprehensive budget planner
for instant download.

Outgoings
List all of your
entertainment expenses
so you have an accurate
reflection of what you
spend each month.

My Budget - Microsoft Excel

Personal Monthly Budget

	Projected Cost	Actual Cost	Difference
PROJECTED MONTHLY INCOME			
Income 1			$6,000
Extra income			$400
Total monthly income			$6,400
ACTUAL MONTHLY INCOME			
Income 1			$3,000
Extra income			$600
Total monthly income			$3,600

PROJECTED BALANCE (Projected income minus expenses) $4,340

ACTUAL BALANCE (Actual income minus expenses) $1,560

DIFFERENCE (Actual minus projected) ($2,780)

HOUSING	Projected Cost	Actual Cost	Difference
Mortgage or rent	$1,500	$1,400	$100
Phone	$60	$100	-$40
Electricity	$50	$60	-$10
Gas	$200	$180	$20
Water and sewer			$0
Cable			$0
Waste removal			$0
Maintenance or repairs			$0
Supplies			$0
Other			$0
Total	$1,810	$1,740	$70

ENTERTAINMENT	Projected Cost	Actual Cost	Difference
Video/DVD		$50	-$50
CDs			$0
Movies			$0
Concerts			$0
Sporting events			$0
Live theater			$0
Other			$0
Other			$0
Other			$0
Total	$0	$50	-$50

In the net
Next to each source of income, list the net
(after deductions) amount you receive
each month. If you don't receive the same
amount each period, work on an average.

Household
Populate this list with the
expenses that are particular to you
and your household and make
sure you don't miss anything out.

Projected expenses
To find your projected monthly
expenses, come up with an average
(eg, divide two months' expenses by
two or annual expenses by 12).

4 SORT Use the **Sort** function under
the View tab to arrange the rows.
Create a spreadsheet for each account.
Now you want to consolidate these
accounts, so open a new spreadsheet
and name it 'Consolidate'.

5 SCOPE Create a row for accounts and
a row for amounts to consolidate. Go
to the Current Account sheet, select the
Balance row, then **Formulas → Defined
Names → Define Name.** Enter the name
'Current' and include the workbook.

6 CONSOLIDATE Do the same for
your other sheets, then in the
Consolidate sheet, under Amount, write
'=Difference'. Arrange your entries with
credit first and debit last and then enter
this formula '=SUM(B2:B3)-B4-B5'.

How to make your mind up!

Not sure which direction to take? The 2007 Office system can help you make the right decision

When you think about it, almost every part of the Microsoft Office system is about helping you make the right decisions. You'll be constantly considering the numbers thrown up in your Excel spreadsheets while you make important choices, and relying on the data stored in your Access databases for informing your plans.

Many small businesses, or indeed homeowners embarking on an extension or similarly costly home improvement scheme, fail to try things out because they sound intimidating. Certainly in the business world, if you begin talking about 'forecasting' and 'financial modelling', people's heads start to spin.

Actually, though, one of the best decision-making tools, particularly for business, is right in front of you – Office Excel 2007. If you've started to keep track of the incomings and outgoings of your organization in a spreadsheet, then you've already got a working model of your business cash flow. You can save a copy of your data and begin populating fields with changing variables (aka, adding figures!), to see what will happen if a certain value goes up or down, or sales increase in a particular area.

Designing the right reports for these applications that return and forecast information is the first step to improving the way you prioritize your resources. And you can take this a step further...

Microsoft Office Visio 2007 is specifically designed to draw up flow charts which can help you keep a project on course, whether you're planning an advertizing campaign or building site. It's a powerful tool which, used correctly at the start of a new project, can provide a long-lasting guide against which to check progress.

Most of us first encountered flow charts at school, and have probably never used them since. But they can be invaluable for keeping track of business processes and helping you identify points where you're not even aware that you're making a decision. Just seeing the workings of a particular department mapped out can help you isolate aspects that need improvement.

The vision of Visio

Microsoft Office Visio is a powerful tool, and you can try it for free

1 TRY FIRST Office Visio 2007 isn't included in Microsoft Office suites; to try it before buying it, either download a trial version in your browser or use the Test Drive environment in your browser.

2 GETTING STARTED You're met with a wizard for starting a new document. There are many templates, and Visio can take information from Excel workbooks or Access databases for updated charts.

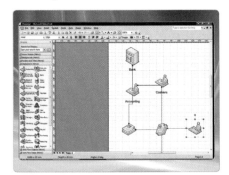

3 PRO TOOLS Visio also includes simple but effective tools for mapping out workflows. You could start with a simple department chain. Then drill down further into each category.

Making the decision

A simple scenario for using Excel to make the right choices

1 POWER SAVE Here's a decision you may have to make at home or at work. Should you supplement your electricity supply with a solar panel? Yes, if it will save money in the long run.

2 GRID COST Start with a simple table for your electricity charges. Add a second column for solar with an extra field for set-up costs. Now you need to research running costs in your area.

3 SOLAR SET-UP Armed with the figures, to ascertain the running costs for one year, use the =PRODUCT function to multiply the unit charge box by the total usage box.

4 COST FOR FIRST YEAR Start a second table for the costs per year. For the first year, link the cell with the total from year one, using the function =E11. Add the set up cost (F8 here) to the total.

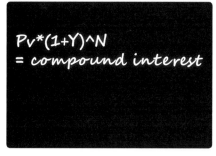

$$Pv*(1+Y)\wedge N = compound\ interest$$

5 FUTURE COSTS You need to factor in price rises (say, 2%). This can be done using the formula for compound interest: $Pv*(1+Y)\wedge N$. Pv = starting amount, Y = inflation rate, and N = number of years.

6 SUBTRACT ONE You don't need to apply the interest multiplier for the first year, so the year 2 running costs for cell I15 is =E11*(1.02*H14). So, in the year two column, use the value of year one.

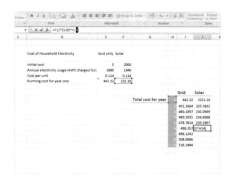

7 REPEAT AS NECESSARY In the Solar column, you don't need to add the set-up cost every year, so use the same formula shifted to the appropriate cells. In this case, =F11*(1.02*H14).

8 TOTAL COST Create a running total table. For year one, link values from the first table. For year two, this example uses =SUM(125+I15). If using link values, use **Fill Handle** to drag over the column.

9 FIND A WINNER Repeat the previous step for the total cost of converting to solar energy. All you need to do is change the values in the first table to create a new price-based scenario.

Turn your own handwriting into a font

Write documents and emails in your own unique hand using an easy scan-to-font conversion service

Who writes letters nowadays – proper letters, that is, of the handwritten Indian ink on thick, quality paper type? Email has obviously become the preferred method of communication, but for all its convenience and ease of use, email is never going to have the touch of character that only a proper handwritten letter conveys.

However, there is a way to fake it – you can create your own font from samples of your handwriting, and then use this one instead of the standard Times or Arial or whatever else you would normally use in an email. YourFonts (www.yourfonts.com) is an online service that has the power to change your handwriting into a TrueType font to use in your documents or emails.

It's your write

First, you need to download a simple template (from $9.95) from YourFonts. You print off this template and then fill in all the boxes – alpha numerics, accented variants, and so on – by hand. The template, which is just two sides of A4 paper, makes it easy to guide your letters with a series of notches on the side. Capitals and ascenders (such as b, d and f) should reach to the top notch, while descenders (such as g, j and p) should reach to the bottom notch, and small letters (such as a, c and e) should fit between the middle notches. Letters that don't quite reach the limits should print well enough, but you need to be careful not to exceed the limits or your letters will be chopped back.

Next you need to scan your template and upload the file to the YourFonts site. If you don't have a scanner, a good digital photograph may work.

Once the templates have been processed by YourFonts, they are changed automatically into a TrueType file format, which you can then install easily into Windows Vista. Click **Fonts** in the Control Panel. In the Fonts folder

PERSONALIZED TEXT Turn your own handwriting into a typeface at YourFonts

you'll see all of your existing typefaces; unfortunately, it's not quite as easy as just dragging and dropping the new one in but it's not exactly rocket science either – you just need to install the font by clicking **File ➔ Install new font**, and then select the new file.

Once it's installed, the new font can be accessed by any application, such as Microsoft Office Word 2007, Wordpad or Windows Live Mail. Note, however, that anyone who hasn't got your font installed on their machine won't be able to see text written in it unless you send it to them and they install it, so it won't always work in email.

One of the best things about YourFonts is the ability to create a custom digital signature, which you can simply import into your documents. This not only looks professional, but can also save you stacks of time if signing for documents that you have to print and return via post. By using a digital signature, you can create PDFs of your documents and then send them via email, slashing turnaround times and saving on postage. ⊞

Sign your emails

Add a handwritten email signature to Windows Live Mail

You can add a signature by using a photographed or scanned image of your moniker and a handy trick in the original Windows Mail. Paste the image into a new email and view the source. Copy this HTML into Notepad and save it as signature.htm. Then in Windows Live Mail go to **Tools ➔ Options ➔ Signatures**, and import the file you made in Notepad.

MAIL TRICK Now you can sign all your emails automatically

Create your own font in five minutes

Use the YourFonts service to make a personalized typeface

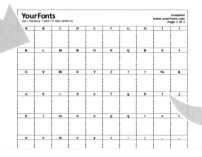

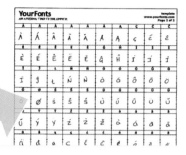

1 PRINT TEMPLATES Go to www.yourfonts.com and you'll find a simple step-by-step formula for creating your own handwritten fonts. To get started, download the PDF of the letters template and then print it out.

2 FILL THEM IN Filling in the template is easy, but there are a few things you need to be aware of. Use a quality, bold pen, and pay attention to the notches on the boxes; stay within the marks or your font may not print well.

3 SCAN THEM The easiest way to get your template back into YourFonts is to use a scanner. Scan the sheets and then save them as JPG files. YourFonts requires the image to be at least 1,000 x 1,000 pixels in size.

Email is never going to have the touch of character that a handwritten letter conveys – but you can fake it

4 IMPORT THEM Go back to the YourFonts website and upload your scanned image. Click **4 Upload Template** and point the website towards your saved image. YourFonts will then do all the hard work and produce a file for you to install.

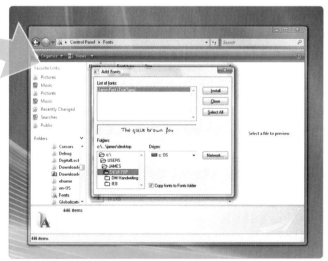

Free of flourish

You can write your letters in a serif style – ie, with detail at the end of some of the strokes – but it's best to keep this minimal as you will risk the letters overlapping one another when words are typed out in full.

5 INSTALL IT Once you've downloaded the font, go to **Fonts** in the Control Panel and select **File → Install new fonts**. Point the dialog at the TrueType file produced by YourFonts. Now your documents can be enhanced with your own handwritten font. Note that recipients will need to install the font to see it.

Edit a film in minutes with Movie Maker

The new version of Windows Live Movie Maker is ready for your creative genius – so what are you waiting for?

 With a code name like Sundance, how could Windows Live Movie Maker fail to tap into your creative talents and help you make fantastic home movies? This video creating and editing software has been completely reworked and redesigned, and is now a lot leaner and easier to use, and it's still free. You can download it from download.live.com/moviemaker.

Lights...

Windows Live Movie Maker is more refined than its cousin, Windows Movie Maker (included with Windows Vista), and it's a lot easier to interact with. One of the best changes is that Live Movie Maker handles more formats, including DVR-S, MPG, MOD, VOB, 3GP, 3G2, MP4, MPEG and MPV2. While it doesn't have its own video and audio capture facilities, you can use Firewire or USB to import your files with the Windows Live Wizard.

Camera...

Live Movie Maker has been designed to work seamlessly with Windows Live Photo Gallery, and you can easily import photos to include in your film. This enables you to create a silent film using only photos for imagery, and the transitions and effects tools to add the words. Live Movie Maker has an option to match the timing of your images with the timing of background music, too.

Action...

One of the reasons Live Movie Maker is easier to use is the fact that the timeline

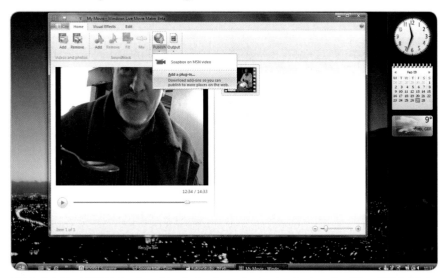

UPLOAD AND SHARE Uploading video is simple – select a plug-in, download it and hit **Publish**

and collection functions have gone. You only work with a storyboard view of your project, and all the files you upload appear in your project automatically. Don't worry whether your various video files are aligned with one another – Live Movie Maker slots them all into a 4:3 aspect ratio so you don't have to fuss. There are still plenty of fabulous transitions and effects available – you can create and edit until you are completely happy with your project. It can take you as little as five minutes to make a silent photo movie, or you can spend several days to perfect every last second of your video epic. It's entirely up to you.

And it's a wrap!

Once you've finished your film you have two choices – you can either upload it directly to the web using sites such as

YouTube or Flickr, or you can save it to your hard drive. The difference is, essentially, the quality. When you save it to your hard drive you'll get a DVD-quality file, which you can then burn to CD or DVD using burning software such as Nero to give to your friends and family. For the inner geek, nerd and hacker in you, you'll be delighted to know that the WIMP format, in which your movies are saved, is a basic XML file, so you can edit your videos in Notepad if you so desired.

The best things about Windows Live Movie Maker are its simplicity and its portability. Anyone who wants to create home movies or presentations, no matter where they are in the world, how much time they have, or how much editing skill they possess, will find this program indispensable.

Edit your home videos

How to use music, transitions, effects and titles

1 IMPORT FILES Download Windows Live Movie Maker, then copy your photos, music and video clips to a folder on your desktop. Launch Movie Maker, select **Add**, browse to this folder and select the files you want to use.

2 ADD TO PROJECT Drag and drop them into your project window in the order you want. Chop and change by selecting the relevant image and clicking **Remove**. You can adjust the length of your clips using **Trim** in the Edit window.

3 ADD MUSIC Choose **Add** in the Soundtrack bar and select the music you want. This can be adjusted to fade in and out using the slider bar. You can only use one track at a time, however. To watch your movie, click the **Play** icon.

4 ADD TRANSITIONS Select the **Visual Effects** tab at the top and this will take you through to Transitions and Effects. To add a transition to a clip or photo, simply select the photo in the project window and the effect you want from the Transition bar.

5 ADD EFFECTS To implement the effect you want, simply choose one from the menu in the Effects bar. Select the photo or video and then the effect you want. To undo an effect or transition select **No effect/transition**.

Direct and document

As it's part of the Windows Live family, you can use the same tagging and rating systems for your movies as you do with your pics in Windows Photo Gallery, so that your favorite clips can be found easily.

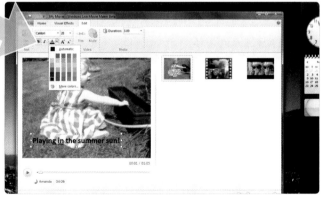

6 ADD TEXT In the Edit tab you can mute the sound of your video, select the display length of your photos and add a text box. To add a text box simply click **Text box** and type the text. Adjust the color, size and font using the boxes provided.

Save an hour a day!

There are loads of different programs available that are designed
to save you time when using your computer – here are 10 of the best

Do you find that you never have enough time to do everything you want? Are you on the lookout for some time-saving programs? Perhaps your friends use different instant messaging programs, for instance, such as ICQ or Windows Live Messenger, and you need both to keep in touch. With applications such as Pidgin and Digsby, you can stay in contact with all your friends from within one program.

Permission to launch

Do you find that constantly navigating your computer to open up programs you use regularly is a laborious process? There are application launcher programs available – such as Rocket Dock – that launch programs from your desktop with just one click. And if you have a good memory for keyboard shortcuts, you can even cut out the mouse click entirely by using AutoHotKey to create your own personalized shortcuts.

Get organized

One of the biggest time wasters in every area of life is disorganization. With programs such as Evernote, however, you can search through all the notes you've been keeping on your computer – be they text documents or handwritten notes scanned in as images – so you need never forget an important date or address again. Keeping your notes on your computer will also help save your workspace from getting cluttered up with confusing scraps of paper, allowing you to sit at a clear desk, which could even save you time when you're not using your PC.

If you have trouble keeping track of all your passwords for the various websites you like to visit, there are applications

available, such as Roboform, that store all of your passwords securely so you don't have to waste time trying to remember them. What sets Roboform apart from simply letting your browser remember your username and password is that you can save a master password to make sure only you have access to your passwords, and you can save

multiple log-in details for the same website – ideal if you have more than one Windows Live Hotmail account, for example. Perhaps the biggest time-saving feature of Roboform, however, is its ability to store your personal details – name and address, for instance – so you can fill in online forms with just a single button click. ⊞

10 applications that will save

1 WWW.ROCKETDOCK.COM
Launch any program from your desktop; drag and drop the application on to Rocket Dock, giving you direct access to your most-used applications.

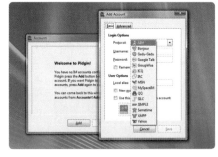

2 WWW.PIDGIN.IM
If you have a number of instant messaging accounts, you can use Pidgin to talk to all of your contacts without switching between programs.

6 WWW.LOGMEIN.COM
LogMeIn is a free remote desktop application that gives you access to your PCs from any other computer that's connected to the internet.

7 WWW.LAUNCHY.NET
With Launchy, you type in the name of a program, file or website you want to launch and press **Enter**; it even guesses what you want while you type.

you time on a daily basis

3 WWW.PORTABLEAPPS.COM
This enables you to run selected applications straight from a USB drive – a web browser with your bookmarks, an email client, even the Open Office suite.

4 WWW.AUTOHOTKEY.COM
With this application you can reduce any task you perform regularly to a keyboard shortcut, speeding up the way you use Windows Vista.

5 WWW.EVERNOTE.COM
With EverNote you can create and organize typed or written memos, and excerpts from web pages, documents or emails, making them easily searchable.

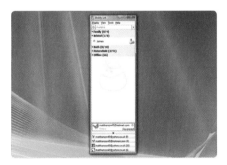

8 WWW.DIGSBY.COM
Digsby enables you to access all of your instant messaging contacts, emails and social networking accounts from one central place.

9 WWW.REMEMBERTHEMILK.COM
This online application helps you manage tasks. You can be reminded when tasks are due via email, SMS, instant messenger and Skype.

10 WWW.ROBOFORM.COM
With Roboform you can fill in online forms with one click and log into websites automatically, without remembering every password.

Plan your wedding – with style and ease

Want to get married in less than a year? Let your PC help to take out the stress factor so that you can enjoy your big day

Wedding preparations can take a year to 18 months, but if the date you've set your heart on is not so far off, it is possible to plan your perfect day in about eight months.

Month 1

Use the Windows Vista calendar to set yourself firm deadlines for when you want to achieve each element, like completing your guest list or booking the cars, and let your Windows Sidebar remind you. Even better, try the Wedding Assistant from www.wedding-assistant.com. It'll keep track of everything for you, and the latest version includes the Fluent interface from the 2007 Microsoft Office system.

Month 2

Getting your venue sorted is now paramount. Going for a big bash in your hometown or an intimate family affair on a romantic secluded island somewhere? Or maybe something in-between?

The internet is your friend at this point. Hunting down local and international

WINDOW SHOPPING Look to the web for some ideas before settling on a dress design

CONGRATULATIONS With the help of a little PC organization, you can enjoy your big day!

I DO Choose where to exchange your vows with care – and factor in guest numbers!

places that offer wedding packages is a lot easier these days, thanks to the web – you can shortlist potential locations using the pictures on their websites, so you'll hopefully only need to visit two or three places to make your final decision rather than spending every weekend for a month checking places out.

Start with a site like www.eventective.com, which lists thousands of registered civil wedding and reception venues throughout the States (should you wish to hold your wedding abroad, type in 'wedding' and the country of your choice into a search engine, but do your research thoroughly if choosing this option!). Make sure you keep notes on any places you visit; a spreadsheet in Excel 2007 or OneNote 2007 can be invaluable here. Most importantly, make sure you keep track of any hidden costs. Some venues may charge extra to keep the bar open beyond midnight, or supply catering but not cutlery or linen, for example.

Month 3
Shopping around online will save you time and money on everything from co-ordinating napkins to the dress itself. There's an incredible array of choice online and, while not everyone is confident enough to buy a dress over the

internet, it may well help to narrow your search. Browsing dress catalogues before you meet with the sales assistant will also give you a clearer idea of what you want – especially if you're not wedded, pardon the pun, to an ultra-traditional nuptial.

In-store assistants can be a mine of useful information from wedding customs to the latest fashions, but they can also be very pushy, and knowing your mind before you meet them will help you make the decisions you want, not what they want for you (and their commission).

Month 4
Now is the time to consider your honeymoon. If you find a bargain break then all the better, but it's an idea to have your romantic getaway booked well in advance – wedding preparations can be exhausting, so you want to be able to relax once you've said 'I do'!

If you're looking for a travel agent that caters specially for honeymooners, don't feel you have to limit yourself to the traditional sun, sea and sand set-up. Responsible Travel (www.responsibletravel.com) was set-up by The Body Shop's Anita Roddick, and is a great resource for those looking for a more authentic once-in-a-lifetime experience. As well as donating money to charity, your guests can buy 'Honeymoon vouchers' instead of gifts, which can be used to ➲

Perfect day

Can your computer really help?

What sort of savings can people make by using their PC?
The average wedding in the US is now circulating at around $30,000. But there are many ways to save. Online stores often give generous discounts on dresses and suits, and most wedding venues now offer virtual tours online.

Can you arrange it all online?
It's best to research online, then check things out in person before booking or buying.

What kinds of services are available online?
Everything! Tap 'wedding' or 'getting married' into a search engine, and you'll be inundated with online wedding guides, each with a comprehensive directory of services. These include customs and etiquette, downloadable seating arrangements, personalized confetti and gift list help. You can even read other bride/groom blogs for advice.

THAT'S IT A little online research can make a big difference when trawling round the shops

pay for flights, accommodation or excursions. Once you've selected the destination, why not put a photo of it on your desktop to keep you going through the months of frantic planning ahead?

Month 5

Whether you're planning to fill the Beaver Stadium in Pennsylvania or make your vows before family members, you'll need to send out invites. Stationery is one area where the canny Windows Vista bride can save hundreds of dollars. Even if you order online, wedding invitations can cost over $7 a card... One option is to email everyone an invite – if you do, you could opt for an ethically aware design from somewhere like www.care2.com. If you think an email invite is a little impersonal,

YOU ARE INVITED Creating your own invitations can be hugely rewarding

you could make your own. You'lll find templates for invitations, place tags and ceremony itineraries at office.microsoft.com. For more on creating your own cards, turn to page 168.

Any high street store should sell art paper or card to print on to for that parchment feel, and you can even create your own seal for the envelopes using the Windows Vista Paint program and www.customwaxnseals.com.

Month 6

Before sending the invites, you should draw up your gift list. Most department stores will keep a list of items your guests can log into and tick off, ensuring no-one doubles up on presents.

It's traditional for the bride and groom to exchange gifts, too. The adventurous bride could try surprising her new husband with a set of tasteful but sexy photographs – www.theknot.com offers a variety of wedding advice, and has a section on boudoir photography.

Month 7

The day of your wedding is drawing nearer but you should have most things under control. While you're getting the final dress fittings sorted, think about your wedding cake and any gifts and

AT YOUR SERVICE Need advice on etiquette or dress choice? The internet can help

decorations – like disposable digital cameras for the tables.

Confirm your bookings – and your flowers – this month. You should have been saving all the important telephone numbers, email addresses and costs in the wedding planning spreadsheet or software you've been using.

One more money-saving tip – many modern brides no longer have dresses made for their bridesmaids and prefer to send them a color sample so they can choose an outfit that suits them as long as it matches the sample.

Month 8

It's time to tie up any loose ends. Collect your dress, check the cake and get those best men down to the tuxedo rental shop

How to create a slideshow

The perfect way to share your memories with family and friends

1 PICK AND CHOOSE In Photo Gallery, select the best shots by holding **Ctrl** and left-clicking on the shots you want. Be ruthless – nobody wants to sit through a 500-image slideshow!

2 BURN DVD Click **Burn** and select **Video Disc**. This will open Windows DVD Maker which will automatically add all the wedding and honeymoon photos you've selected to a new project.

3 THEME Choose a style for the menus and intro. There are several themes included – this example shows the Special Occasion look. Pick the image or video you want to play in the menu.

CUT THE CAKE Not the atmosphere! Make you don't miss a trick with an organized schedule

for their fittings. Keep track of who's doing what with another spreadsheet or planning software like iDo Wedding Couple Edition (www.elmsoftware.com/ido). Keep a checklist of things to do (like hair appointments) open in the Notes gadget for Windows Sidebar.

The intense world of wedding planning can make the sanest people go nuts, so let off steam with the Flash game Wedding Bouquets (www.novelgames.com – search for 'wedding bouquets').

Then good luck with it all!

SORT IT OUT You did stick to the original plan, right? Then the last month should be easy

And when you get back home

Even after the honeymoon, there are things to do...

1 THANK YOU VERY MUCH
Keep track of who sent what by making notes and using the Windows Vista search function.

2 PREPARE THE CARDS
A personalized thank you card, with a picture of your guest, will make them feel appreciated.

3 SORT AND SHARE
Use Windows Vista Photo Gallery to sort your honeymoon shots before sharing them online.

4 EDIT THE MOVIE
Edit your wedding movie in Windows Movie Maker for lasting memories.

5 SHARE THE MEMORIES
It's easy to burn the wedding video or a photo slideshow to disc using Windows DVD Maker.

4 MUSICAL MAYHEM Now you can customize how you want the fades to appear, and what music you want. You can also select the Menu text option to give a name to your wedding slide show.

5 TRIPLE-CHECK Before you click on Burn, make sure you have a blank DVD in the drive and preview your slide show to check it through. Then hit the button, sit back and enjoy.

LOVE IS ALL AROUND Be sure to capture that all-important confetti moment

The perfect holiday...

Don't get caught up in the pre-holiday horrors – Windows Vista can make your planning as simple as making a cup of tea

You're probably sceptical about how well you can plan a holiday on your PC... Remember the last time you started to plan a holiday? And how, after five minutes, you were ready to give up and do something simple, such as rewire your house.

Not only do you have to manage the basic details such as accommodation, flights and passports, but you also have everybody else's opinions and views to take into account – which usually results in an overwhelming desire to book a one-way flight for one.

Fortunately, it doesn't have to be this way. You can use Windows Vista and Windows Live to whip everything into shape, without having to do the majority of the donkey work yourself.

Whether you're planning to go away with a group of friends or gather the family together, you need to get everyone involved to agree on the budgets, the locations and the activities. Windows Live (home.live.com) is your knight in shining armour. Use your Windows Live ID, such as the one you use to sign into your Hotmail account, and create your holiday by clicking **Events** under the More tab on the main page. **Edit Event** updates the event information on the website instantly, so everyone can see exactly what's happening, and if anything has changed or been missed out. It's a great way to keep track of fussy details such as food allergies or malaria tablets.

Get organized

When you're searching for hotels, don't be too quick to go for the cheapest deals. Use a website such as www.holidaywatchdog.com, which is packed with reviews from holidaymakers, to read about the best and worst resorts.

If you're planning to travel to far-flung destinations such as Africa or South

CHECK IT OUT Use websites such as Holiday Watchdog to assess hotels before you book

America, it's also a good idea to pay a visit to the US government website (www.usa.gov and click on Americans Abroad). There you'll find loads of information about passports, visas, vaccinations and health precautions. Upload links to these sites and the relevant information to your Windows Live site as you go, so that everyone else is privy to them, too. You could use a

Working with Windows Live

Create the ultimate holiday planner online

1 CREATE EVENT Once you've registered with Windows Live, click **More ➜ Events**, then click **Create your own**. Ensure you click **Only people who are invited can view this event**.

2 INVITE GUESTS Now you go to your main page. Click **Invite Guests** and enter their names and a message. This is a good time to give people deadlines so they know what to do and when.

3 UPDATE EVERYONE You may need to keep everyone informed of a sudden change or important requirement. Click **Send update ➜ Everyone invited to the event**. This updates everyone, instantly.

In real life...
Event planner

Tamsin Oxford, Contributor, *Windows Vista: The Official Magazine*

I found Live Events a lifesaver when I planned a massive family gathering. People from all over the world had to converge at the airport, and getting the timing right was a nightmare. To avoid panic, I booked the transport for everyone and put the times up on the website so everyone knew where we were meeting and when. It meant that 20 relaxed and excited people arrived on time for the flight instead of a bunch of bickering couples!

program such as Office OneNote 2007 to store all the links that meet your criteria, and add relevant screen clippings by pressing **Windows + S**. Don't worry about sorting it out – OneNote can help you to annotate and order these sites once you've finished the initial leg work.

When you're done, leave it for at least 24 hours – you'll need this time to regain perspective. When you're ready, go through all the options you've listed and re-read them until you've found your top three, then put these on to your Windows Live site for people to select from. That way you can say goodbye to hundreds of email hours trying to make everyone happy – just pick the ones that get the most votes. Websites such as www.travelex.com are handy to see what currency you need and what the exchange rates are – again, put a screen clipping of your destination's currency and rates on to your Windows Live site for everyone to reference.

Final touches

Lists are the holiday planner's best friend. Use either Microsoft Word 2007 or Notepad to draw up lists of things you mustn't forget, such as a camera, clothes and so on. Your tickets, passport and wallet are the most essential items, so use Outlook 2007 to set reminders and sync with your phone so that they both remind you to check that you've packed them. Post your list on your website and send an update so others can check their lists against yours or even remind you of something you've forgotten.

Now all you need to worry about is how much factor 20 you might need...

Seven holiday tips

Keep your holiday on track

1 DELEGATE Instead of shouldering all the searching and calling, ask others to help. It can take hours to go through all the offers, so use teamwork.

2 EMERGENCY Email yourself important information such as flight details, passport numbers and credit card phone numbers in case your wallet or purse is stolen.

3 MAKE A DATE Check your passport expiry date and any required vaccinations two to three months prior to departure.

4 CHEAP NOT CHEERFUL Check that any cheap deal covers airport tax, and that you won't land at an airport miles from your destination. Paying for a long cab drive from the airport is not a great way to start a holiday.

5 LITTLE THINGS If you're traveling with small children, make sure your rental car includes a car seat and that it's guaranteed never to have been in an accident. Also, check with your hotel that they provide travel cots and childminding services or a crèche.

6 PICTURE PERFECT Put your digital camera in a watertight bag, take spare batteries and check that the recharger will fit the sockets at your destination.

7 RELAX AND ENJOY! Something invariably doesn't go quite according to plan so, instead of letting it ruin the experience, let it become a part of it.

4 CHOOSE PARTICIPANTS In Options select **More options → E-mail publishing** and tick **Turn on e-mail publishing**. You can choose who is allowed to join in and create a password.

5 ADD A MAP Use the blogging tool to provide your members with news. You can even insert a map by going to **Edit event → Add map** so people can take an aerial gander at their destination.

Card creativity

Indulge your ingenious side and produce the kind of greetings cards you've always wanted to give...

Can't find the perfect greeting card? Well, make your own and save money! All you need is Office Word 2007, Office Publisher 2007, your imagination and a printer.

Both Word 2007 and Publisher 2007 offer excellent choices for producing cards and the ability to be creative with photos, Clip Art and fonts. If you're using Word 2007, you can use the ready-made templates from http://office.microsoft. com and customize them with your own photos. A great idea is to scan in children's artwork, or your own, and insert the scans into one of the downloaded templates. It couldn't be easier but the results look fantastic.

Sometimes, however, you may prefer to create a more personalized design and the pre-designed templates just aren't quite right for what you have in mind. If that's the case, it's easy to be a bit more inventive in Publisher 2007; follow the 'Create a party invitation' walkthrough on how to make a fabulous invitation with Clip Art or your own photography. While many choose to design in Word 2007 because of its familiarity and simplicity, Publisher 2007 offers more features suited to design and production, so it's worth experimenting with if you are aiming at a more professional finish.

Word 2007 may not have the elite power tools at Publisher's disposal but it has some versatile – and easy to use – options. You can have great fun using Word Art to revolutionize your text and enhance a particular theme. Why not create a card with its very own word search on it? Go to www.teacherly.com and enter your words into the Wordsearch creator – then copy and paste the puzzle into your card design. Not only will the recipient appreciate your efforts, they'll have fun trying to find all the words! Once you've got a handle on designing, you can save your own layouts as templates.

Print options

If you have a home printer check what thickness it can print and do a test run to see if the ink dries properly and doesn't bleed. Some laminate cards will only print well with specific photo inks. You don't have to go with printing at home though... If you're creating your own wedding or party invitations, submitting your designs to a printer will often work out cheaper than printing at home and you get a wider choice of paper stock. Just make sure you get plenty of quotes. And don't forget to factor envelopes and postage into your costs. (Turn to page 170 to find out how Windows Vista makes address labels easy.) Then you can get on with organizing the party!

Create a BBQ party invitation

Let everyone know you're having a sizzlin' hot party!

1 CHOOSE DESIGNS Open Office Publisher 2007 and in the Getting Started section scroll through the options. When choosing the design don't worry about the images as you'll replace these with your own.

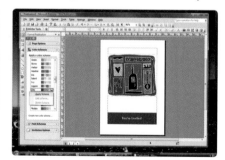

2 SELECT OPTIONS In the left column, under Format Publication, go to **Invitation Options ➜ Page Size** and select the size that you want for the design. Then go to Color Schemes and Font Schemes to choose these.

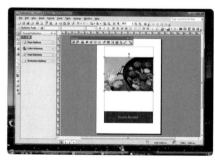

3 INSERT IMAGE To insert an image, click on the card image and the Picture formatting bar will appear. Select **Insert Picture**. If you've chosen a template that does not have an image, select **Insert ➜ Empty picture frame**.

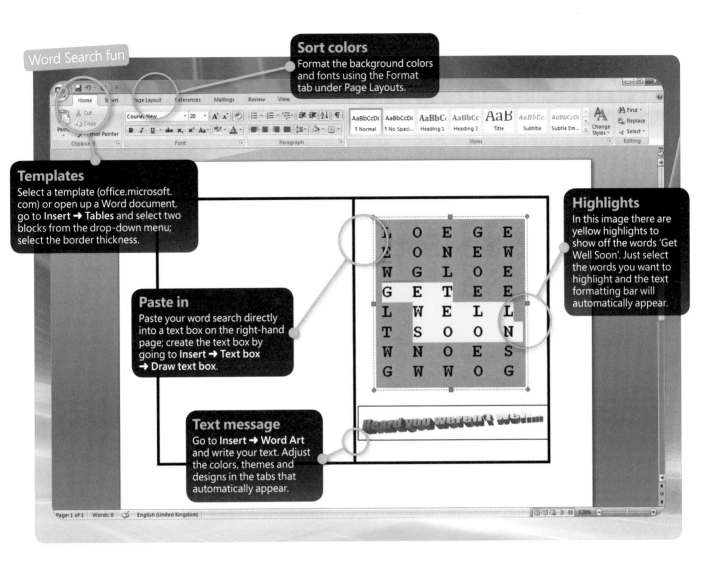

Word Search fun

Sort colors
Format the background colors and fonts using the Format tab under Page Layouts.

Templates
Select a template (office.microsoft.com) or open up a Word document, go to **Insert → Tables** and select two blocks from the drop-down menu; select the border thickness.

Highlights
In this image there are yellow highlights to show off the words 'Get Well Soon'. Just select the words you want to highlight and the text formatting bar will automatically appear.

Paste in
Paste your word search directly into a text box on the right-hand page; create the text box by going to **Insert → Text box → Draw text box**.

Text message
Go to **Insert → Word Art** and write your text. Adjust the colors, themes and designs in the tabs that automatically appear.

4 SIZE IT UP Using the green dot to rotate and the black cross to adjust size, you can then move and resize the picture to fit the frame as you want it. Just be careful of stretching the picture and making it look unnatural.

5 MAKE ADJUSTMENTS Use the numbered tabs at the base of the screen to go through to the next pages where you can add different images and text. Using the **Format Picture** option you can create unusual colors and stains.

6 ADD STUFF Add backgrounds by going to **Format → Background** and change fonts in **Format → Styles**. You can also include images/text from Word 2007 – **Format Publication → Change Template → Import Word Documents**.

Send all your cards in an hour

Sending out Christmas or thank you cards doesn't have to be time-consuming with Windows Contacts

We've all done it... staring at a pile of Christmas cards in the corner and putting them out of our minds until we have to spend the night before the mail deadline painstakingly writing and addressing them. Well, now you can still do it the night before but instead of it taking all night, it will take you an hour. And you can watch TV at the same time!

To start with, you'll need to store all your contacts in Windows Contacts, possibly the best invention since the Delete key. Windows Contacts has the ability to add pictures and file formats for storage and integration with other applications. It works beautifully with Windows Mail and Microsoft Office Outlook, and it can

COMPLETE CONTROL You can customize the layout of Windows Contacts to suit your style

also export information to other applications. To find it, go to **Start ➜ All Programs ➜ Windows Contacts**. If this is your first foray, click **New Contact** and enter the information you need – anything from family details to private notes and email addresses. Use

the **Organize** button to tailor the way your Contacts appear and how you want to categorize them. Once you've entered all your contacts, click on **New Contact Group** and give it a name. You can add as much or as little information about the group as you wish, and then you can select the contacts you want to have on your address labels. Now this group is ready to be used to create your labels – see the guide opposite.

Missing persons

If you've missed anyone off your Christmas or thank you list, Windows Contacts can instantly draw contacts from Office Outlook, Windows Mail and Windows Messenger. To make sure you haven't missed anyone, be sure to go through all your emails.

Labels need not all be plain white blobs sitting on plain white envelopes; thanks to office.microsoft.com you can choose from loads of fabulous label templates. If you are doing Christmas cards, try a sprig of mistletoe; or for wedding photos you might want to try two linked rings.

"Wow"
Auto updates
Whenever contacts are updated in Windows Live Messenger they are updated in Windows Contacts. Just uncheck the option to encrypt Windows Live Messenger under Security

PRESENT TENSE Sending out thank you cards for gifts can now be a pain-free process

Labels made easy

Follow these simple steps to making labels

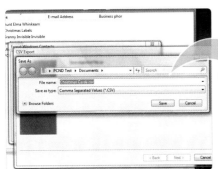

1 EXPORT IT In Windows Contacts select **Export → CSV → Export**. In the box enter the name of your file, select **Save → Next** and then check **First name**, **Last name** and the address boxes. Uncheck all the others and click **Finish**.

2 DESIGN IT In Word 2007, click **New → Labels → Mailing and Shipping → Holiday** and select some labels. In the top-left, delete the text, then click **Mailings → Select Recipients → Use Existing list**. Choose the file you saved.

3 MERGE IT In the **Start Mail Merge** group select **Edit Recipient List**, choose the names you want to include and click **OK**. Place your mouse in the top-left label and click **Insert Merge Field** and check the **Address Fields** box.

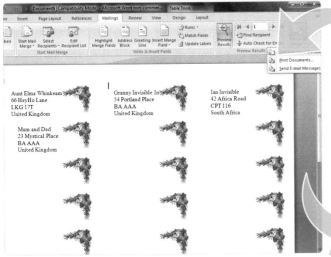

4 TAILOR IT Select each element you want on your label – First name, Last name, Street 1 and so on – and click **Insert** each time. These will appear consecutively on the label. Then go into the label and put spaces between each section so they print as you want them to.

5 PERFECT IT To use the same fields and layout for each record, click **Update Labels**. This is your chance to adjust the layout and spacing to get it just right. Once you have finished, click on **Preview Results** to see your final labels.

Lovely labels

Fortunately Office Word 2007 has made printing labels extremely easy, with customizable measurements and several pre-set formats for the most common sizes, so there's no excuse for not mailing your cards right away.

6 PRINT IT Click **Finish and Merge → Print Documents → Merge to printer → Print → All** to print the records you have chosen, then click **OK**. If you need to make changes click **Finish and Merge → Edit Individual Documents** and click **OK**.

Sort out your family!

Don't struggle to keep track of household arrangements –
Windows Live Calendar can organize your home life

We've all done it – forgotten someone's birthday or a vital appointment because we have too much other stuff going on. It's frustrating and can be the cause of some unpleasant family fights. So why not dump those pieces of paper stuck to your fridge and use your Windows Live ID to snag yourself the simplicity of Windows Live Calendar instead?

It's just good news all-round – you don't have to pay a penny to use Live Calendar and it's extremely easy to set up. Enter Windows Live by going to http://home.live.com – if you have a Windows Live ID (such as a Hotmail account or Windows Messenger login), use that to sign in, otherwise click **Sign up** and follow the instructions. Once you're in, go to **More ➜ Calendar** to open up the Calendar window. You can view your schedules by week, month or day, and you can drag and drop your

KEEPING TRACK It's easy to stay on top of plans and it takes seconds to add new entries

appointments if you need to reschedule. You can even use Windows Live Calendar to arrange major social events, complete with tracking invitations, RSVPs and thank you messages.

Tucking in

To start with, you probably want to get all the birthdays, appointments and daily drudgeries into your Live Calendar. Your

Hotmail and Messenger contacts' birthdays can be easily imported and you can link to your Outlook 2007 and third-party online calendars, such as Apple iCal and Mozilla Sunbird, too.

To add new appointments, click on the date you want and a '+' symbol appears

Combine your calendars

Get all your calendars merged seamlessly into one perfect place

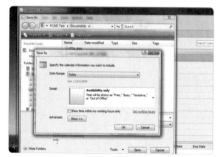

1 IN FROM OUTLOOK To export your Outlook calendar, save the data as an ICS file. Click on **Calendar ➜ File ➜ Save as ➜ More options.** Select the date range and the level of detail you want.

2 NO STRINGS ATTACHED Go to **Advanced ➜ Show** and uncheck **Include attachments within calendar items**; Live Calendar does not support attachments as yet. Click **OK ➜ Save.**

3 SIZE MATTERS Right-click the ICS file you just saved and select **Properties.** Check its size on the General tab. If this is greater than 10MB export your calendar again using a smaller date range

STAY ALERT Set reminders to go to your email and Messenger so you won't miss anything

in the bottom-left corner. Click on it to add the details of your schedule. What's even better is that you can set the Calendar reminder service to send alerts via Messenger or email.

You can add as many calendars as you want by going to **New → Calendar**. Customize and name each one – for example, 'Jenna's tap dancing lessons'. These can be viewed in the main screen but you can control the permissions for each so you can keep a surprise birthday party secret while still taking advantage of all the tricks Live Calendar has to offer.

Sharing is caring

If you don't want to bear the sole responsibility for updating and

maintaining your Live Calendar, you can designate your partner as co-owner. To do this, click on **Share** and select the calendar you want to share, then click on **Share this calendar** and choose what you want them to see – from to-do lists to events. Select **Share your calendar with friends and family → To** and either write out their email addresses or select the contacts from the drop-down list. Under **Choose what people can see in your calendar**, select the level of access you're happy to give them. Then click **Add a new person** for each family member. This is also a stunning way of keeping in touch with family overseas. They can use it to add in their own birthdays and special occasions, and you can have access to their calendars, too. It certainly makes things a lot easier when planning big family get-togethers.

Windows Live Calendar is eminently customizable, too. You can color code all the entries to match the different family members and it automatically updates so that anyone who's signed up to get your calendar updates actually does. Now you just have to find a way of dragging yourself away from the calendar long enough to actually go and get on with all those tasks it was just reminding you about...

Smart start

Six simple ways to get the most out of Windows Live Calendar

1 FACEBOOK Transfer Facebook events to your Windows Live Calendar. Open www.facebook.com/home.php#events.php, which shows your events once you've logged in. Click on **Export Events**. This gives you a URL. Then go to your Live Calendar, click **Subscribe**, select **Subscribe to a public calendar** and paste in your URL. Click **Subscribe** to calendar.

2 AD-FREE Get rid of the banner ad by creating or joining a Windows Live Group. Every group has a built-in calendar that you can integrate into any other calendar – including the one that is linked to your Hotmail.

3 WHO'S FREE? Set up a calendar for each family member so you can compare them and see who's free. Check the box for their calendar and it shows up on yours.

4 INVITATIONS Click **New Appointment → Details** and fill out everything your guests will want to know. Then select **Attendees,** enter their names and email addresses, and click **To → OK.** Then go to **Details → Invite.**

5 TO-DO Use the To-Do list to plan and finalize events or sort out your household. Go to **To-Do list → Add a to-do** and select **Add more details**. Here you can set a reminder and a priority rating.

6 CUSTOMIZATION Don't settle for the standard layout and design. Go to **Options** and choose one of the many themes available to personalize your calendar.

4 FIRST DATES Sign in to Live Calendar and click on **Subscribe**. Select **Import from an ICS file → Browse**. Locate your ICS file and click **Open**. Click **Import into a new calendar** and enter a name.

5 IN WITH THE OLD To add your ICS file to an existing calendar, select **Import into an existing calendar**. Select a calendar and under **Prevent duplicates** choose the appropriate option.

Print your own illustrated children's book

Use your PC to create something special for your children to share with friends and family – without being rejected by a publisher!

Toys aren't always enough to keep the kids amused. An online game can provide some entertainment, but you don't want Junior playing them all day. So indulge their creative side by helping them make a book.

You need a subject, so sit down with your children to discuss ideas. Next, you need supporting material, such as text and images, related objects and so on, so plug in your scanner and fire up Windows Vista. Scan in any artwork and save those images and any digital pictures in the order they'll appear in the book, such as Picture 1, Picture 2 and so on. Type your text into Microsoft Word 2007; if the kids are old enough, let them do it. They'll learn useful keyboard skills and you can put your feet up, too.

Once the text and illustrations are on your PC, decide on the book's format. If

CREATIVE KIDS Scan in kids' art for your book

TEXT TIP Position text wherever you want it and select **No Fill** to show the background

you're printing to letter size, you could have landscape pages, or two small portrait pages per sheet. Consider how you'll place the material. Storybooks, for instance, are often laid out as two landscape pages, with a picture across both and text on top. Or you could put images on the left and text on the right.

Select a layout

Choose **Page Layout → Orientation → Landscape** and adjust the size by going to **Page Layout → Size**. To make your cover and illustration pages, open a new Word document, go to **Page Layout → Margins → Custom margins** and change the values to 0. Then go to **Insert → Picture** and select an image – adjust the image using the arrows on the edges of the image. Insert your headline by going to **Insert → Text Box → Draw Text Box**. Choose your font, color and size, then under the Format tab go to **Text Box Styles → Shape Fill → No Fill**. Now you should just see your text on your picture. If there's a box outline, go to **Shape Outline → No Outline**. Save all full-

page images separately to keep the formatting. Now choose **Insert → Text Box → Draw Text Box**, and draw it in the center. You can always use some of the pre-formatted styles. Paste your text in, then select **Format → Shape Fill** and use a Color, Picture, Gradient or Texture to add a background.

Send to print

You could use a service such as www.lulu.com to print your creation as a bound book. Or you could print the pages at home using high-quality paper and have them professionally bound. A photo book, from somewhere such as www.smilebooks.com, is a stunning option for a more luxurious gift. ■

Be a designer

Design your own book page layouts using Microsoft Word

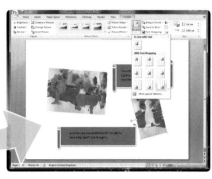

1 INSERT AN IMAGE Choose **Insert →
Picture** on your first page. Go to
Arrange → Position to set where you
want your image to sit. Go to **More
Layout Options** to play around with
the various settings.

2 ENTER TEXT Choose **Insert → Shapes**
to choose the shape for your text box.
Drag it where you want it and choose a
color from **Shape Styles**. Insert a text box
and write text. Choose **No Fill** to keep
the background color.

3 EDIT IMAGES Use the green rotation
tool that appears beside an image to
rotate it and the Crop tool in **Format →
Size** to get it the correct shape and size.
Under Format, go to **Arrange → Position**
to allocate a zone to your first image.

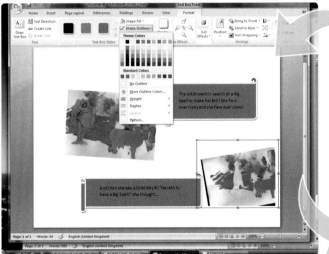

4 POSITION IMAGES
Insert a second image
and use the Arrange tool
to position it, or create
your own: go to **Insert →
Text Box → Draw Text
Box** and click and drag
where you want it, then
go to **Insert → Image**
and the image appears
in the box.

5 FINESSE BOXES Remove the fill and border from the text
box and the image will sit perfectly on the page. Using
this technique you can add as many different boxes as you
want to a single page of your book.

Font fount

**Microsoft Word 2007 comes packed with loads of
pre-set fonts for headings, body text and boxes, so
before spending hours looking for the right fonts,
simply let Word do the work for you.**

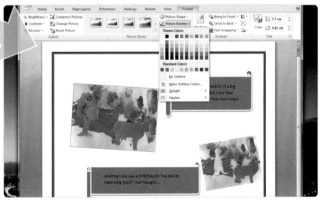

6 USE BORDERS To add a page border, go to **Page Layout →
Page Background → Page Border**. To add a picture border,
simply click on the image and go to **Format → Picture Styles
→ Picture Border**.

Host a great party

If you really want a party to end with a bang, you've got to put some preparation in before the big night

Elsewhere in this book, you'll find plenty of ways of using your PC and Windows Vista to help you and your social life – from organizing email accounts, to sending out cards or invites. But now you've invited everyone, you've got a party to put on. Fortunately, Windows Vista can help again.

Even if you've sent invites, it's a good idea to put the event up on Windows Calendar (find Windows Calendar in the Search menu). To add an event, scroll to the appropriate area on the left, select a date and time, select **New Appointment**, then give the event a name and location.

To add friends to your contact list, go to the top menu, click **View → Contacts**, create your new contacts and include their email addresses. Once this is done, add **Attendees** to the Participants list and click **Invite**. This will attach your calendar to the email, so that when your friends open it, the event is added to their Windows Calendar.

Check out office.microsoft.com/en-us/templates for 'party' or 'celebration' invites and, when you've filled your details in, attach this to your invitation email by clicking **Insert** in the top menu

If the party is a little more mature, you need to consider your drinks order

and selecting **File attachment** from the drop-down menu.

If you're hosting a barbecue or outdoor party, make sure you have the latest weather reports by checking out a weather gadget from gallery.live.com. If the party's going to be held indoors, you need to think about clearing space and maybe putting some decorations up; again, Microsoft templates come in useful if you want to put up themed pictures of the birthday boy or girl.

It's an idea to order your other party accessories online, as the savings can be incredible. There are many online party favor companies to choose from.

If the party is a little more mature, you need to consider your drinks order. Try to buy from a place that offers sale or return, and if you want to make savings, pop to a site like www.freemania.net to see if they're running any relevant coupons. You can make savings on your food order at this kind of site, too. If you don't want to overdo it on the drink supplies, you could try opening up an Excel 2007 spreadsheet and entering drink choices against the names of your guests – beer, wine, spirit, soft drink. Make an educated tally of how many

PERFECT PARTY Thanks to Windows Vista, planning an event is easy

drinks people will consume and then, with a few formulas, you will be able to work out quantity required and costs.

Sights and sounds

Now you need to look at your music collection. If your playlist is a little outdated, now is the time to download. Try a site such as www.mtv.com/music/downloads to access a variety of free MP3 downloads and drag your tunes out of the ice age and into the 21st century. You might want to consider equipment, too. If you're having a kids' party or pumping tracks aren't your thing, your

everyday sound system will suffice but, if you want a bit more boom in your bass, you may want to rent better speakers. Just type 'PA, sound equipment, rental' along with your location into a search engine and you should get plenty of companies to choose from.

Alternatively, returning to the outdoor/barbecue theme, you could treat yourself to some outdoor speakers that you can position in your backyard to pump out the sounds. There are plenty on the market now that are portable and waterproof. You'll need to couple these speakers with a media

extender, such as an Xbox 360, to access all the songs stored on your PC.

Hopefully, you and your friends will be trying to capture all the fun at the party on camera, so make sure you download your shots to the PC, ready to share with everyone else over the internet – you can tag them in Windows Photo Gallery so that you know which party they're from, and who's taken them.

Till then, get in the mood by making a party music mix or go to www.allrecipes.com and click on **BBQ and Grilling** for skewer-friendly menus or **Drinks** then **Cocktails** for knockout punches.

Make the ultimate playlist in Media Player

If you've tagged your tracks, you can make soundtracks for any mood

1 DETAIL When you burn music to your PC, take the time to add some more data to it, to aid searching in the future. Right-click on a single track or a group of songs, and select **Advanced Tag Editor**.

2 IN THE MOOD In the ripping process Windows Media Player fills in most of the fields automatically, but there are other important fields. Select a mood and any other data about the track.

3 PLAYLIST To quickly make a playlist perfectly suited to your mood, right-click on the playlist tab in the left-hand pane. In the resulting menu click **Create Auto Playlist**.

4 CRITERIA In the following menu is a list of criteria you can add, to narrow down your music into a playlist. Click the first green plus sign and a list of criteria is presented. Click **More** for a full list.

5 MOODY BLUES The option to set by mood is in the following menu. Click it to agree, then the option to choose from moods will be available. You can add more criteria, otherwise hit **OK**.

6 MEGA MIX Now you've made your playlist, you can add cross fading and auto levelling. Go to the **Now Playing** tab, then **View ➜ Enhancements ➜ Show Enhancements**.

Get more out of your laptop battery

With a little inside knowledge, it's easy to stretch some extra life from your notebook battery, enabling you to work for longer when on the move

Working on the move has never been easier, but laptops are still slaves to the electricity network. A modern laptop's advanced features drain battery life to the extent that you can only get a couple of hours out of it before it turns up its toes.

However, it's possible to get significant improvements by good practice and a few software tweaks. To help you get the most from your battery, we've found the seven easiest ways to power up your PC.

1 Dim your screen
It takes serious amounts of battery power to keep your display looking clear and bright. Saving this power is simply a question of turning the brightness down. The screen brightness button is usually a second function of one of the F keys, represented by a sun symbol with up and down icons. To use it, hold down the function key and choose up or down.

BYE BYE WI-FI Disable wireless connections when you're not using them to save power

2 Change power settings
Windows Vista comes with power features that enable you to eke out the best performance when you're plugged into the mains, and optimize battery life when on the move. Type 'power options' into Start Search and choose **Power saver**. The Windows Mobility Center has more methods for saving battery life. These include powering off the monitor and kicking into sleep mode quickly.

3 Switch off Wi-Fi
One of the biggest battery sappers is the wireless networking capabilities built into most laptops. Wi-Fi drains the battery by constantly drawing power and, when not connected, looking for networks. If you're not using a wireless network, turn this device off. Many laptops have a function button to turn off the wireless adaptor manually to save waste, but older laptops often don't have this. If so, go to Control Panel, access the **Network Connections** menu and disable your wireless connection.

4 Turn off peripherals
USB peripherals can put a big drain on your PC, because your motherboard has to power them. USB sticks, mice and webcams are common offenders, so copy all your data across and eject your devices as soon as possible, and put up with laptop trackpads over your USB mouse. Many laptops have function buttons to turn off their webcam, which drains the battery if given the chance.

5 Eject your disc drives
Having a disc spinning in the drive is a huge drain on resources, and many programs constantly do this. Simply eject your discs before you switch to battery power to gain vital extra minutes from your working day.

6 Invest in some hardware
Most laptops come with a six-cell battery, but many manufacturers offer eight- or even 12-cell optional upgrades, which can double your power. The

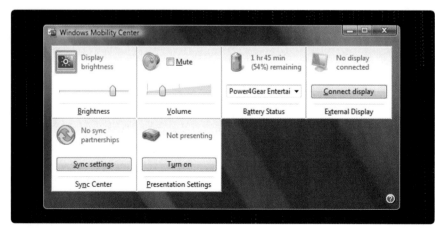

MOBILE HOME The Mobility Center offers several ways to cut power consumption on the move

LOOKS DON'T MATTER It makes sense to use less power-hungry appearance options

alternative to expensive laptop batteries are products such as the Philips Portable Power Pack, which gives you valuable extra hours for all your devices. The Philips is a compact battery unit that has adaptors for most laptops and cell phones, which is portable enough to be placed in a bag and has enough capacity to double the length of your charge.

7 Disable features

Windows Vista has some great built-in features, but many put demands on your system that are unnecessary when working on the move. Take the simple measure of turning off Windows Aero and the Windows Sidebar when you're on the move to make Windows Vista even more efficient.

LONG LIFE A few adjustments to your settings and your laptop battery will last a lot longer

Tweak your power options

Get extra battery life with Windows Vista power options

1 EXPLORE To check which power plan you're using, search for 'power options' in Start Search. The following menu shows all plans, with options for extra economy or better performance.

2 SAVE The Power saver setting enables you to switch to a power-friendly mode with just one click. Many laptop manufacturers supply their own power settings, tailored to the individual laptop.

3 CREATE Adapt the power plans to suit you by clicking **Create a power plan**. In Advanced settings you can change the options, from the power to USB devices to what resources are assigned to tasks.

Share your files across the world for free

Never be caught without important files again – make your documents accessible online with Windows Live Sync

Thanks to Windows Vista, which makes storing digital photos and movies easier than ever, we keep more of our important files on our PCs. Although having all our digital memories, music and work in one place is extremely useful, sometimes we need to access those files from a different location. Carrying them on removable media such as USB flash drives is not always a viable option.

Windows Live Sync is part of the Windows Live free suite of tools. It enables you to share your documents online so that they can be accessed from any computer that's connected to the internet.

You can quickly access your synchronized folders by right-clicking on the Windows Live Sync icon in your Notification Area. A menu will appear listing all the folders that you are sharing between computers, and clicking on one of them will open up the folder in Windows Explorer.

This means you'll never have to worry about being without your files again. Want to show a relative your holiday photos on their computer, but forgotten your digital camera? With Windows Live Sync this is no longer a problem. Simply download and install Live Sync and then access your account from their computer. The only limit to what you can share is that each file has to be under 4GB in size, and you can only have up to 20 synchronized folders that can hold 20,000 files each – which should be more than enough for most people.

Copy cat

Live Sync can also serve as a rudimentary backup solution, because it downloads and stores the files on each computer you've installed it on, meaning you'll have multiple copies of the file saved in different locations. This could be a life saver if one computer ceases to work.

By automatically updating the files you select to share between computers, any changes you make to the file on one computer are shown on all computers linked to your Live Sync account, so you always have access to the most recent version. Unlike online storage solutions such as SkyDrive, where files are stored on the internet, Live Sync keeps all files on your local computers – handy if you have a slow internet connection. ⊞

SHARE CENTRE Keep files synchronized across as many PCs as you like with Windows Live Sync

Exchange files
How to create a folder of files that update automatically

1 DOWNLOAD AND INSTALL To use Live Sync, download and install it from sync.live.com. You are asked to enter an email address and password that will be tied to your Sync account, which you use to access your files from anywhere.

2 CREATE A FOLDER Click **Sync website** in the taskbar's Notification Area. To share files with other people click **Create a shared Folder** and add files. Then send out email invitations. You can only access personal Folders from your account.

3 ADDING FOLDERS After you have chosen what type of Folder you want to make, select the folder from your PC that you wish to add to Live Sync and select **Create Folder here** or, if you wish, you can create a new folder.

Any changes you make to the file on one computer will be shown on all computers linked to your Live Sync account

4 PICK AND CHOOSE Install Live Sync on any computer and log in. Select the Folder you wish to synchronize with, click on **Sync with a new computer** and then select the computer you want to have access to the Folder. Then choose a folder on the new computer to store the synchronized files in.

Turn them on

Don't forget that in order to take advantage of Windows Live Sync, you need to keep all the computers which you want to synchronize files to switched on and connected to the internet.

5 WHEN YOU WANT Select **Automatic synchronization** for the computers to update their Live Sync folders every time you connect to the internet. With **On-demand synchronization** you update the files manually, giving you more control over what files are shared, and when they are updated.

Be a student entrepreneur

Unleash your inner business guru and pay your way through college with help from Windows Vista

Starting your own business while still studying may sound like a pipe dream, but thanks to a growing interest in student development and technology it is achievable.

Before you can even start dreaming about paying your way through college you need an idea, and you need to be sure that it will work. At Business.Gov (www.business.gov) you'll find an entire section dedicated to helping you work out whether your idea is commercially viable. If you want to improve on your concept, or get some inspiration, attend lectures dedicated to student entrepreneurship. Many universities have student entrepreneur societies with mentors and advisors to help you. Events

BUSINESS SCHOOL Starting a business while studying broadens your employment prospects

Get your business going

Five tools to make creating, running and promoting a business a lot easier

1 WINDOWS SIDEBAR AND GADGETS
Keep vital data such as calendar notifications and to-do lists close by, so you don't need to waste time opening websites or programs to get the info.

2 WINDOWS VISTA ROI CALCULATOR
There's loads of business features in Windows Vista Business edition. Use the return on investment calculator at snip url.com/2ssdx to see if it's worth buying.

3 WINDOWS SPEECH RECOGNITION
If you work better while pacing your room, or need to use the keyboard for research instead of writing, this will make your life a lot easier.

such as Entrepreneurship Week (entrepreneurshipweekusa.com) also give you the opportunity to meet up with potential investors and mentors.

You need a realistic business plan, which is a breakdown of your business, its objectives, its strategies and so forth. There are lots of business plan templates available for free from Microsoft Office Online (office.microsoft.com); or you can go to Bplans.com where there are sample plans for you to try out. A good template includes sections such as an executive summary, a description of the business opportunity, your strategies and your target market. If you create a solid plan then you'll have a clearer idea as to your overall business strategy, including how much it's going to cost.

Fearsome finance

Getting a business off the ground costs money – the one thing you won't have a lot of while at college. You can cut corners without losing sight of your goal but you need to be inventive. Events and seminars are the places to meet potential investors, so go to as many as you can. Other ideas include using PCs provided by the college for your market research and plans, getting second-hand equipment (or trawling Freecycle), and doing research to make sure you use the cheapest suppliers. Again, you can get loads more ideas from Business.Gov.

A strong IT (Information Technology) strategy will help you to communicate with customers and improve service. You can also respond to requests quickly with email and manage business info more efficiently. In short, there are few businesses that can work without one and it doesn't have to cost the earth.

Accounting software, along with email and word processing, is essential. Microsoft Office Accounting Express 2009 is a good accounting program, and is available as a free download (office. microsoft.com/en-us/accountingexpress). See page 44 for more. Recognized systems like Microsoft Office and Windows Mail mean that your files will be compatible with most other businesses, and that you're running a secure system; after spending hours designing and emailing your company newsletter or product list, the last thing you want is to send everyone a virus, or an attachment they can't open. You can also use chat tools such as Windows Live Messenger to stay in touch with other entrepreneurs, to ask advice at all hours and even talk to your customers.

Taking off

Be realistic about how much time you can spend on your business – you still have to attend lectures, work on assignments and pass tests. If you have something that is flexible and expandable, let it adjust to your studies and not the other way around. It's easy to get caught up and lose sight of why you started in the first place.

4 BACKUP AND RESTORE CENTER Automatic File Backup, in most editions of Windows Vista, can schedule backups to your choice of location, such as a network, external hard drive or DVD.

5 INSTANT SEARCH Don't waste time hunting for documents, applications and random notes you have taken – Instant Search for them instead. It's as simple as typing in the keyword. Easy.

Top tips for success

The very successful Peter Jones, of the UK's *Dragon's Den*, gives advice

1 MENTOR Approach someone in a similar field to you and ask them for advice. You'll gain a mentor who can offer guidance and vouch for your abilities.

2 WORKING There's nothing like learning on the job. Work hard at making every aspect of the business a success. This is easier if you worked for a mentor before.

3 BE UNIQUE Think about how you can be different to – and better than – competitors. This can be achieved by a unique product, customer service, promotional activity, the type of customer you chase and so on. Don't under-price yourself.

4 CASH FLOW The best entrepreneurs keep a tight lid on expenses and re-invest profit to improve their business.

5 IDEAS Keep your imagination flowing and think of things that you would like to do. It is only from using our imagination that we come up with ideas. Make your dreams become a reality, and don't be put off by any obstacles.

Boost your career and get a pay rise

If you're trying to climb the corporate ladder, your PC can help you achieve your goals and gain that elusive promotion

Climbing the career ladder can be an ordeal. It's like the 'Travelator' from *Gladiators*, making you run harder and harder without seeming to getting anywhere at all. However, with a little cunning, and Windows Vista, you can get organized and earn yourself a Bill Gates-sized paycheck.

First you need to know what you want to achieve. Look at all your options – even if you have no intention of leaving your job. You may find that the same role in rival companies is better paid, and this can be used as ammunition when you go to your boss. Check vacancies at www. monster.com or www.usatoday.com.

Unfortunately, few people are in the position of being able to go to their boss,

AIM HIGH Windows Vista and the Office system can help you on the road to promotion

Be more productive with Windows Mail

Set it up in five easy steps, and start enjoying efficiency benefits

OPEN UP Open Windows Mail and click **Tools ➔ Accounts ➔ Add**. You can set up as many accounts as you like, so you can use it for your home email accounts as well as your business ones.

WORK FROM HOME Give your business account a recognizable name so you'll be able to identify it. If you do this, you'll be prompted to enter the full email address for your work email.

CHOOSE A SERVER Determine the address for the server your work email runs from. Choose the server from the list and add the prefix to the address, such as pop3.company-name.com.

demand a pay rise and walk out with swollen pockets. If you're going to get that promotion or pay rise, you're going to have to work for it, and this is where Windows Vista comes in.

Dave Berry, advisor for the Careers Advice Service in the UK, recommends you think about how you can increase your work performance. "Boosting your productivity is a great way to get noticed. Come in a little early and stay a little late, and your boss will see and appreciate that," he says. You can use Microsoft Office 2007 to increase your productivity, and free up time for important things. That may be more work if you're out to impress, just a more efficient workplan.

Microsoft Office Outlook 2007 has had a complete overhaul, making it a great place to centralize your work. It now comes equipped with the To-Do bar, which sits to the right of the screen and acts like a personal organizer.

Darren Strange, UK product manager for Microsoft Office, advises using these tools to your advantage. "Start using the To-Do bar in Office Outlook 2007," he says. "Don't let your diary push you around: take control and start blocking out time to get priority tasks done."

When you get an email, it can be dragged to the To-Do bar. Items on the

POWERFUL ALLY Make a presentation in PowerPoint 2007 and impress your boss

bar can then be added to your calendar, given priority flags and sent to other people just by dragging them.

Darren also champions new developments in Microsoft Office PowerPoint 2007, which he believes can help impress the boss, and get you on the fast track to promotion. "Put an end to death by PowerPoint and start to create more interesting presentations," he recommends. "Use the SmartArt feature to change boring bullet lists into diagrams that mean something."

Making contact

Windows Vista is packed with features designed to make you more productive. Try using a few of these and see how your performance increases. ↻

Expert tip

Use your own human resources, says Microsoft's Allister Frost

ONE KILLER TIP
Impress your boss by responding quickly to their emails. Disable desktop alerts for all emails (in Outlook, select **Tools → Options → Preferences tab → E-mail options → Advanced E-mail Options** then clear the Display a New Mail Desktop Alert box). Create a rule to display a desktop alert only when you receive a new email from your boss. Then jump into action as that alert appears!

GENERAL ADVICE
Office Outlook is a great career-enhancing tool. A tidy inbox will help you respond efficiently. Keep all emails succinct, using helpful subject lines and highlighting actions. Only send emails to the boss when you have to – a chat by the coffee machine will do your career more good in the long run!

NAME AND PASSWORD Now enter your username and password, which Windows Mail will use to verify your log-in details. Click **OK** again and enter your details again to access the account.

GOOD TO GO Now when you hit **Send and receive**, the server you have set up in accounts will be downloaded to Windows Mail. Now you can stay connected away from the office.

CLEAR MESSAGE Ignore junk emails and cut to the chase with an organized inbox

No one can function without email these days, and any time spent away from your inbox can lead to disaster. You could set Windows Mail to receive your work email at home – this means in times of crisis, you can come to the rescue while others flounder. Alternatively, you could set up a web mail service, such as Windows Live Hotmail, and have your

messages forwarded. Being able to pick up messages while you're out of the office saves time, and could prove vital one day.

You can further increase your productivity by using the Windows Sidebar feature. Check out gallery.live. com for thousands of Sidebar applications designed to make life easier. There's also the Microsoft Office Outlook gadget,

which brings your inbox to your desktop, which can save considerable time.

Windows Vista comes with a plethora of programs designed to increase your productivity. Eliminate wasted time looking for numbers in address books and on bits of paper by centralizing your data in Windows Contacts. The Windows Contacts program feeds into a Sidebar gadget, which enables you to have your colleagues' details within easy reach.

If your work relies on breaking news and developments, then web feeds can help. Look for feeds on your favorite news sites and add them to Internet Explorer by clicking the orange logo. Any feeds you add are automatically added to Microsoft Office Outlook as well.

If you feel that you and your colleagues aren't communicating well, or you need an easy way to share information, Windows Meeting Space could be the answer. This enables you to set up conferences where you can chat, share and edit files conveniently. It can be done over any wired or wireless local (LAN) or wide area network (WAN). If used properly, Meeting Space can really improve your department's performance.

TAKING OFFICE Time-saving features in Microsoft Office mean you can ponder your next move

Get together with your colleagues

You don't have to be in the office to hold a meeting

START Open Windows Meeting Space, and instruct your colleagues to do the same. You'll then find a simple menu giving you the options to start a new meeting, join a meeting, or load invitations from a file. Choose **Start a new meeting**, then give the meeting a password for security reasons.

INVITE Click on the **Invite** menu tab to view all the people on your network who are using the Windows Meeting Space service. Click the tick boxes for the people you wish to invite and they'll be sent notification of the meeting. When they accept their name will appear as attending in the right-hand pane.

SHARE Windows Meeting Space enables you to share programs in unprecedented ways. Click **Share a program** on your desktop and a list of options will be displayed. If you click **Give control**, others can take over your PC and make changes as well – great for demonstrations and group work.

While Windows Vista can help increase your productivity and get you organized, sometimes you need a little extra help to get further up the career ladder. Dave Berry constantly deals with people who are struggling to break through the promotion barrier. "People often get in touch because they feel unable to move on," he says. "They may have been in that role for a long time and need some extra training, perhaps with IT, for example.

"Occasionally people lack experience when they have to move to management or customer-facing roles," says Dave.

Foot in the door

If experience is all you're lacking, this can be a frustrating barrier to reaching the upper echelons of your profession. Voluntary work is not only great experience, but rewarding as well – www. volunteer.gov lists vacancies in the US and www.bunac.org (British Universities North America Club) has information on voluntary jobs both home and abroad.

If you're serious about getting a promotion, it's a good idea to think about the skills you currently use and could bring to another role. "People often take

If your work relies on breaking news, web feeds can really help you out

their skills for granted," says Dave. "It's easy to say 'I'm just a sales assistant', for example, without thinking of the vast number of skills this requires. Play to your strengths and give yourself credit for what you do. In every job there are loads of transferable skills that you can take to bigger and better roles."

Dave advises to make a skills' inventory to help identify your unique selling points. This can be done simply in Microsoft Office by making a spreadsheet or document listing all the skills you have to offer. This can help to convince your boss – and yourself! – that you do have the ability to work at higher levels of

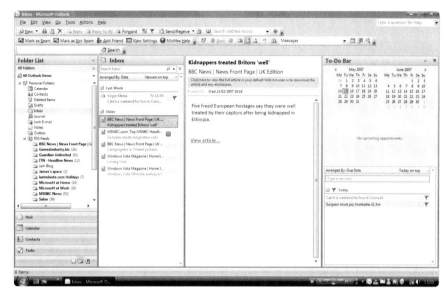

TIME SAVERS From RSS feeds to clever gadgets, Office Outlook 2007 is full of handy features

responsibility, or that you're worth that pay rise you've been looking for.

If you have to apply for your promotion formally, you may have to update your CV. With a little work, you can really sell yourself. Try using Microsoft Office Word 2007 to redesign it, making sure it's clearly laid out. Don't be afraid to leave white space, which will make it much easier on the eye and use contrasting bold fonts on section headings.

While Office Word 2007 empowers you to express yourself however you like, don't be tempted to include flowery borders or, the cardinal sin, clip art. Keep your CV simple, and make sure you fill it with details of the skills you've obtained from every job. Also remember to stick to the salient points – your résumé is your first point of contact and you need to stand out from the crowd; the interviewer can always ask for more detail in the interview itself...

With a good CV you'll be able to make it to an interview, and that promotion will finally be in sight. Interviews are nerve-racking and, if you haven't had one in a while, you could be unprepared. Make sure you think about the skills you identified in your CV, and think of real-life situations where you've used them. Employers will always ask you to give examples, so don't exaggerate or you'll

READY RESUME Struggling to write your CV on a blank page? Start with a template...

suffer from an attack of the blank mind.

It's also important in an interview to show you've done some background research on both the company and what the role entails – make a start at www. hoovers.com, which holds profiles and information about companies across the US. During the interview, also remember to ask questions – you need to show why you're keen to get the job.

For further advice on different areas of the application process, go to www.usa. gov and follow the Jobs and Education trail. Check out all the helpful information at the Career Resource Library to see what you can do to boost your chances.

With a little help and know-how, it's not too hard to get that promotion or pay rise, and turn the career ladder into a money escalator. Good luck!

Appendix

You've discovered what Windows Vista
and the 2007 Microsoft Office system
can do – now you'll want to install them

Installing Windows Vista

Choosing the right edition

Whatever your needs, there's a version of Windows Vista that's perfect. Which one is best for you?

"Wow"
Find out more

If you're still not sure which edition of Windows Vista is the right one for your needs, log on to www.microsoft.com/windows/windows-vista/discover for more info

Microsoft has made not one version of Windows Vista, but four main editions (as well as a 'starter' version for emerging markets, one for global organizations, and special '64-bit' versions of each for heavyweight PCs!). Whichever edition you go for, you can

easily change: Microsoft has put every version on the same disc, so if you decide you want a more powerful edition you don't need to trek to the shops. Instead, just contact Microsoft, pay for the upgrade and unlock the version instantly.

On the opposite page you'll find details of the four main Windows Vista editions, along with a rundown of the specific features. Home Premium is the best version for most people, but then the all-singing, all-dancing features of the Ultimate Edition are difficult to resist...

A whole lot more

As you'll discover, it's similar enough to Windows XP that you won't feel lost when you use it, but there are some major new features, new programs and new tools designed to make your PC more powerful, more productive and

more in tune with your life. It's an impressive achievement.

Windows Vista is an operating system, acting as a middleman between your PC's hardware and software. So when you want to print a document from your word processor, Windows Vista tells the hardware what to do; when you need to find a file, Windows Vista searches your hard disk, and so on. But it's more than just an interpreter...

Windows Vista comes stuffed with software that enables you to do all kinds of useful things without shelling out for extra programs; web browsing and email, home entertainment, DVD burning, photo editing, video editing and much more. It also comes with a range of security tools, although you'll still need to invest in an anti-virus program.

The Windows Vista user interface

Solid security

Iron-clad protection for your PC

Bolstered security is arguably the most important element in Windows Vista. For instance, the Windows Firewall is now two-way, monitoring outbound and inbound network communications (previously it was inbound only). Windows Defender, Microsoft's anti-spyware tool, is turned on by default, offering real-time protection against malicious software. Similarly, Internet Explorer runs in a 'protected' mode that forces you to grant permission for any action that could be 'suspect', such as downloading and installing software.

Windows Vista also boasts User Account Control, which pops up whenever Windows is about to perform a process that could be damaging. The screen goes black, then freezes, and up pops a dialog box for you to choose between continuing or cancelling.

UPGRADE The move from Windows XP to Windows Vista is usually very smooth

strikes you as soon as you hit the on switch. The familiar green Start button has morphed into a blue orb and the Start menu itself is organized differently. The Desktop still sports a taskbar with a Notification Area to the right and an optional three-icon Quick Launch area next to the Start button, but that's where the similarity ends. Icons are now high resolution and 3D; the taskbar is semi-transparent, as are the borders of windows, and you'll find a bunch of 'gadgets' nestled in a strip running vertically down the right side of the desktop. The overall color scheme is subtle, soft and very easy on the eye.

As you'd expect, virtually everything in Windows Vista is customizable. More surprising, perhaps, is that some familiar tools and shortcuts have moved. For instance, if you right-click the desktop in search of the Properties dialog box – as you might do to adjust screen resolution,

CLEAR VIEW You can turn off transparency, but why would you when it looks so good?

change the wallpaper and tweak the graphics driver settings – you'll find no such menu. Instead, there's a Personalize option that fires up a hefty Control Panel-style window comprising seven main headings, a separate 'task' list and some links to related features.

The elements covered in this book should help you to maximize the benefits that the operating system has to offer.

Windows Vista – the four main editions compared

So what are the differences between each edition of Windows Vista? Here are the salient features...

Features

Feature				
Manage your kids' access to the PC using Parental Controls	✓	✓	✗	✓
Back up files to a network device	✗	✓	✓	✓
Stay secure with Windows Defender and Windows Firewall	✓	✓	✓	✓
Find documents with Instant Search	✓	✓	✓	✓
Browse the web with Windows Internet Explorer 7	✓	✓	✓	✓
Enjoy the new look Aero desktop and Flip 3D	✗	✓	✓	✓
Get on the move with Windows Mobility Center and Tablet PC support	✗	✓	✓	✓
Share documents with Windows Meeting Space	✗	✓	✓	✓
Use your PC as an entertainment center with Windows Media Center	✗	✓	✗	✓
Protect against hardware failure with business backup features	✗	✗	✓	✓
Business networking and Remote Desktop	✗	✗	✓	✓
Protect against data theft with Windows BitLocker Drive Encryption	✗	✗	✗	✓

Installation preparation

If you're worried about making the upgrade to Windows Vista, a little prep work is a good idea...

Imagine being mere seconds away from finishing an installation and the worst happens – a power cut, lightning strikes your house, aliens land on the roof or, more mundanely, your hard drive fails.

No matter how unlikely it is that anything will go wrong, you should never risk all your photos, emails and other treasured mementos, or indeed important business documents, to chance, particularly when it's so easy to protect them using Windows Backup.

You'll find Windows Backup in **Start ➜ All Programs ➜ Accessories**, though if you're running Windows XP Home, you need to install the utility first – you'll find it in the VALUEADD\MSFT\NTBACKUP folder on the installation CD.

If you want an even easier option, dumping My Documents and any personal folders on a single DVD or CD takes less than half an hour.

Fight the temptation to tidy up My Documents before backing up – just be selective when you restore the data.

Check where more obscure programs store files by checking their **File ➜ Save** menu, and don't forget any save points for games; they're usually in their own folders in Program Files.

If you've bought online applications, grab the keys and passwords for these as well (and the actual files). And, if other members of your household use the same machine, you need to do all of this for each account.

Other areas you should take note of are your internet favorites, email account settings and website passwords. It's also worth taking note of the programs in the Start Menu, because it's easy to lose more obscure utilities.

Easy transfers

The manual approach isn't the only choice, though. Windows Vista introduces Windows Easy Transfer, a new program that makes it really easy to copy all the important settings over.

You should never risk files, particularly when it's so easy to protect them

While you can use it to get files off an old PC and on to your new Windows Vista machine – either by connecting their USB ports with an Easy Transfer cable or connecting them both to a home network – you can also use it to back up a computer before installing Windows Vista on it.

It doesn't support every program, and you'll still need to reinstall lots of stuff once you've got your new system in place, but it's a lot easier than painstakingly tracking down long-forgotten set-up details.

> ## "Wow"
> ## More stable
> Service Pack 1 has been designed to remove up to 75 per cent of all reported system failures from crash reports that relate to Windows Vista, helping to make it even more stable

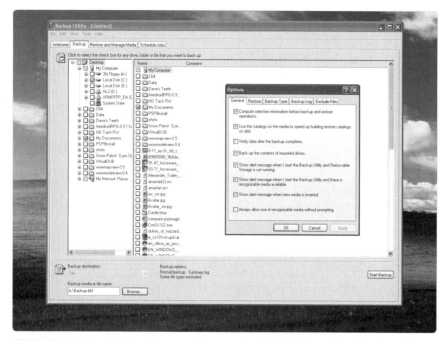

HELPING HAND Forget a laborious manual approach – let the Backup utility take the strain

And if you're migrating to a new PC...

Using Windows Easy Transfer really is easy

1 GETTING STARTED Place the Windows Vista disc in your old system, wait for the Install Windows screen, and click **Transfer files and settings from another computer**.

2 TO TRANSFER Click **Next → Close All** to close running programs. Choose how to transfer data; an Easy Transfer Cable is best, but this example uses Use a CD, DVD or other removable media.

3 PICK A DRIVE Easy Transfer can use USB flash drives or a network drive. If you don't have either, click **CD**. Pick a CD or DVD writer from the list, and password-protect your files.

4 WHAT FILES? You can click **All user accounts, files, and settings** to transfer the lot, but that requires lots of space (say, a network drive). If using DVDs, click **Advanced options**.

5 WHICH SETTINGS? You'll see a tree of every group of files and settings that Easy Transfer can move, with the size displayed. Browse the list, clearing check boxes for entries you don't need.

6 BURN DATA Place a blank, writable CD or DVD in the drive specified, and click **Next**. Windows Easy Transfer will copy the checked files and settings – prompting you to replace as required.

7 AT THE NEW PC Put the first disc in a drive. Click **Start → Computer**, choose the drive containing the disc you've inserted; double-click on the **Migration store** file it contains to import the transferred data.

8 NAME CHECK Your PC may not have the same user account names as your old one, so you'll be asked which new accounts should be used for each old one: Pick an existing account from the old computer and click **Next**.

9 LET'S DO IT Click **Transfer** and switch discs as prompted. When complete, click **Show me everything transferred** for a list of every file and Registry setting added or changed. Everything should have copied over, so just click **Close**.

Starting the install...

It may seem a scary thing to do but replacing the operating system of a PC isn't anywhere near as difficult as it used to be

If you aren't buying a brand new PC with Windows Vista pre-installed, there are three ways to upgrade your PC to Windows Vista:

1 An 'in-place' upgrade of an earlier version of Windows. This preserves your old programs, files and settings.

2 A clean installation over an existing version of Windows, erasing your previous version and your old files, favorites and settings.

3 A clean installation on a new or formatted hard disk or hard disk partition, with or without a dual boot.

Option 1 is not recommended as there are four concerns. First, there's no way back, so if you don't like Windows Vista, you're stuck. Second, there's a risk that the upgrade will fail and you'll lose data. Third, any existing problems on your PC may be carried over, including viruses

and spyware. Finally, your current system may be running 'under par', and this could affect post-upgrade performance. A fresh installation will get the best out of Windows Vista.

Windows Easy Transfer

Option 2 is fine so long as you back up everything you need from Windows. Windows Vista formats (wipes clean) the hard disk during installation, so your data will be gone. Your installation of Windows Vista will be free from performance and security issues, but you'll need to install your old software again. Windows Easy Transfer makes it much easier to configure your new version of Windows like the old one.

Option 3 doesn't delete the old version of Windows; it simply installs alongside in a different location. If you only have one hard disk, you can either

install a second disk or split it into two (or more) partitions – separate sections that behave like distinct hard disks. This way, you leave your previous version of Windows on one partition and install Windows Vista on the other. You can use your old version of Windows whenever you like by selecting it from a menu when you reboot. You can launch the Windows Vista set-up routine either by accessing the DVD from within Windows XP or by booting directly from the DVD.

The walkthrough looks at accessing the DVD from within Windows XP. If your hard disk isn't partitioned, Windows Vista can't do it for you without erasing data. There are two ways round this. You can either install a second hard disk, which removes the need for partitioning, or you can invest in a third-party disk partitioning program (choose the NTFS file system option, not FAT32). 🪟

It's only 12 steps to installation heaven

Just to prove how easy it is to install, here's every major step

1 MAKE SPACE If you intend to install Windows Vista on a hard disk partition next to your existing edition of Windows XP, create the partition using a third-party tool. If you have a second hard disk, you don't need to worry.

2 NO MESS The installer gets straight to the point. If you haven't already run the Upgrade Advisor, which is recommended (see page 191 for further details), you can do it from this screen; otherwise, click **Install now**.

3 CHOOSE METHOD If you launched from within Windows XP, either select **Upgrade** to replace Windows XP (keeping your files, etc) or **Custom (advanced)** to install a clean copy to a separate hard disk or disk partition.

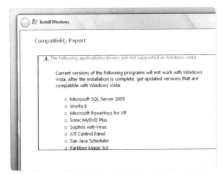

4 SAFE THAN SORRY By way of an illustration, here's what happens when you try to perform an upgrade without first remedying compatibility issues identified by the Upgrade Advisor. There's no way forward here so retreat.

5 GET ON Pitfalls aside, Windows Vista should now install smoothly with no further intervention from you for a while. Your PC will reboot a few times. When you see the **Press any key to boot from CD** option during a reboot, don't do this.

6 CHOOSE PASSWORD You'll be asked to specify your regional settings – Windows Vista defaults to US settings – and thereafter to create a User Account. This is the master account that Windows Vista will use by default.

7 NAME THIS KIT Give your PC a name. This will become important if and when you connect to a network. Choose a name that's not already on any network that this computer will join. You can also select a desktop background.

8 PLAY IT SAFE Now specify some basic security settings. It's best to go for the default **Use recommend settings**, because this turns on the Windows Firewall and configures automatic updates and problem reports.

9 WHERE AM I? You'll be asked to review international time settings and to specify how the computer will be used. This is to help with your Windows networking settings, although you can adjust the Network setup later.

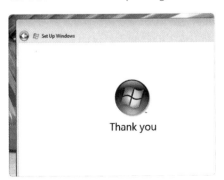

10 READY TO ROCK All that remains now is to hit the **Start** button to run some final automated configuration. Your PC will reboot and, if you have upgraded Windows XP, fire up Windows Vista for the first time.

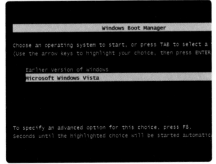

11 WHICH WINDOWS? If you selected a separate hard disk or hard disk partition (step 3), you will be presented with a boot menu. The 'earlier version of Windows' is Windows XP. Use the **arrow** and **Enter** keys to select.

12 HERE WE GO Finished! Your new desktop appears on your screen for the first time, displaying the wallpaper you chose in step 7. Welcome to the world of Windows Vista. Is it a wonderful world? You'll soon find out...

Keep your PC running like new

Windows Vista is packed with tools to keep your computer reliable and in top condition

The best part about having a new computer (apart from showing it off) is the super-fast, slick way that it will perform. Unfortunately, after a year or so, your shiny new machine may start to slow down. The good news is that Windows Vista is packed with great applications that are designed to keep your PC running at its best.

Staying up-to-date is one of the best ways to keep your PC secure, and with Windows Vista it couldn't be easier. Now most homes have an internet connection, Microsoft feeds important updates through Windows Update. Security patches are updated automatically, but improved support for graphics cards and hardware are optional, so make sure you check Windows Update regularly.

It's important to monitor the programs that are loaded when Windows Vista

"Wow"
Keep a schedule

Thanks to Task Scheduler, Windows Vista can automatically run tools when you are away from your PC. Go to **Start → All Programs → Accessories → System Tools → Task Scheduler**

THE LATEST THING Use Windows Update to keep your PC working as well as possible

starts. A lot of programs automatically demand to be started up when your PC boots, and for the most part this is completely unnecessary – and the effort involved in opening all these programs at once can slow your boot time to a grinding halt. To combat this, use Windows Defender (see page 98 for more) to manage these programs and make sure that only the essential ones, such as security software, are loaded.

Driving speed

The state of your hard drive is another important factor when it comes to keeping your PC working like it's 'fresh out of the box'. When your hard drive becomes cluttered, it takes longer for Windows to retrieve your files, and this can make a big difference to the way it runs. Use the Disk Cleanup utility to get

rid of unwanted files that may be affecting your PC's performance.

It's also important to defragment your hard drive regularly, so that all the clusters of data are grouped together, and the disk doesn't have to work so hard to retrieve your information. Getting round to defragmenting can be difficult because it's very time-consuming, but in Windows Vista you can schedule it to run at a time when your PC is idle.

If your PC is still suffering, try ReadyBoost to give your system extra oomph. Most USB drives and SD cards are configured for this. Just insert the drive/card, choose ReadyBoost from the auto-run menu, and you can put up to 4GB of memory aside for system processes. If you're running a system with limited RAM, you can gain a lot of speed by using the ReadyBoost feature.

In real life...
Keep it clean

**Jo Membery
Operations editor,
Windows Vista: The
Official Magazine**

I'm the last person in the world to look for extra work but I'm a convert to the fact that a little bit of time spent spring cleaning my PC reaps such significant performance rewards. A few checks make for a sparkling system – and Windows Vista does a lot of the hard work for me!

Keep your PC running smoothly

Five Windows features to keep your PC happy

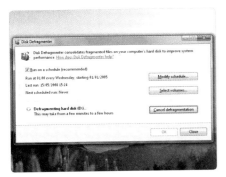

1 DISK DEFRAG The defragmenter makes sure your information is stored logically, making less work for your hard drive when retrieving and reading files. Use this regularly, and schedule it for times when you won't be using your PC.

2 DISK CLEANUP Get rid of wasteful temporary files and free up space using Disk Cleanup. Making sure that your hard drive is in order will keep your PC running smoothly; you'll be shocked by how much space you can save.

3 WINDOWS UPDATE Keeping Windows up-to-date is an easy way to boost performance. Updates for drivers are being released all the time, but aren't downloaded automatically, so check Windows Update for releases.

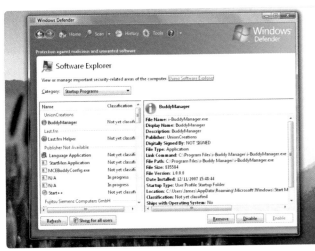

4 WINDOWS DEFENDER As well as being your first defence against internet nasties, one of the best features of Windows Defender is its ability to monitor start-up programs. Make sure non-essential programs aren't slowing down your start-up time by disabling them here.

It's important to defragment your hard drive so the disk doesn't have to work so hard to retrieve information

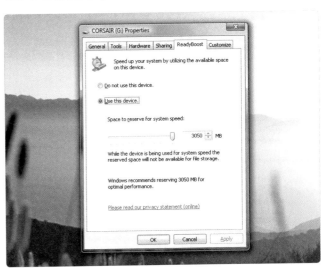

Stop unwanted programs

Here's another way of stopping unwanted programs at startup... Click **Start**, type 'msconfig' then hit the Startup tab; you'll see a list of programs. Uncheck next to the program's name to stop it loading at startup.

5 READYBOOST If your PC is sluggish, then ReadyBoost can provide some instant oomph to your system performance. Plug in a USB drive configured for ReadyBoost and allocate up to 4GB of space to take the pressure off your system, and keep Windows Vista operating at its best.

Love your computer!

Don't put up with poor performance, crashes or other PC hassles – with a little home maintenance your PC can run like a dream

Computers can seem intimidating and complex, forever misbehaving for no apparent reason, and refusing to respond no matter what efforts you make to try to get things working again. After a while it's tempting just to give up, and simply accept that Internet Explorer hangs occasionally, you can't view particular videos any more, your computer's performance is simply rubbish, or whatever your own personal list of PC problems might be.

This hands-off approach to PC maintenance has its appeal, at least for a while, as you fool yourself into thinking that taking the time to keep things in order will make little difference to the computer's daily operation. But the reality is very different. What actually happens is that you start adapting the way you use your PC to work around the ever-increasing list of bugs. So you'll have to reboot before you launch this application, view those videos with a different media player, turn down the quality settings on your game to get the same performance – the list goes on. While others get on with using their computer for work and fun, you'll be following complex workarounds to perform the simplest of applications.

Sound familiar? Then maybe it's time to do things differently. Stop living with irritating problems, and make an effort to fix them. It doesn't have to be difficult; Windows Vista can uncover a solution to some issues automatically, others can be fixed with a registry tweak, and most of the rest can be solved in five minutes... You'll be surprised at the results.

RECONCILIATION Start to love your PC again by following our hints and tips

In real life...
Ready for revival

Nick Odantzis Writer, *Windows Vista: The Official Magazine*

My PC started to really annoy me, crashing now and again, and I just assumed that this is what happens to PCs eventually, so I considered buying a new system to fix the problem, even though mine was only a year old. Luckily, I found out that all I needed to do to bring it back to life was to follow a few simple steps. It's saved me £400.

Performance

There are many reasons why your PC might boot slowly, crawl during the day, or take an age to shut down. Fortunately Windows Vista monitors most of these issues…

Hold down the **Windows key** and press **E** to launch Windows Explorer, click **System Properties**, select **Windows Experience Index** then click **Advanced Tools**. If Windows has spotted problems, it lists them under **Performance issues**. Click the links for details, such as a driver slowing things and consider updating or removing it.

If Windows doesn't report a problem, it could be that one of your programs is grabbing a lot of memory or processor time. To find out, press **Ctrl** and **Left Shift** and **Esc** to launch Task Manager. Select the **Processes** tab, then click **View → Select Columns** and ensure that **CPU Usage, Memory – Private working Set, Handles, USER Objects** and **GDI Objects** are checked.

Now, any time your PC seems slow, launch Task Manager, click the **Processes** tab and select **Show**

processes from all users. Click the column headers to sort by an element, so the most active process is at the top. You'll see what's using the most memory, processor time or resources. If it's a non-essential application, think about removing or updating it.

Task switching

The average PC has at least 40 processes wanting to run at any one time. Your processor can't execute all of these simultaneously, so it runs each one for a short period of time, then switches to another, sharing processor time.

The problem here is that, by default, Windows can give tasks as little as 20ms before changing. While this keeps the system responsive, it also wastes time in switching tasks. To try to change this, type 'System' into **Start Search** and click on **System → Advanced System Settings → Performance Settings → Advanced**, and set the 'Adjust for best performance of' value to Background services. If games or other programs respond slowly, switch back, but otherwise leave this setting

Expert tip

Big up your previews

The preview windows you get when you hover the mouse over a Taskbar are great. If you find them a bit small, try the free Vista Thumbnail Sizer (http://snipurl.com/guag8) to enlarge them (or add a fade-in effect). This only works with Windows Aero enabled, and mucks around with internal stuff in explorer. exe, so use at your own risk.

active to squeeze more power. Some people report copying across networks as particularly slow. The Windows Vista Remote Differential Compression (RDC) scheme can improve performance but doesn't work everywhere. Enter 'OptionalFeatures' into **Start Search** and press **Enter** to view the Windows features box. Clear the **Remote Differential Compression** box and click **OK**. Turn it back on again if you notice no real difference.

Maximum speed

Slick tricks to help your PC work faster

1 VISUALS Click **Start**, right-click **Computer**, select **Properties → Advanced System Settings**. Click **Performance Settings**. Click **Visual Effects**; Adjust for best performance.

2 POWER Click **Control Panel → System and Maintenance → Power Options**. If this isn't a laptop and you haven't tweaked settings to save energy, select the **High Performance** plan.

3 DRIVER To find your graphics driver performance settings, click **Control Panel → Adjust Screen Resolution → Advanced Settings → [graphics card name] → [control panel button]**.

Security

Windows Vista, your browser, Microsoft Office and all the major applications have important security settings, and it's not always obvious when they're set incorrectly. But there is a quick way to find out if you have any vulnerabilities. Run a copy of the Microsoft Baseline Security Analyzer (MBSA) and it checks your User Accounts, looks for weak passwords, makes sure things are updated, and more, all in about three minutes.

MBSA should be an essential part of everyone's security toolkit. You'll find it at Microsoft TechNet (snipurl. com/2bjf3) – follow the link for MBSA 2.1 and download the appropriate file. You'll probably want MBSASetup-x86-EN.msi for 32-bit Windows Vista, or MBSASetup-x64-EN.msi if you have the 64-bit version. See the PC security check below for more details.

ANALYZE THIS The Microsoft Baseline Security Analyzer checks your PC for vulnerabilities

Free tools

There are similar free services available online that can scan your PC and report weak spots, open ports, firewall problems, whatever they might be. Try Hacker Whacker (www.hackerwhacker. com), Audit My PC (www.auditmypc.com) or PC Flank (www.pcflank.com) and make sure your system doesn't have any wide-open security holes.

Checking potential weak points is a good place to start, but even if they're

Get a PC security health-check

Sort out security issues with the Microsoft Baseline Security Analyzer

1 QUICK START Launch the Microsoft Baseline Security Analyzer (see above); click **Scan a Computer**. Ignore the configuration options – the default settings are fine. Click **Start Scan**.

2 TAKE TIME MBSA starts checking your system settings. This can take a few minutes, even on a fast PC, but when it's complete you get a full report on everything the program has found.

3 FIX PROBLEMS MBSA is aimed at professionals, so problems aren't always described that clearly. Scroll down the list, clicking on any **How to correct this** links for detailed advice.

all closed, your PC can still be infected – especially if you're one of the millions who hasn't installed a decent antivirus program, firewall and perhaps a spyware blocker. Obviously, it's your decision, but if you don't protect your system properly, all your files, email messages and passwords are at risk. Which is a shame, especially when you can get very good security tools for no cost at all.

Turning on Windows Defender, for instance, provides basic anti-spyware protection. Launch Windows Defender, click **Tools ➔ Options**, and make sure that it's set to run daily scans at a convenient time.

Some commercial anti-spyware tools are available in free versions, too, such as SUPERAntiSpyware (www. superantispyware.com) or Spyware Doctor (www.pctools.com). You could opt for a more comprehensive free anti-virus solution such as Avira AntiVir (www.free-av.com), avast! anti-virus (www.avast.com) or AVG Free (free.avg. com). And Comodo (www.comodo. com) has free antivirus, anti-spyware and firewall tools – just download the one you need.

Quick fixes

Your security software will have a much easier time if you don't turn off the protection that Windows Vista offers already. It's a bad idea to turn off User Account Control (UAC). Yes, you lose the annoying prompts by doing so, but along with that goes Internet Explorer Protected Mode and other useful things, leaving your computer far more exposed to malware.

The best approach is to keep UAC on. Type 'User' into **Start Search** and open User Accounts. Click on **Turn User Account Control on or off**, then make sure that the box is checked. If it really does bother you, though, there is a

compromise. Launch REGEDIT and go to HKEY_LOCAL_MACHINE\SOFTWARE\ Microsoft\Windows\CurrentVersion\ Policies\System. Double-click **ConsentPromptBehaviorAdmin** on the right, set its value to **0** (use 2 later to restore the default), and click **OK**. Now UAC continues to run, which means features such as Internet Explorer Protected Mode remain active, but it doesn't display any annoying prompts. You're not as safe as you could be, but this is a far better option than turning it off altogether.

➡

Super tip

Prompts be gone!

The Windows Security Center flags up security issues. But what if you've installed anti-malware and it's not been recognized? If you're sure you don't need the Security Center prompts, click **Control Panel ➔ Security ➔ Security Center ➔ Change the way Security Center alerts me**, and select **Don't notify me, but display the icon.**

PROMPT ACTION If you find UAC annoying, you can switch off the prompts it creates

Stability

Does your PC keep crashing, displaying error messages or locking up for no apparent reason? This quickly becomes frustrating, but Windows Vista tracks all these problems and helps you find the cause.

Click **Control Panel → Problem Reports and Solutions**, and Windows checks online to see if there are known fixes for any of your problems. Click any links in the Solutions To Install or Information About Other Problems sections for ideas on what to do next.

If Windows doesn't uncover anything, you can always try a little detective work of your own. Type 'perfmon' into **Start Search**, then click Perfmon.exe in the search results to launch the Reliability and Performance Monitor. Select Reliability Monitor in the Monitoring Tools section and you'll see the system stability chart, a graph showing how well (or badly) your computer is performing over time. It's amazing just how useful this can

MEMORY TEST Adding more RAM can significantly improve your PC's stability

be. Look back over the graph and you might find your stability has been falling over time, indicating things are getting

worse. But when did this start? Scroll back to see. The stability chart also records any new software you add to

Uncover the crash culprits
Work out what's really causing your PC problems

1 LOOK CLOSER Press **Ctrl**, **Shift** and **Esc** to launch Task Manager, press **View → Select Columns** and check **Handles, User** and **GDI Objects**. Click the Handles column header twice, so the highest numbers are at the top to give a rough idea of resources used.

2 RESOURCE HOGS Typical applications use just a few thousand handles, user or GDI objects. If you see a process that's using maybe 10,000, and the numbers keep rising, the drain on Windows resources may cause a crash. Search online for the process name.

3 REVEAL CLUES Type 'Event Viewer' into **Start Search**, then launch it from the program list and click on **Custom Views → Administrative Events**. Scroll down the list of recent errors for more clues on what's behind any recent errors and crashes.

the system, so you might find the problems began on the same day that you installed a new antivirus program, for instance. Armed with this clue you can try updating or removing the offending program, and there's a very good chance that your stability problems will disappear.

Back to basics

If Windows can't help with your constant crashes, it makes sense to go back to basics and think about what actually caused the system instability in the first place.

A lack of resources, for instance, can cause all kinds of odd problems. If your PC is short of RAM (1GB or less), adding more may well help. It's surprisingly cheap (around $20 for 1GB), and tools such as the Crucial Memory Advisor (www.crucial.com) can help you choose the right memory type.

If you're short on hard drive space, perhaps with less than 4GB free, that can also contribute to stability issues. Uninstall any unwanted programs and then launch Disk Cleanup (type 'Disk Cleanup' into **Start Search**) to free up some space, and perhaps consider adding another hard drive. Buy a fast model and it'll improve your performance, too.

It's possible that some applications may be conflicting with others. Uninstall anything you don't need, and use Windows Defender to stop unnecessary programs loading at start-up (launch Defender, click **Tools →** **Software Explorer**, click an unwanted application and select Disable).

Your older programs may be unreliable because they don't include the latest updates. Check the author's website to see if there are new versions available, or use UpdateStar (www. updatestar.com) to check all your applications automatically.

Sometimes following guides online can lead to serious instability, usually because the authors don't tell you everything you need to know. For example, sometimes you'll read that turning off your paging file, or fixing its size, leads to better performance. But choose the wrong size and your computer will soon start crashing. Type 'System' into **Start Search and click on System → Advanced System Settings → Performance Settings → Advanced → Change** and make sure that **Automatically manage paging file** has been checked.

Expert tip

Keep it clean!

To keep your PC stable, clear junk and keep it clean. Try PC Decrapifier (www.pcdecrapifier. com) to remove irritations that come installed, and Revo Uninstaller (www.revouninstaller. com) to remove applications. And always create a system restore point when installing software, so it's easy to roll your settings back.

CRASH COURSE Use the Reliability Monitor to track down the cause of crashes

Annoyances

Some of the best Windows tips are simple tweaks that overcome common annoyances.

If Windows Explorer doesn't recall the settings you choose for individual folders, press **Alt** then **Tools ➜ Folder Options ➜ View**, and check the **Remember each folder's view settings** box. If that doesn't work, your folder settings are probably corrupt. Launch REGEDIT, go to **HKEY_CURRENT_USER\Software\Classes\Local Settings\Software\Microsoft\Windows\Shell**, right-click **Bags** in the right-hand pane and click **Edit ➜ Delete ➜ Yes**. Erase the BagMRU key as well, then reboot.

If Windows Explorer stops displaying your DVD drive, or thinks it's a DVD-ROM, launch REGEDIT, navigate to **HKEY_LOCAL_MACHINE\System\CurrentControl Set\Control\Class\{4D36E965-E325-11CE-BFC1-08002BE10318}**, and delete the UpperFilters or LowerFilters settings in the right-hand pane. (These settings only – deleting UpperFilters.bak, say, doesn't help.) This usually works at the expense of whatever application added the faulty filters; if a DVD-related program now stops working, you'll have to reinstall it.

Old and new

Old applications don't always run well under Windows Vista. Try right-clicking the program shortcut, select **Properties ➜ Compatibility**, check the **Run this program in compatibility mode** box and select Windows XP (Service Pack 2), or Windows 98 if it's very old. Click **OK**.

To access your network connections in Windows Vista, type 'ncpa.cpl' into **Start Search** and press **Enter** for information.

If you miss the way Windows XP enabled you to change resolution or tweak settings just by right-clicking the desktop and selecting Display Settings, Windows Vista can do the same. Launch REGEDIT, browse to **HKEY_CLASSES_**

ROOT\Directory\Background\Shell. Right-click Shell, select **New ➜ Key** and call it Display Settings. Double-click (Default) in the right-hand pane and enter 'Display Settings' in the Value Data box. Right-click Display Settings in the left-hand pane, select **New ➜ Key** again; call this key 'command'. Double-click this new key's (Default) value and enter: 'rundll32 shell32.dll,Control_RunDLL DESK.CPL,@0,3'. This is case-sensitive. Click **OK**, right-click the desktop to find Display Settings.

Faster, easier searching

Speed up searches with this handy little tweak

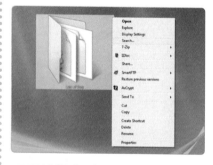

1 SEARCH Service Pack 1 removes the right-click search option from folders. To get it back, run REGEDIT, go to **HKEY_CLASSES_ROOT\CompressedFolder\shell\find, HKEY_CURRENT_USER\Directory\shell\find** and **HKEY_CURRENT_USER\Drive\shell\find**; delete LegacyDisable keys.

2 LOCATE If you don't store documents under the Users folder, index their location for fast searches. Click **Control Panel ➜ System and Maintenance ➜ Change how Windows searches ➜ Modify ➜ Show all Locations**, and check the folders to index. The more there are, the longer indexing takes.

3 LANGUAGE For easier searching, launch Explorer, click **Tools ➜ Folder Options ➜ Search** and check **Use natural language search**. Now enter searches such as 'Email from Bill Gates', 'Music by Duffy', or 'Documents modified yesterday' and Windows Vista will find exactly what you need.

Disaster recovery

Most PCs are crammed with valuable data, from practical things such as usernames, passwords or email addresses, to personal items such as digital photos. It only takes a moment of carelessness, a software bug or virus, though, and you could lose the lot.

Fortunately, there are ways to recover. If Windows doesn't load, for instance, the new Startup Repair tool might help. Boot from the Windows DVD, click **Repair My Computer**, select your installation and click **Startup Repair** to give it a try. If you don't have a DVD, hold down **F8** as Windows boots, select the **Advanced Boot Options** screen and click **Repair your computer**.

If Startup Repair doesn't work, perhaps not recognizing your drive, reboot and launch your BIOS setup program (press **Delete, F2**, or whatever else it recommends when you turn your PC on). If your motherboard battery is failing, you might find its hard drive settings have been corrupted, and a quick tweak will get you started again.

The real secret to disaster recovery is to think ahead, and prepare for the worst. If you spend an evening preparing your personal PC disaster recovery toolkit, you'll be ready for just about anything.

For instance, your hard drive is divided into partitions, structures that tell the PC where it can start booting Windows. But if these are corrupted, Windows won't load, and Startup Repair will be unable to fix things. Try downloading a copy of the free PartedMagic (partedmagic.com), which you can use to create a bootable CD or DVD that will get your PC working again.

Be prepared

Maybe you've forgotten your password, and can't log in. Oops! You can prepare for this by creating a password reset disc (**Control Panel ➜ User Accounts and Family Safety ➜ User Accounts ➜ Create a password reset disk**). If there is ever a problem with your password, just press **Enter** and you're prompted for the disc and can log on. Though beware – this means anyone else can, too, if they get hold of the disc, so keep it safe. Without

System restore

Step back in time

If registry corruption or a dodgy new driver are preventing your PC from working properly, there's a way to recover. Type 'System Restore' into **Start Search**, launch System Restore and restore settings to a time when the PC was working well. By default, System Restore uses up to 15% of your hard drive for backups; this can be increased.

the password reset disc, you'll need to download tools such as the Offline NT Password & Registry Editor (home.eunet.no/pnordahl/ntpasswd) or Login Recovery (www.loginrecovery.com) to try to reset it again.

If your PC boots, but some files have been wiped, a good undelete program can recover them quickly. SoftPerfect File Recovery (www.softperfect.com/products/filerecovery) or Undelete Plus (undelete-plus.com) are good.

Run regular backups
Keep everything backed up in case disaster strikes

1 BEGIN BACKUP Back up your data every few days. Type 'Backup' into **Start Search** and launch the Backup and Restore Center. Click **Back Up Files** to copy your data elsewhere.

2 CALL ON COBIAN OK, so that's not exactly a 'five-minute fix'... Try Cobian Backup 9 (snipurl.com/2bjn5); this offers more control over the data you back up. Click **Task ➜ New Task ➜ Files** to start.

3 QUICK SAVE Backups don't have to be of your entire system. Drag and drop Contacts and Favorites folders to the Files Screen to save email addresses and URLs in minutes.

How to be comfortable in your new office

There are eight editions of the 2007 Microsoft Office release – which version is right for you?

Things were simpler in the old days. Take coffee, for example: you'd go to a diner and ask for a cup of Joe. But now it's all skinny this and double-decaf that with extra froth. It takes longer to order your coffee than it does to drink it.

Now, call us conspiracy theorists but the world's biggest coffee company, Starbucks, is based in Seattle – and so is Microsoft. Coincidence? Well, if Microsoft hasn't been inspired by the coffee king, why else would it replace

Office Standard and Office Professional with not one, not two but eight versions of the 2007 Office system?

As with modern-day coffee options, the idea is to have something for everyone, but all that choice can be confusing if you're not sure what you need... Never fear! The chart below analyzes every version of the 2007 Office release so that you can easily see which version is right for you. Whether you're on a tight budget or ruling a giant corporation, planning a major business event or taking notes in a lecture, there's

PICK AND CHOOSE Whatever your requirements you'll find a suite to suit

an edition for you. So no matter if you're a struggling student or a director of a globe-straddling organization, you can pick the right edition.

2007 Microsoft Office editions explained

Eight great choices, but what comes with each package?

	Microsoft Office Basic 2007	Microsoft Office Home and Student 2007	Microsoft Office Standard 2007	Microsoft Office Small Business 2007	Microsoft Office Professional 2007	Microsoft Office Ultimate 2007	Microsoft Office Professional Plus 2007	Microsoft Office Enterprise 2007
Word 2007	Yes	Yes	Yes	Yes	Yes	Yes	Yes	Yes
Excel 2007	Yes	Yes	Yes	Yes	Yes	Yes	Yes	Yes
PowerPoint 2007	No	Yes	Yes	Yes	Yes	Yes	Yes	Yes
Outlook 2007	Yes	No	Yes	Yes*	Yes*	Yes*	Yes	Yes
Publisher 2007	No	No	No	Yes	Yes	Yes	Yes	Yes
Access 2007	No	No	No	No	Yes	Yes	Yes	Yes
InfoPath 2007	No	No	No	No	No	Yes	Yes	Yes
Groove 2007	No	No	No	No	No	Yes	No	Yes
OneNote 2007	No	Yes	No	No	No	Yes	No	Yes
Communicator 2007	No	No	No	No	No	No	Yes	Yes

* Outlook 2007 with Business Contact Manager

How to try out the 2007 Microsoft Office release

Want to find out more about the 2007 Microsoft Office suite? The best way is to get hands-on and try it for yourself. Follow these steps to see how

You can try all the features of the 2007 Microsoft Office system for up to 60 days absolutely free, and you don't have to uninstall your current software to do it. It's an easy way to experiment with the features without interfering with your current work, although we suspect that your old applications will find themselves unused before long... And when you decide to make the upgrade permanent, you can buy the suite you want online and simply carry on using the software you've already installed.

Trial run

How to try before you buy

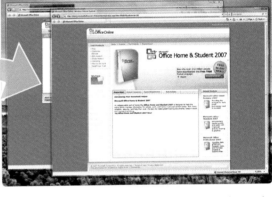

1 BEFORE WE BEGIN Go to the Office homepage – office. microsoft.com – and click on **Try in your Browser**. You'll be prompted to download and run a helper application, which allows you to use the major applications straight away in a new window.

2 PICK A SUITE Click on the **Product Comparison** tab to see which one you need, then choose **Download Now**. You need a Windows Live ID; if you don't have one you can register here.

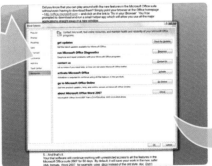

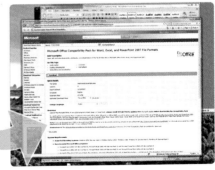

3 TRIAL KEY You need the Trial Key to activate your Microsoft Office trial. (It also gets mailed to your Windows Live address.) You can use the applications 25 times before you need to activate them.

4 ACTIVATE Once downloaded and installed, you must activate. If you pay for a full version, you're sent a new Key. Then follow **Office ➜ Options ➜ Resources ➜ Activate Microsoft Office**.

5 THAT'S IT By default, the software will save your work in XML format – readable in older versions of the Office suite by downloading the Compatibility Pack from www.microsoft.com.

The Office Ready PC Programme

Now you can experience the superb features and advancements of the 2007 Microsoft Office system before you buy!

Great option for work & home

Here's why you need the 2007 Office system

1 FAST WITHOUT FURIOUS **The 2007 Office system has been** designed far more intuitively than its predecessors, so it's easier to find what you need as you work.

2 TIME MANAGEMENT **Outlook 2007 has the wonderful** Business Contact Manager that sorts all of your tasks, flagged emails and appointments into the To-Do Bar so you have instant access and you can drag and drop them into your calendar.

3 GET CREATIVE **With Microsoft Publisher 2007 you can create** publications for print, email and the internet with plenty of templates, fonts and formats.

4 PROFESSIONAL PRODUCTIONS **Documents, presentations and** plans are quickly created and have a slick professional finish, without fuss or panic.

5 ANALYZE THIS **Excel 2007 has great tools to filter, sort and** visualize data, so complex info can be analyzed far faster.

The 2007 Microsoft Office system delivers better results faster. However, as with any new technology, you might want to try before you buy, and this is where the Office Ready PC Program steps in...

A Microsoft Office Ready PC is a computer with the Microsoft Office Ready PC image installed. This single image can be converted to one of the following 2007 Microsoft Office suites: Office Basic 2007, Office Small Business 2007, and Office Professional 2007. So, when you buy a new PC, particularly for business, ask if it is a Microsoft Office Ready PC – if it is, you'll get the functionality of one of the Office editions for free, for 60 days. This is a perfect opportunity to assess the features and make sure the software is the right choice for your home or business use. And you won't be disappointed. The list of features in Office Professional 2007 is very impressive, including the new intuitive

MOVE IT Looking for a new laptop? Think ahead and get one with Office pre-installed

interface, formatting features, the ability to preview changes to work before committing to them, enhanced graphics and photo, fax and scan capabilities...

Getting activated

To start with, you need to activate your trial software, which requires an internet connection. If you do not activate it now, the programs will remain locked. See the walkthrough opposite for step-by-step instructions on how to activate.

If you decide not to go ahead and purchase the 2007 Office system, the software automatically locks at the end of the 60-day period. You will, however, be able to access your documents and saved files if you transfer them to a PC with the right software installed.

If you decide to stick with the software, all you need to do is purchase a media-less license kit (MLK) for the version of Office you want to buy. You can get this from your retailer or online if it is within 90 days of buying your PC. The key you then enter to activate your software determines which components are unlocked. So if you bought a key for Office Professional, then you will be given all of the programs for that option, but if you bought a key for Office Basic, you would only unlock Outlook, Excel and Word. If you change your mind again, you can purchase another key that will unlock other additional programs.

Purchasing a Microsoft Office Ready PC is the ideal way to experiment with top-of-the-range technology and to purchase it according to your own business needs and budget.

Activate an Office trial

Have a quick try; this example shows Office Professional 2007

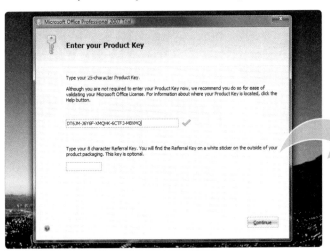

1 NUMBER CRUNCH Enter the 25-character Trial Product Key into the Setup dialog box. This key will have been provided along with your new Office Ready PC or generated when you clicked on the trial icon.

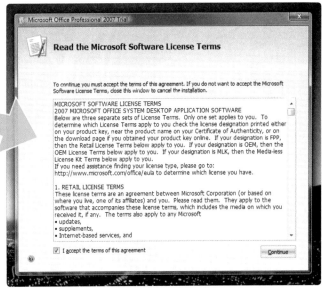

2 SIGNING ON Once you have entered the key, click **Continue** and the End User License will appear. If you are happy with this, you should click **I accept the terms of this agreement**, then click **Continue** to move on to the next step.

3 MAGIC MOVES Once you have accepted the license agreement, the Activation Wizard will appear on screen, ready to take you through the entire process. It's all very simple; you need to select **I want to activate the software over the internet** and then click **Next**.

It's a perfect opportunity to make sure the software is the right choice for you

4 STEPPING OUT At the end of the activation process, you will receive a notification that indicates the date when the trial expires, along with confirmation of a successful activation. Now you're ready to enjoy 60 days of computing pleasure before you need to make your final purchasing decision.

Index

Index

Get more from your PC

GET STARTED
How to install Windows Vista and get to grips with the new programs and features

BLOGS
Read opinions from magazine staff and other site users – or even start your own blog

DO MORE
Discover how to use Windows Vista to get more from your everyday interests and activities

MESSAGE BOARDS
Have your questions answered by our friendly and informed community

www.windowsvistamagazine.com

What do you think of this book?

We want to hear from you!

To participate in a brief online survey, please visit:

...and enter this book's ISBN number (appears above barcode on back cover).

Tell us how well this book meets your needs—what works effectively, and what we can do better. Your feedback will help us continually improve our books and learning resources for you.

Thank you in advance for your input!

Where to find the ISBN on back cover

ISBN: 000-0-0000-0000-0

Example only. Each book has unique ISBN.

Microsoft®
Press

Stay in touch!

Choose the Right Book for You

Plain & Simple

- Easy visual approach shows the simplest ways to get things done
- Full-color guide features easy-to-follow steps and screenshots
- Just the basics—no jargon, no hassle

Step by Step

- Build exactly the skills you want
- Take just the lessons you need, or work from cover to cover
- Easy-search CD includes practice files, complete eBook, and helpful resources

Inside Out

- Comprehensive, in-depth reference for intermediate to advanced users
- Features hundreds of timesaving solutions, troubleshooting tips, and workarounds
- CD packs custom resources and a fully searchable eBook

Resources from Microsoft Press

Plain & Simple

Windows Vista *Plain & Simple*
978-0-7356-2268-5

2007 Microsoft® Office System
Plain & Simple
978-0-7356-2273-9

Microsoft Office Access® 2007
Plain & Simple
978-0-7356-2292-0

Microsoft Office Excel® 2007
Plain & Simple
978-0-7356-2291-3

Microsoft Office Outlook®
2007 *Plain & Simple*
978-0-7356-2294-4

Microsoft Office PowerPoint®
2007 *Plain & Simple*
978-0-7356-2295-1

Microsoft Office Word 2007
Plain & Simple
978-0-7356-2293-7

Microsoft Expression® Web
Plain & Simple
978-0-7356-2519-8

Step by Step

Windows Vista *Step by Step*
978-0-7356-2269-2

Windows Vista *Step by Step
Deluxe Edition*
978-0-7356-2532-7

2007 Microsoft Office System
Step by Step, 2nd Edition
978-0-7356-2531-0

Microsoft Office Access 2007
Step by Step
978-0-7356-2303-3

Microsoft Office Excel 2007
Step by Step
978-0-7356-2304-0

Microsoft Office Outlook 2007
Step by Step
978-0-7356-2300-2

Microsoft Office PowerPoint
2007 *Step by Step*
978-0-7356-2301-9

Microsoft Office Project 2007
Step by Step
978-0-7356-2305-7

Microsoft Office SharePoint®
Designer 2007
Step by Step
978-0-7356-2533-4

Microsoft Windows®
SharePoint Services 3.0
Step by Step
978-0-7356-2363-7

Microsoft Office Word 2007
Step by Step
978-0-7356-2302-6

Inside Out

Windows Vista *Inside Out
Deluxe Edition*
978-0-7356-2524-2

2007 Microsoft Office System
Inside Out
978-0-7356-2324-8

Advanced Microsoft Office
Documents 2007 Edition
Inside Out
978-0-7356-2285-2

Microsoft Office Access 2007
Inside Out
978-0-7356-2325-5

Microsoft Office Excel 2007
Inside Out
978-0-7356-2321-7

Microsoft Office Outlook 2007
Inside Out
978-0-7356-2328-6

Microsoft Office Project 2007
Inside Out
978-0-7356-2327-9

Microsoft Office Word 2007
Inside Out
978-0-7356-2330-9

Microsoft Windows
SharePoint Services 3.0
Inside Out
978-0-7356-2323-1

Other Titles

Breakthrough Windows Vista:
Find Your Favorite Features
and Discover the Possibilities
978-0-7356-2362-0

So That's How!
Timesavers, Breakthroughs,
& Everyday Genius for 2007
Microsoft Office System
978-0-7356-2274-6

Beyond Bullet Points:
Using Microsoft Office
PowerPoint 2007 to Create
Presentations That Inform,
Motivate, and Inspire
978-0-7356-2387-3

Take Back Your Life! Using
Microsoft Office Outlook 2007
to Get Organized and Stay
Organized
978-0-7356-2343-9

The Best of Windows Vista:
The Official Magazine
978-0-7356-2579-2